MW00640331

FORAGING THE MOUNTAIN WEST

Gourmet Edible Plants, Mushrooms, and Meat

Thomas J. Elpel and Kris Reed

Dedicated to Katie Russell, Professional Wilderbabe—

Thanks for a moment in time.

HOPS Press, LLC
12 Quartz Street
Pony, Montana 59747-0697
www.hopspress.com
www.wildflowers-and-weeds.com

Foraging the Mountain West

Copyright: 1st Edition. June 2014. 5,000 copies printed.

ISBN: 978-1-892784-36-0

Help refine this book! Please e-mail suggestions, corrections, and comments to us through the current address posted on our web site at www.hopspress.com. We will do our best to incorporate your input into future editions.

Legal Note: This guide is intended to aid in the identification, harvesting, and processing of edible wild flora, fungi, and fauna. Be sure to corroborate your findings with other sources before you consume. Also keep in mind that every field guide has errors, and every person who uses a field guide makes errors. Misidentification, accidents, allergies, and unforeseen events and complications can lead to unfortunate outcomes. You, the reader, must take full responsibility for your choices before you consume anything. The authors are not responsible for your accidents.

Publisher's Cataloging-in-Publication Data
Elpel, Thomas J. 1967-
    Foraging the Mountain West / By (Author), Thomas J. Elpel;
    By (Author), Kris Reed

    Includes bibliographical references and index.
    ISBN: 978-1-892784-36-0 $30.00 Pbk. (alk. paper)
    1. Wild Plants, Edible. 2. Plant Identification. 3. Wild
    Foods—Rocky Mountains.
    I. Elpel, Thomas J. II. Title.
    QK98.5.A1 E47 2014 581.632 LCCN: 2014904979

This book is printed in the USA with soy-based inks on recycled paper with 100% post-consumer waste. Remember to recycle your papers!

HOPS Press, LLC
12 Quartz Street
Pony, MT 59747-0697
www.hopspress.com
www.wildflowers-and-weeds.com

The authors, Thomas J. Elpel and Kris Reed. For consistency in style, the final text is written in Tom's words, although Kris provided much of the draft content.

Table of Contents

Region Covered i
Nature's Banquet 1
Plant Identification 101 11
Foraging Basics 17
Caretaker 25

Salads and Greens.. 39
Edible or Poisonous? 43
   Siberian Elm: Invasive or Inviting? 45
   Cattails: Food from Swamp Muck 47
   Wild Asparagus: Defend your Territory 55
   Milkweed: The Other Asparagus 57
   Tumble Mustard: Wild Broccoli 63
   Dandelion: Supermarket of the Lawn 66
   Sow Thistle: The Bigger Dandelion 72
   Salsify: A Forgotten Delicacy 75
   Goosefoots: Better than Garden Greens 78
   Stinging Nettles: Food that Bites Back 84

White Clover: Always a Lucky Find 88
Sorrel and Dock: Sour or Astringent? 90
Violets: They're not all Purple 94
Brook Saxifrage: Mountain Lettuce 96
Plantain: White Man's Footsteps 98
Thistles: Food with a Security System 100
Prickly Pear Cactus: Good Green Slime 105
Purslane: A Delicacy Underfoot 109
Watercress: Available in any Season 112
Greens in Winter: Foraging for Hope 114

Rooting Around 119
Edible or Poisonous? 125
Bitterroot: Spirit of Montana 127
Spring Beauty: Potato of the Rockies 131
Common Camas: Slow Cooking 136
Glacier Lilies: Too Pretty to Eat? 143
Yellowbells: Chiming in Springtime 146
Burdock: Eating an Invasive 148
Sego Lilies: Food with Fashion 151
Brodiaea: What to Call It? 155
Wild Onions: Diverse and Delicious 157
Yampa: Twins are Normal 159
Biscuitroots: Facts versus Reality 161
Harebells: More than Meets the Eye 163
Worth Mentioning 166

Fabulous Fruits 169
Edible or Poisonous? 175
Gooseberry and Currant: Berry Good 179
Huckleberry: Worth Dying For 182
Salal: Purple Power 186
Wild Strawberry: Flirting with Desire 188
Blackberry & Raspberry: Aggregates 190
Wild Rose: Totally Hip 194
Cherry and Plum: From Flesh to Pit 196
Serviceberry: It's Got Substance 204
Black Hawthorn: Packed with Pectin 207
Apple and Crabapple: Feral Fruits 211
Blue Elderberry: The Mother Lode 218
Oregon Grape: The Ungrape 222

Kinnikinnick: Almost Food 227
Buffaloberry: Winter Harvest 229
Worth Mentioning 234

Seeds and Nuts 237
Edible or Poisonous? 238
Sunflower: World Traveler 241
Amaranth: Grain of the Ancients 245
Grass: The Seeds of Civilization 249
Pine Nuts: Insanely Nutritious 255
Black Walnut: In a Nutshell 262

Marvelous Mushrooms 267
Edible or Poisonous? 270
Tree Mushrooms: First Rite of Spring 273
Morels: Lose your Morals 275
Meadow Mushroom: Familiar Favorite 279
Shaggy Mane: Self-Destructing 282
Giant Puffball: Wild Tofu 284
King Bolete: Fit for Royalty 287

Hunting and Scavenging 291
Hunting 101: Sticks, Rocks, and Spears 294
Crayfish: Inland Lobster 298
Common Carp: Disdained but Delicious 300
Roadkill: It's What's for Dinner 309
Dumpster Diving: Living the High Life 323
Gleaning: An Age-Old Tradition 327

A Foraging Lifestyle 329

Bibliography 333
Index by Genus 335
Index by Common Name 336

Region Covered

Foraging the Mountain West is optimized to the chunk of inland ge-ography spanning from the Rocky Mountains west to the Sierra Nevadas, then north to the Cascades and into Canada, encompassing everything from the valley bottoms to the mountain tops. It is a hardscrabble land-scape where normal weather includes too much of everything: too hot, too cold, too windy, too wet, too dry, and too smoky. The uniqueness of this environment necessitates a text that reflects the realities of foraging here, and this is the first comprehensive field guide to fill that role.

In addition, most of the plant, fungi, and animal species covered in this guide are found far beyond the Mountain West. Moreover, we uti-lized a patterns-based approach to help the reader recognize individual plants and their uses, as well as many of their closest kin.

For example, there are about 200 species of gooseberries and cur-rants (*Ribes*) around the world, including about 55 species in North America. Rather than featuring just one or two species as separate entries, this field guide combines all gooseberries and currants in one description, with photos of multiple species to show the range of variation. That way the reader is empowered to recognize other species anywhere in North America or halfway around the globe.

Slicing and dicing for a stir-fry. This group meal, prepared on a canoe trip, included wild harvested cattail stalks, morel mushrooms, and wild onions, plus tomatoes and a jalapeno pepper foraged from a grocery store dumpster.

Nature's Banquet

I checked the time, then pocketed my watch and thrust my digging stick into the ground. The tuberous little spring beauty roots lay close to the surface, so it wasn't hard to dig them. But they were small, the biggest a half-inch in diameter. These comparative "giants" were not hard to identify, since older plants grow multiple stems. A first-year spring beauty grows only a single stem from a potato-like tuber too small to bother with, but with each passing year the plant sends up additional stems and the tuber grows larger. Two or three stems are also not worth bothering with, but the presence of four, five, six, or more dainty flowering stalks emerging from a single point in the soil signifies a tuber that will likely have some substance.

I wanted to learn how to survive and thrive in nature with the resources at hand.

Thrust a sharpened stick into the ground beside the spring beauty, and lift up underneath it to bring the little treasure to the surface. It almost seems like

1

a shame—all those years of growth to produce a tuber that is, at best, painfully small. But I was determined.

I had a lot of grand dreams and goals as a teenager and young adult, and learning to survive and thrive in the wilds, to "live off the land," was perhaps my most personal ambition. My father introduced me to my first wild edible plant, known as "miner's lettuce," just like every other green plant eaten in mining camps. Only this "wild" plant grew in an empty lot down the street from my childhood home in Los Altos, California. While my father piqued my interest in wild edibles, it was my grandmother who inspired my life long interest in botany and foraging.

Every summer, Mom and Dad loaded their six kids in the big blue Suburban and drove north to Montana to be with Grandma Josie. She lived up Granite Creek, or "Granny Creek," as we knew it, near Virginia City, in southwest Montana. Dad flew home after two or three weeks to go back to work, and Mom spent the summer with all of us kids at Grandma's house.

Grandma didn't own a television, and radio reception was non-existent up the canyon. Videos and video games hadn't been invented yet. We spent our summers playing in the creek, walking through meadows and woods, and picnicking in the mountains. Grandma had taken a few classes on wild edible and medicinal plants, so we were always collecting along the way. We gathered and dried herbs, including peppermint, blue violets, or red clover for tea. We also gathered edible weeds like lambs quarters and purslane from her garden, dandelions from the pasture, and wild fruits as they came into season. Gooseberries and chokecherries thrived in patches along Granite Creek. Wild strawberries and dwarf huckleberries grew in the mountains.

Grandma Josie nurtured my interest in edible and medicinal plants and wilderness survival skills.

We moved to Montana not long after my father died of cancer, and I attended junior high and high school in Bozeman. I went to Grandma Josie's house just about every other weekend and as much as possible through the summers. Grandma and I often picked up roadkill deer. We brought them home and skinned and butchered them. We kept the good meat for ourselves and gave the scraps to the dogs.

I foraged for wild edible plants and hunted squirrels with sticks and rocks.

Grandma had a good library, where it was easy to get caught up in stories about the mountain men, the hunters and trappers who left civilization to eke out a living in the wilds of the early West.

I also discovered the writings of Tom Brown, Jr., where he described being tutored in wilderness survival and tracking skills by a displaced Apache Indian living in New Jersey. His stories fueled my imagination and my passion for learning to live in harmony with the land—to survive and thrive like a native with little more than my bare hands. That is what ultimately led me to bring a watch along to record how many spring beauty roots I could dig up in one hour with a digging stick.

While I was still in high school, Grandma Josie moved from Granite Creek, on one end of the Tobacco Root Mountains, to Pony, at the other end of the same range. I followed her, and as a young adult, I eventually bought land and built a house two blocks away from her's.

One hour of picking dwarf huckleberries (Vaccinium scoparium) yields about one cup of fruit.

The Tobacco Root Mountains were my backyard, and I saw little reason to go elsewhere. With fifty thousand acres of forests, meadows, mountains, and lakes to explore, I had the perfect playground to perfect my survival skills. I started close to home and gradually penetrated deeper and deeper into the hinterlands, slowly developing my skills at navigation, shelter building, fire-starting, and foraging.

From reading survival books, particularly Tom Brown's, I thought that a person should be able to survive and prosper anywhere. Brown implied that nature was like a banquet where a person could go out and feast. I was inspired to hone my skills until I could walk out the door with only a knife—or perhaps without it—and find everything in nature I needed to survive.

Foraging was by far the most challenging skill. Year after year I tried to survive by digging up roots, eating whatever greens or berries were in season, and by throwing sticks and rocks at small prey. I eventually learned to stay adequately sheltered and warm, but my foraging efforts were dismally unsuccessful. I didn't seem to get much of a return compared to the effort expended, so I started doing timed studies to quantify how much food I was harvesting per hour of effort expended.

Wild greens didn't count in these studies; while rich in nutrients they did little to satiate my appetite. I was going after food with substance—things like starchy roots, seeds, and delicious fruits. Strangely, it didn't matter what I harvested. I always came up with a similar result. An hour of determined effort consistently yielded a single cup of food. And that didn't include preparation time, such as carefully scrubbing and removing all the dirt from each little root in freezing cold mountain streams. My wild dinners were delicious, but clearly I was expending more calories than I obtained for my labors!

My timed studies ultimately taught me a lesson in geology. Like many of the little mountain chains that make up this portion of the Rocky Mountains, the Tobacco Roots were formed from a giant blob of molten magma that slowly rose up through the earth's crust about 73 to 78 million years ago, during the Late Cretaceous. The molten mass gradually cooled into mountains of granite as it pushed up through and accelerated the erosion of older sedimentary and metamorphic layers.

Granite makes spectacular mountains and scenery, but not particularly good soil for nurturing edible plants.

Unfortunately, granite makes poor soil. The crumbling, weathering rock breaks down into sand with few nutrients and almost no water-holding capacity. The mountains here may be covered in lush, green forests, and buried in snow for eight or nine months of every year, but it is a cold desert. There is nothing left after the snow finally melts into the soil; the ground is immediately dry. The forest understory consists of little more than dwarf huckleberries rooted in sand, with fruits so small that a person could starve to death while gorging on an insanely abundant patch.

The trees here grow so slowly that upon cutting a one inch-diameter sapling for a bow stave, I counted fifty years of growth rings! The soils don't just affect the plants, either. There are few rabbits in the Tobacco Roots, and the red squirrels are scarce and skinny. Grizzly bears sometimes venture north from Yellowstone National Park, but they don't stay in the Tobacco Roots. There isn't enough food to support them, either. In retrospect, this wasn't the most promising place to support a hobby, passion, and career of wilderness survival and foraging, but perhaps I am more stubbornly persistent than most people. When I finally explored beyond the Tobacco Roots, I discovered that the same or similar roots and berries grew three times as large in places with sedimentary or volcanic ash soils. I finally began to learn the secret of foraging in the Mountain West!

The granite soils and paucity of resources characteristic to my local mountains are recurrent throughout much of the Mountain West, from the Rockies to the Sierra Nevada and Cascade ranges. Yet, there are also pockets of amazing abundance. Some places are simply better to forage than others.

And yet, at its best, the West is inherently scarce. Plop yourself down at some random place and season, and it is unlikely that you will find much for food. But, if you do come to terms with the inherent scarcity, then you can begin to find and enjoy the pockets and bursts of abundance. As native peoples knew, you have to be in the right place at the right time to take advantage of each wild crop. Western tribes were nomadic for a reason. They walked from food source to food source, as each crop came into season throughout the year. I discovered

Nature is like a banquet, but in the West, the table is very long, and you have to be in the right place at the right time.

that nature truly is like a banquet, but in the West, the table is very long, and you have to be at the right place at the right time.

The funny thing is that, while I aspired to be as proficient in my survival skills as any native person, there weren't really any natives here. The Rocky Mountains were still swaddled in ice long after the first immigrants migrated across the Bering Land Bridge and spread out south and east across the continent. There are a few scattered archaeological sites from these Paleo Indians dating back to 12,000 or 13,000 years ago along the east slope of the Rockies. Native peoples lived near here about 9,400 years ago, after the mammoths were extinct and the ice was gone. They left behind an extensive complex of cooking pits and earth ovens, which were used for cooking small game and seeds. But climate change brought dramatically drier conditions 6,000 or 7,000 years ago, and the Northern Rockies were largely abandoned until the Kootenai, Salish, and Pend d'Oreille Indians migrated in from the north and west in the 1500s.

With the aid of Spanish horses in the 1600s, the Shoshone migrated into Montana from the Great Basin, hunting bison and becoming the dominant tribe in the area. Other tribes migrated into the area as European settlements on the east coast pushed Native Americans west in a domino effect that extended all the way to Montana. The Crow migrated in from the east in the 1600s, followed by the Blackfeet, Gros Ventre, and Assiniboine in the 1700s. With the acquisition of guns and horses, the Blackfeet became the dominant plains tribe in the 1700s.

The Shoshone were largely pushed back over the continental divide into Idaho, but still ventured into Montana hunting and foraging. By 1800, southwest Montana was a crossroads frequented by the Lemhi Shoshone, Bannock, Nez Perce, Flathead, Crow, Sioux, and Piegan Blackfeet, but nobody called it home and stayed here all year long.

The Northern Rockies were largely abandoned until the Kootenai, Salish, and Pend d'Oreille Indians migrated in from the north and west in the 1500s.

In 1805, Lewis and Clark spent four months ascending the

Missouri River within present-day Montana before encountering a single human being. Sacagawea's people, the Shoshone, were hungry enough that when one of the expedition's hunters shot and gutted a deer, a Shoshone man went straight for the gut pile, gobbling down the bloody entrails as quickly as he could squeeze the contents out the other end. Perhaps being as proficient as a native isn't quite as glamorous as I had imagined it to be!

As a now middle-aged man, I have to admit that I am not as hardcore as I once was, and my priorities in life have changed somewhat. I continue to hike and camp and occasionally push my skills to new levels, and I don't mind sleeping on hard ground. But I also appreciate a stable and diverse food supply that doesn't require an hour of labor for every cup-worth of harvest. I no longer feel like I am cheating if I bring food along on camping trips.

Oddly, I feel more native to the Rockies more now than ever, having dropped my beliefs and accepted the reality of it. Fifty-thousand acres is not enough to survive on when the worthwhile crops are

growing in another mountain range three hundred miles away! Here in the West, native peoples kept a mental map of what grew where and when it was in season, migrating hundreds of miles, sometimes more than a thousand miles, over the course of a year. In that spirit, I too have developed a mental map of food resources spanning several states.

Rather than trying to survive on dwarf huckleberries a mere eighth-inch in diameter, I know when and where to find the big ones, so that I can gorge myself like a bear until I can stand no more. I know when and where to dig up camas bulbs in the spring, and where to look for pine nuts in the fall. I have learned

Rather than trying to survive on dwarf huckleberries, I learned to go where the fruits are bigger.

the place and time to find morel mushrooms and tree mushrooms in the spring and king boletes in mid-summer. I know when and where I can shoot carp with primitive bows and arrows or lift trout out of the streams with my bare hands. Every year I fill in the map a little more, finding new stomping grounds to harvest, and sometimes learning new ways to harvest and prepare plants that I formerly dismissed.

Like my ancestry, many of the wild foods I harvest are not indigenous to this landscape. Everything from carp to goosefoot greens, plantain leaves, and purslane are all transplants from the Eurasian continent, and may not be truly "wild," so much as merely untamed, inhabiting niches around places of human habitation and disturbance. And in some cases, even our cultivated crops go feral, as asparagus, plums, apples, and black walnuts become naturalized in favorable landscapes. Where do we draw the line between that which belongs in a foraging book and that which doesn't? Should "wild" asparagus be eliminated because it isn't a wild plant at all, but a domestic crop that sometimes thrives on its own along ditch banks and roadsides? I don't think so. It's all part of nature's banquet and essential to foraging in the Mountain West.

Some friends and I were harvesting Nanking cherries from a bush planted along the sidewalk in front of the YMCA in Dillon, Montana. Several people stopped to ask us what we were picking. Some had watched the fruits ripen and fall to the ground for years, not knowing what they were. I was initially shocked that these people could not recognize a cherry. But more than anything, I realized that foraging isn't just something that happens on a wilderness survival trip; it is a way of life and a means to connect with the landscape wherever you are. If foraging cherries in town is a novel experience, then let's include it in the field guide to encourage more urban foraging.

My own mental map of food resources is hardly limited to wild foods in wild places. Traveling west, I know of an apricot tree in a parking lot in Missoula, Montana where the fruits splatter all over the ground because nobody picks them. I also pick blackberries

My mental map of "wild" food resources includes feral fruit trees and rich grocery store dumpsters across several states.

around Riverside Park in Spokane, Washington, and all kinds of fruits farther west. I even have favorite places to pick oranges, lemons, and dates down in Arizona and California. Wherever I travel, I constantly keep an eye out for something, anything, that might be good to forage, and add it to my mental map. I check that resource again each time I pass through, and sometimes try to coincide my travels with the ripening of the local crops.

This act of foraging is satisfying in more ways than just the thrill of eating fresh or wild foods. There is also the thrill of self-sufficiency, of being able to provide for oneself without being enslaved to the system of working a forty-hour week for money to exchange for food provided by multi-national corporations. The greater the independence you can achieve, the greater the thrill of freedom.

Following my grandmother's lead, I still butcher roadkill deer. It is my preferred method to fill the freezer. I always expected to become a hunter, but it hardly seems necessary when there are thousands of perfectly good carcasses laying on the side of the road every year. There is nothing better than free, organically grown venison, and I can obtain it any time of year, without a gun, and without competing with other hunters. Fortunately, it is now legal to pick up roadkill game in the state of Montana, so I can continue to utilize the resource and write about it, too.

Not surprisingly, my mental map of food resources includes a few dumpsters spread across several states.

Dumpster diving is increasingly common, and each recession recruits new dumpster divers when

I always expected to become a hunter, but it hardly seems necessary when there are thousands of perfectly good carcasses laying on the side of the road every year.

ordinary, dignified people go to new extremes to find ways to feed their families. Most people find jobs again, eventually, but that doesn't mean they stop dumpster diving. Why waste money on food, when perfectly good groceries can often be obtained for free? Being a forager is all about being an opportunist and going where the food is. It is what

It is my hope that the reader can become more native to this place, not as it was in the past, but as we know it today.

subsistence cultures all over the world have always done. Once initiated, it is hard to forget the taste of freedom from the corporate machine. And so, this foraging guide wouldn't be complete without a few basic instructions on dumpster diving, and other tips and tidbits for self-sufficiency.

It is my hope that you the reader can benefit from this book to become more native to this place, not as some romantic idea of the past, but as we know it today. This guide is intended to help you learn about and cultivate a deeper connection with the surrounding landscape in all its forms, from the edible weeds in your garden and the forgotten fruits down the street, to the truly wild foods in the backcountry, to the obscene wastes of corporate agriculture and food production. In getting educated about the resources and issues, we become aware and more empowered to make a positive and more sustainable difference in the world, and that is ultimately the most critical survival skill of all.

Thomas J. Elpel
Pony, Montana
March 1, 2014

There are at least fifty species of huckleberries and blueberries (*Vaccinium*) in the world, yet there is no need to identify every species or any species. Familiarize yourself with the broader pattern of variation among the genus, and you can feast on huckleberries from here to China!

Plant Identification 101

The human brain is a marvelous glob of grey goo, capable of accomplishing extraordinary tasks once it has been programmed to do so. For example, the brain can compute complex calculus equations once it has been properly programmed with years of addition and subtraction, multiplication and division, algebra, and finally calculus classes. Plant identification is somewhat similar, but a lot more fun!

To the beginner, nature can look kind of green, without many distinguishing characteristics, like a green blur seen from a car window. But learn some plant identification skills, and that green differentiates into an intricate mosaic of diverse individual plants. With time and experience, plants become so distinct that you will recognize them at high-

Plants often seem like a green blur to the beginner.

way speeds. The human brain is capable of sorting all that information while you are driving along, even while you are lost in thought or conversing with a fellow passenger. You may find, as I do, that any plant you don't know stands out as prominently as if there were a gigantic billboard with an arrow pointing right at it.

Botany in a Day introduces plant family patterns.

Acheiving a useful level of plant identification can happen very quickly with the aid of a few simple tricks, beginning with family patterns, as introduced through my book *Botany in a Day: The Patterns Method of Plant Identification* and my children's book, *Shanleya's Quest: A Botany Adventure for Kids Ages 9 to 99.*

For example, there are about 3,500 different species in the Mustard family, and all have 4 petals and 6 stamens (with 4 tall and 2 short), and all species are more-or-less edible. With that much information you could be hiking across the middle of Africa and encounter some plant you have never seen before, but recognize it as a member of the Mustard family. Try it. Does it taste good? If so, add it to a salad. Plant family patterns can be that simple. Read more on pages 39-41.

The Parsley family can be recognized by its distinctive umbrella-like "compound umbels," as shown on the facing page. The Parsley family includes some wonderful edible plants, but it also includes poison hemlock and water hemlock, the deadliest plants in North America. Find a plant with the Parsley family pattern and you know it is essential to identify the species before eating it.

Similar patterns exist for the Rose family, Aster family, and the many other plant families covered in *Botany in a Day* and *Shanleya's Quest.* Read about family patterns in the books, then play the *Shanleya's Quest Patterns in Plants Card Game* to memorize the patterns through games like Memory, Slap Flower, and Crazy Flowers. The books and game are available from **www.hopspress.com**.

Shanleya's Quest teaches family patterns in a fun story and card game.

Plant Family Patterns

Mustard Family

watercress
Nasturtium officinale

rockcress
Arabis confinis

dame's rocket
Hesperis matronalis

wallflower
Erysimum asperum

Parsley Family

western sweet cicely
Osmorhiza occidentalis

nineleaf biscuitroot
Lomatium triternatum

poison hemlock
Conium maculatum ☠

water hemlock
Cicuta douglasii ☠

Rose Family

wild rose
Rosa woodsii

wild strawberry
Fragaria virginiana

largeleaf avens
Geum macrophyllum

shrubby cinquefoil
Potentilla fruticosa

Aster Family

Nuttall's sunflower
Helianthus nuttallii

oxeye daisy
Chrysanthemum leucanthemum

blanket flower
Gaillardia aristata

alpine sunflower
Tetraneuris grandiflora

While *Botany in a Day* and *Shanleya's Quest* focus on plant family patterns, *Foraging the Mountain West* dives into greater detail on a fewer number of closely related plants.

For example, within the Rose family there are about 700 species of *Rubus* around the world, including raspberries, blackberries, salmonberries, thimbleberries, dewberries, cloudberries, and more.

One challenge to identifying individual species is that plants can be as variable as people. Consider, for example, Arnold Schwarzenegger, Nelson Mandela, and Sandra Bullock. Which one would you include in a field guide to identify humans? How would you know if you had the right species if your sample specimen is Danny DeVito and your field guide has a picture of Angelina Jolie? Plants can be that variable, and some species even have separate males and females.

It is easy to assume that each species is totally unique and readily definable, as if God made a raspberry and then a blackberry and so forth down the line, but biology is messy enough that even taxonomists frequently struggle to agree on what constitutes a species. Distinguishing one species from another can be like trying to distinguish Dallas, Texas from Fort Worth. The city centers are recognizably different, but the suburbs blend together such that it is nearly impossible to distinguish one city from the other without an arbitrary sign marking the boundary. Fortunately, such precision is often not necessary. Being able to narrow the identity down to Dallas-Fort Worth may be all that is needed to get your bearings.

As for raspberries and blackberries, each species of *Rubus* looks and tastes different, yet they all have a similar aggregrate fruit, as covered on pages 190-193. Some species are easy to recognize indepenently, while others can be challenging to distinguish from one another, even for professional botanists. Rather than identifying any one species of *Rubus*, it is more useful to learn the range of variation within the genus to be able to recognize all of them.

Being able to recognize the aggregate fruits common to all species of *Rubus* is more important than knowing which species this is.

For each plant entry covered in this book, we have covered the broadest patterns useful to the forager. In the case of "wild" asparagus, that is only one species, *Asparagus officinalis*. For milkweeds, we cover two species and urge the reader to approach other species with caution. In many cases, such as *Rubus*, the whole genus is treated as one unit. As for apples, we strayed outside the *Malus* genus to describe the many related, minaturized apple-like fruits that are found in the wilds or along city streets. And in the case of wild mustards, we feature a few key species but encourage the reader to learn the whole Mustard family pattern. Be sure to consult *Botany in a Day* for more useful whole-family patterns.

Mistaken Identity

The most common error in plant identification is our natural tendency to see what we want to see. Anyone who has navigated the backcountry with a topographic map has experienced this phenomenon. Matching the landscape to the map is skewed by the desire to find the answer. The answer may be found with great confidence, but that doesn't always make it right. Fortunately, precision is often not required, and it doesn't matter if you are on one side of a hill or another.

The most common error is our tendency to see what we want to see.

For example, I once ate what I thought was some type of wild strawberry, but it turned out to be a false strawberry (page 176). No big deal. The fruit was bland and not very interesting, although definitely not poisonous.

But sometimes accuracy does matter. For instance, edible milkweed shoots resemble and often grow among poisonous dogbane shoots. In such instances, we included photos and text to help the reader distinguish the plants from one another. Fortunately, the worst case scenario is usually not catastropic, as detailed on pages 59-60.

As you will see through the pages of this book, there are many poisonous plants in the world, but only a handful that are truly dangerous or deadly, such as water hemlock, poison hemlock, monkshood,

The most poisonous plant in the world may be a species of monkshood from India, *Aconitum ferox*. Our western monkshood, *A. columbianum*, as shown here, is much less toxic, but still not something to mess with.

and death camas. These toxic species could potentially be mistaken for edible plants, as detailed throughout the book. In this case, being wholly positive of your identification isn't enough. It is equally important to be correct. Fatalaties from dining on wild plants are exceedingly rare, but possible if one mistakes a deadly plant for an edible one.

Fortunately, it is easy to avoid an untimely demise with a little bit of commonsense. Make it a priority to learn to identify the most dangerous plants first. Study them thoroughly in this text and other field guides, and keep an eye out for them, then examine the live plants in detail.

In addition, avoid jumping too quickly from identification to foraging. If you have identified a plant using one book, then take the time to look up that plant in one or several other books to verify your findings and learn more about it. Come back and look at the same plant tomorrow. Are you still confident of your identification, or were you just seeing what you wanted to see?

Still sure of yourself? Try tasting a little bit. Does it taste good? Don't make yourself eat anything that doesn't taste right, just because you read that it was edible. You may have the wrong plant!

Hunter-gatherers typically worked only two or three hours per day.

Foraging Basics

Deer eat when hungry, rest when tired, or play when feeling frisky. Animals don't work and have jobs, and neither did our species for most of human history. The world was a grocery store where food was seasonably available and free for the taking. As observed by anthropologists, hunter-gatherers were the most leisured peoples on earth, typically working only two or three hours a day for subsistence.

Think about it. Land was free. A house could be thrown together from sticks off the ground. There were no mortgage payments. The utility bill consisted of picking up firewood. Running water could be found in the closest stream. There were no crops to plant, no weeds to pull, and no fences to build. People lived, more or less, like deer, foraging when hungry, sleeping when tired, and playing when frisky.

Hunter-gatherers were typically reluctant to adopt agriculture because farming was more work than foraging. But farming can support a larger population on less land, so agricultural societies ultimately displaced hunter-gatherer societies around the world.

Fortunately, we can reclaim our heritage by becoming foragers once again. And if you are feeling trapped by your job and expenses, then foraging could be the first step in regaining your freedom to live life more like a deer. From urban jungles to mountain tops, there is plenty of food that is free for the picking. The following guidelines will get you started.

Edible or Poisonous?

Browse through any field guide to so-called "edible" plants, and you will discover many serious warnings, such as these:

"The fruit is edible, but the leaves and seeds are poisonous."

"The leaves are toxic, however, the leaf stems may be eaten."

"The fleshy fruit is delicious, but the seeds contain cyanide."

"The starchy tuber is edible, however, the toxic green skin must be removed."

"Excess consumption of the raw nut could be fatal, but it is edible and choice when properly prepared."

"The spicy fruit is considered edible, but could cause nausea, vomiting, abdominal pain, and burning diarrhea if consumed in excess."

"The seed contains cyanide, but is edible when properly cooked."

Are you excited to start foraging now? Are you inspired to start identifying, harvesting, and eating these novel foods? What sounds most enticing? Everything listed above is true. Those are the facts. Here is the reality: in the order presented, the text is describing cherries, rhubarb, apples, potatoes, cashews, hot peppers, and lima beans.

Through the pages of this book we introduce wild foods that are as deadly as apples, as terrifying as potatoes, and as scary as lima beans. Moreover, in addition to introducing foods as toxic as cherries, we also provide instructions to prepare and eat some of the poisonous parts, in this case the cyanide-laden cherry pits.

That's the funny thing about poisonous plants—many of them are quite edible, and some of them are as delicious. For example, alfalfa sprouts contain canavanine, which the body mistakenly incorporates and utilizes to produce malfunctioning proteins. If you are afraid of alfalfa sprouts, then this book is probably not for you!

Granted, there are also poisonous plants that are not edible. Most

Death by apple is possible, but not very efficient.

taste bad enough that the forager is unlikely to consume enough to even become ill. And most poisonous plants are mild enough that it would take a heroic effort to die from them. And yes, there are also a few poisonous plants that are actually dangerous and potentially deadly. Therefore, each section of this book includes a realistic overview of the poisonous plants one might encounter while foraging.

Too Much of a Good Thing

Many wild foods are highly nutritious and edible when eaten in moderation, but like anything, too much of a good thing can be detrimental. For example, cherry pits and apple seeds contain amygdalin, also known as laetrile or Vitamin B17. Amygdalin is beneficial in small amounts, but it is also breaks down into toxic cyanide, as discussed on pages 196-197. However, the lethal dose for a normal, healthy adult would require hundreds of seeds, so there is little need for concern. Death by apple is possible, but not very efficient. Other plant constiuents often cited for concern are oxalic acid and nitrates.

Oxalic Acid: Many wild and cultivated plants contain oxalic acid or oxalates, including beet greens, chard, spinach, amaranth, goosefoot, purslane, sorrel and dock, woodsorrel, and rhubarb. In sufficient quantity, oxalic acid imparts a nice lemony-sour flavor. For example, a few sorrel leaves can liven up a bland salad.

In small doses, oxalic acid combines with calcium and other minerals, blocking nutrient uptake, and creating oxalate crystals, which may contribute towards kidney stones and gout. However, for poorly understood reasons, our bodies also produce oxalic acid, and in much greater quantities than what we consume in plants. One person is known to have died after consuming several bowls of woodsorrel soup, but his organs were already failing from poorly managed diabetes and a lifetime of drinking and smoking. Any normal, healthy adult would struggle to consume enough oxalic acid to cause measurable damage.

A bigger concern is needle-like calcium oxalate crystals, which can cause swelling, choking, and an intense burning sensation in the mouth and throat and permanently damage the liver and kidneys. Calcium oxalate crystals are found in rhubarb leaves, but are otherwise unlikely to be encountered in the Mountain West.

Nitrates: Many wild plants can accumulate nitrates from the soil when grown in soil enriched with excessive manure or chemical fertilizer, especially in extended dry conditions, without rain or irrigation. Nitrate accumulation can also occur in many cultivated plants under similar conditions, including spinach, corn, celery, broccoli, and wheat. Nitrates are not a concern for normal, healthy adults.

However, infants have immature digestive systems unable to handle nitrates. Caution is advised when feeding infants anything other than breast milk. Nitrates from wild or cultivated vegetables are not considered a threat to people over four months of age. Read more about oxalates and nitrates in John Kallas' excellent book, *Edible Wild Plants: Wild Foods from Dirt to Plate.*

Delicious, Palatable, or Acquired Taste?

Many wild foods are indisputably delicious the first time you try them. For example, huckleberries, goosefoot greens, or watercress are all quite tasty. Other foods may taste good or bad depending on when or where they are harvested or how they are prepared. And some wild foods take time to grow on a person.

For instance, if you haven't eaten dandelions then you may be disappointed when you try them, especially if you harvested dark green leaves late in summer. On the other hand, try dandelion leaves early in the spring when there is lots of moisture, plus cool days and cloudy weather to cut down the sun's intensity, and you might find that dandelion leaves are downright palatable. In fact, you may discover that dandelion leaves taste better and better over time, until even the dark leaves are delicious.

Americans generally prefer sweeter, blander foods than people from other parts of the world, which can be a disadvantage when learning about anything new. For example, the European mountain ash (*Sorbus aucuparia*) is planted as an ornamental tree in many towns across the Mountain West. The trees are somewhat related to apples, and if you look close at the fruit, you'll see that it somewhat resembles a miniaturized apple. The fruit is theoretically edible, and there are many books and websites that list it as edible. I've tried eating it many times, and it always tastes bitter and nasty. I've also added lots of sugar and made jam out of it, and it still tastes nasty.

Thus I was greatly surprised to meet a woman who ate mountain ash fruits like they were candy. This red-headed gypsy dancer grew up in Estonia where foraging was a way of life, rather than a mere hobby. She grew up eating mountain ash berries and couldn't get enough of them!

In that sense, whether or not a plant is "edible" can depend greatly on who is doing the eating. The wild foods chosen for this text are based on our personal biasis.

Photo by Matt Lavin

European mountain ash berries taste awful to me, but some people like the flavor.

Allergic Reactions

Poison ivy (*Toxicodendron rydbergii*) can be locally abundant in the West.

Allergies can vary significantly from person to person, and anyone with known allergies should be cautious when trying new foods or handling unfamiliar plants.

For example, many people, myself included, are not allergic to poison ivy, while others are mildly or severely allergic. I once led some friends through a poison ivy patch on walkabout in Arizona. I recognized the plant, but it was winter, there were no leaves on the plants, and we had to get through the canyon. It seemed like a minor concern at the time, but one of my friends is so allergic to poison ivy that she had to be hauled out of the wilderness a couple days later. She was covered in massive rashes that took weeks to heal.

She is so allergic to poison ivy that she even gets a rash from mango juice. Mangos, poison ivy, and cashews all belong to the Cashew family, and all three contain some amount of urushiol, the oil that causes contact dermatitis. She can eat mangos, but she is allergic to the juice on her skin.

Interestingly, some people who are allergice to poison ivy actually eat small amounts of the plant early in spring to build up immunity. Caution is advised, however, since an allergic reaction could cause the throat to swell shut and result in asphyxiation.

The bottom line is this: be cautious in exploring new foods if you have any known allergies. Go slow if you are allergic to anything from poison ivy to peanut butter, gluten, pollen, pine pitch, or pet dander, and remind your friends to do the same.

Silver sagebrush (*Artemisia cana*) produces lots of pollen. Be cautious when foraging if you have any known allergies.

Artificial Hazards

Foraging is a great way to obtain free, healthy, highly nutritious, totally organic, naturally grown foods—aside from incidental contamination from pesticides, road dust, or other artificial pollutants. Property with persistant and known toxins may be labeled, but it is often not, so it is important to apply

Potential toxins are not always this clearly marked.

some commonsense when foraging. Avoid grazing where there are inexplicable patches of bare ground, sickly looking plants, or significantly questionable waterways.

Also watch for signs of recent herbicide use, which is common along roads and trails, sometimes even in remote places. Green dye is often mixed with the herbicide to show the applicator what has been sprayed, but the color doesn't last long. However, herbicides have a strong chemical smell, somewhat like fertilizer, and the odor can linger for days.

Most herbicides are selective, killing broadleaf plants, but not grasses. Unhealthy, curly looking leaves and droopy tops are a potential

indicator for herbicides. Avoid foraging in areas that have been recently treated.

There is also some concern about foraging along busy roadways where plants might be contaminated by exhaust and other road toxins.

Nevertheless, most foragers harvest along all but the most obviously polluted roadsides, because that is frequently where the food is available and accessible. Realistically, most contaminated wild foods are probably no worse than anything purchased at the store.

The most toxic place I've ever foraged was a public apple orchard where the fruit had a white crust on it from all the pesticides!

This aspen tree absorbed herbicides that were applied to kill weeds on the ground.

Fair Game: Where to Forage

To pick or not to pick? That is the question. Foraging is easy when you own or rent a parcel of land with edible plants and mushrooms, but what happens beyond your own postage stamp property?

Wild and feral foods can be found just about anywhere: city parks, vacant lots, college campusus, cemetaries, along sidewalks and road-sides or rivers and streams, on public lands, and behind "No Trespassing" signs. How do you know what is and isn't fair game?

Most public property, such as federal and state land, is open to foraging, unless specified otherwise. Private property posted with threatening signs, on the other hand, is probably not a good place to forage. In between these extremes, there are many public-private spaces where the rules or courtesies are not so obvious.

Foraging often requires a judgement call based on the particular situation. For example, an apple tree with a branch overhanging a city sidewalk is generally considered fair game. In rare cases, however, individual landowners may have a different opinion. Partly it is a matter of courtesy. Picking from a branch that overhangs a solid wooden fence is probably okay. But if the fence allows the homeowner to watch you harvesting fruit from their living room, then it might be better to ask. Besides, they will likely let you pick a lot more fruit than what is merely available from the sidewalk. Be courteous and offer to rake up any fallen fruit while you are there.

Parking lots are a similar issue. I know of some nice orange, grape-fruit, and lemon trees at a conference center in an Arizona town, more than a thousand miles away from my Montana home. Strangely, I seem to pass by there once every few years when the citrus is ripe. Arriving after hours, I made a judgement call and decided it was okay to help myself. I did that several times before finally arriving during business hours, at which time I asked and was granted permission to pick the fruit.

In general, any neglected food source is a good candidate for foraging, but permission may be required. If the situation doesn't feel right for helping yourself, then ask away, and you will probably be rewarded.

Free grapefruit, oranges, and lemons harvested from a parking lot in Arizona.

National Parks

Foraging is not allowed in many of our national parks, but there are some exceptions. In Yellowstone National Park, for example, it is presently legal to harvest edible plants, mushrooms, and berries for one's own daily consumption. Visitors can forage in the park (away from high traffic areas) and utilize plants, mushrooms, and berries in meals, but cannot harvest extras to take home or sell. Park regulations can change at any time, so it is important to inquire about current rules before foraging. Also, some park rangers may not be aware of this provision, so check online or at the backcountry office for current regulations, and bring a copy along in case someone doubts you.

Picking serviceberries (*Amelanchier alnifolia*) in Glacier National Park.

The act of taking can be an act of giving.

Caretaker

Reduced to a dictionary definition, foraging is merely "the act of looking or searching for food or provisions," or "the acquisition of food by hunting, fishing, or the gathering of plant matter." Reduced to soulless words, the forager is merely a consumer and nature is a place to plunder, pillage, and take from without giving anything back.

Our culture teaches us that we are separate from nature. We draw lines on the map designating nature preserves that are partitioned off from zones of human habitation. At home or "in nature," our relationship with the planet is measured according to degrees of harm.

If we take only a little bit from nature, then nature can recover from the impact, and our actions are "sustainable." Taking too much is "unsustainable." We damage nature and therefore must allow sufficient time for nature to recover. The best that we can achieve in life is to minimize our impacts and become less bad.

Based on this worldview, the grizzly bear is also a mere consumer, raping and pillaging the environment for berries, roots, and salmon. But a grizzly bear eating and pooping huckleberries is planting the seeds and fertilizing them. A grizzly digging up glacier lilies is cultivating the soil to make more glacier lily habitat. And a grizzly dragging salmon out of the water is feeding insects, birds, mammals, and trees with nitrogen-rich carcasses. Like grizzly bears, we can be caretakers of the land, foraging and enriching the world as we go.

Foraging versus Farming

It is often said that there are too many people to justify foraging and "living off the land." That may be true, but as Sam Thayer points out in *The Forager's Harvest*, what do people "suppose that we live off of now?" Overall, farming produces more food per acre of land and can support a larger population, but only at the cost of eradicating whole ecosystems to re-purpose the land.

Farming can wipe out nearly every indigenous grass, herb, flower, shrub, tree, beetle, spider, wasp, bee, fly, moth, butterfly, mole, mouse, snake, rabbit, wren, hawk, elk, bison, lion, tiger, and bear—in order to grow one crop like soybeans. Meanwhile, rich soil built up through natural biodiversity is steadily lost to erosion, and puts the land at risk of desertification. As Miles Olson points out in *The Compassionate Hunter's Guidebook*, it is far more ecologically sustainable to leave the ecosystem intact and harvest its surplus.

For example, deer reproduce very quickly and can easily over populate without predators or hunters to keep their numbers in check. Harvesting a surplus deer is as sustainable as picking an apple off a tree. And harvesting a road-kill deer is as sustainable as gleaning a fallen apple from the ground. Either way, there is no loss to the ecosystem from this act of foraging.

Archery practice. Harvesting the surplus from an intact ecosystem is far more sustainable than plowing it under to grow crops.

On the other hand, there is the people population problem. There are already more than twice as many humans on the planet now than when I was born in 1967, and there are more all the time. Foraging alone cannot feed the masses, and therefore farming is required. In addition, it is theoretically more sustainable to eat vegetarian than to consume meat, which is more resource-intensive. For example, it takes about six pounds of corn to produce just one pound of beef, so it is more sustainable to forgo the steaks and just eat corn.

Sand dunes form at the edge of a farm field in Idaho.

While mathematically true, it doesn't account for the fact that beef is primarily raised on grass, not corn, and here in the Mountain West, most of the land isn't suitable for farming anyway. Plowing to plant supposedly eco-friendly crops is the surest way to make the soil dry up and blow away. It is far more ecologically appropriate to leave the native grasses and forbs in place and harvest the natural surplus, which is primarily meat.

Some people would counter that cows are horribly destructive in the West, and that the only ecological answer is to remove all livestock and return the land to its "natural" state. But ecologically, cows are largely indistinguishable from bison. The difference is that cattle are managed by humans and bison were managed by wolves.

Just as grizzly bears caretake the land they feed upon, so do bison and wolves. The threat of predation from wolves encourages bison to stick together in herds for security. The herds destroy anything in their path, trampling organic matter, seeds, and manure into the soil. In other words,

Bison grow the grass that feeds them.

they efficiently plant the seeds, fertilize them, and mulch the ground with organic matter to keep the seedlings from drying out. Then they move on to greener pastures, allowing new growth to flourish.

In contrast, cows managed by humans tend to scatter too widely to trample organic matter into the soil, and they linger too long, grazing the same tender grasses again and again. Organic matter doesn't get recycled into the soil and new seedlings dry out before they can establish. The space between the grass slowly widens and the land turns to desert. Rangelands that once supported thousands of animals now support only dozens. In this way, human management has created vast deserts all over the world, and we are now in the process of creating an American Sahara through our blindness and mismanagement.

Animal impact is required to plant seeds and fill in the bare ground.

Ironically, according to some estimates, our country produces no more cows now than there were bison to begin with, suggesting that all money and labor invested in ranching is meaningless. The meat would be there whether or not people went through all the trouble to build fences, put up hay, calve and medicate the animals, and make mortgage payments.

Mother Nature is pretty talented at building soil, optimizing biodiversity, and producing a sustainable surplus. Farming may be able to feed more people per acre of land, but most of

Grass seedlings emerge from a hoof print in the desert.

the Mountain West isn't suitable for farming. Ranching could be sustainable, but usually isn't, and isn't necessary, either. Therefore, foraging for the natural surplus of plant and animal foods is arguably the most productive and only truly sustainable way to manage most of our regional ecosystem.

Farms are still necessary, and there are niche environments where the climate is suitable for growing crops without fear of the soil blowing away. And as John Kallas points out in *Edible Wild Plants: Wild Foods from Dirt to Plate*, farming and foraging can compliment each other. Farming disturbs the soil and favors the growth of many wild plant foods such as goosefoot, amaranth, mustards, and mallow.

These "weeds" can be highly prolific and even out produce the cultivated crop, yet farmers expend vast time and resources to control the weeds through pulling, spraying, or plowing. But as Kallas points out, the weeds could be harvested by foragers for personal consumption or donated to the needy, or even sold as a cash crop.

The bottom line is that foraging shouldn't be dismissed as a viable and significant food source, and the environment could benefit from more foraging and less farming and ranching, especially here in the Mountain West.

Orache (*Atriplex hortensis*). Many farm weeds are choice edible plants.

Foraging for Awareness

Bison may grow their own grass and grizzly bears may plant their own huckleberries, but neither is committing a conscious act. Given adequate time, plant and animal species co-evolve to fit each ecological niche until Mother Nature unconsciously optimizes biological productivity. Adding or removing species can throw the natural balance out of whack, and it can take thousands or millions of years to again achieve an optimal balance. Unfortunately, we humans have been scrambling ecosystems all over the planet for a very long time, with devastating consequences. Now we are altering the entire planet through climate change. Our actions imply that we are not yet a conscious, self-aware species, or we would make different choices.

Ironically, self-awareness is rooted in environmental degradation. Our woes are self-inflicted, and the more we devastate the planet, the more we become conscious of our actions. Now we are in a race against time. We face the unsavory prospect of destabilizing the climate and losing half of all life on earth this century. The question is, can we become self-aware in time to halt the devastation, or do we need to destroy the entire planet in order to become aware enough to save it? As a prospective forager, you are on the front lines of consciousness, with the potential to cultivate awareness and make a difference.

Our track record isn't much different from cats and rats. In Hawaii, for example, cats and rats have wiped out about half of all native bird

Do we need to destroy the planet to become self-aware enough to save it?

species. Many species might have been able to adapt to cats or rats over long periods of time, but not both simultaneously. Nevertheless, Mother Nature will re-establish a sustainable equilibrium over time. The remaining bird species will adapt or evolve to live in a world of cats and rats, and they will also evolve to fill the ecological niches left vacant by extinct species. The process could take millions of years, but Mother Nature will figure it out.

Like cats and rats, our species has upset the balance in established ecosystems around the world. For example, aside from some over-sized eagles, the Maori people were the first serious predators to colonize New Zealand. Foraging for dinner was as easy as clubbing a flightless moa, and some species weighed up to five hundred pounds! They ate hundreds of thousands of them, and within a century all nine species of moa were nearly or entirely extinct. It was a great party while it lasted, but the Maori didn't leave much for their descendents, forcing them to work harder to survive.

Similar extinctions closely followed the arrival of human beings in places such as Australia, Tasmania, Madagascar, and North and South America. For example, 73 percent of all large mammals in North America went extinct shortly after the arrival of humankind at the end of the last ice age 11,500 years ago. The casualties included two species of peccary, the sloth, two types of llamas, an indigenous camel, horse, and moose, two species of deer, one species of antelope, two of musk oxen, the mastodon and mammoth, saber-toothed tigers, a giant beaver, a giant capybara, a tapir, the spectacled and short-faced bears, a cheetah, and an armadillo.

If our ancestors were conscious, sentient beings, then they would have stewarded their resources more wisely and to the betterment of all. Consider how easy life would be today if foraging consisted of clubbing five-hundred pound flightless birds! But our ancestors killed off all the easy animals, making life harder for future generations.

However, humans don't just evolve bio-

Building a fish trap. Killing off the megafauna made survival more challenging for those to follow.

logically, we also evolve technologically and culturally. Left with a world where all the easy game was gone, people had to innovate more sophisticated weapons and hunting strategies to harvest animals that were more cautious and fleet of foot. They also resorted to greater dependency on plant foods.

Over time, many native peoples also developed an ethic of stewardship, often characterized by rituals and taboos, that enabled them to achieve balance with the ecosystem, or what was left of it. In other words, stewardship wasn't necessarily a conscious act, but arguably an unconscious act that seemed to work. Many peoples developed sustainable lifeways that persisted until a new change came along, in this case agriculture.

Oddly, our species probably wouldn't have ever moved beyond the Stone Age if it were not for human-caused environmental degradation. Numerous anthropological studies have shown that hunter-gatherers typically work only two or three hours per day for subsistence, and Stone Age life can be astonishingly leisurely. Real estate is free, and a house can be built out of sticks lying around on the ground. There is no home mortgage, no interest, no taxes, and no need for a job. There

Using the fish trap to catch trout in a small stream. Hunter-gatherer cultures typically work two to three hours per day for subsistence.

are no crops to plant or weed or defend from animals, nor is there any need to process and store food in the fall to last all year long. Food and water are free for the taking, and paying the power bill is a matter of picking up sticks for firewood.

Our ancestors didn't generally embrace agriculture as an easier way to live, because it wasn't. Farming was more work and often resulted in poorer nutrition. But farming was sometimes necessary to ensure a more reliable food supply than could be obtained through foraging, and farming could support a larger population. Cultures that adopted farming grew in size and ultimately assimilated, displaced, or eradicated foraging cultures.

Continued population growth led to new and more challenging environmental problems, resulting in more complicated social and technical answers, but also a glacial emergence of awareness of ourselves and our actions. Quoting from my book *Roadmap to Reality—Consciousness, Worldviews, and the Blossoming of Human Spirit*:

> *The hunters who killed off the last flightless moa couldn't know it was the last one, and probably perceived the find as a moment of great luck or magic anyway. However, with written records and long distance communication, we are becoming aware of our actions, recognizing for the first time that we cannot just hunt wildlife, we also have to manage populations and habitat for sustainability.*
>
> *This awakening can be traced back to one moment more than any other: June 3, 1844. Feather collectors started hunting the great auk, a flightless seabird, in 1785 for stuffing pillows and mattresses. The industry systematically wiped out every auk on every island from Scotland to Iceland, until the day two fisherman, Jon Brandsson and Siguror Islefsson, killed the world's last breeding pair—and smashed their single egg—at Eldey Rock.*
>
> *Like an embarrassingly stupid criminal act, the event was recorded and added to our collective consciousness. The tragedy doesn't fade away, even though it happened more than one hundred fifty years ago.*
>
> *The demise of the great auk marked the beginning of a shift towards wildlife management. Human cultures started evaluating what it would take to maintain sustainable population levels. The result is that deer and dozens of other species that were once scarce from unlimited hunting are now abundant. Wildlife managers consciously adjust hunting policies and manage habitat to maintain desired population levels.*

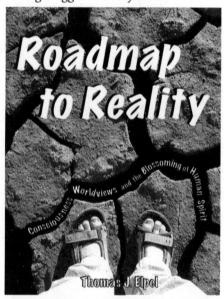

Roadmap to Reality. Environmental problems lead to increasingly complicated solutions and the gradual emergence of awareness of ourselves and our relationship to the planet.

Our overwhelming population growth has led to environmental catastrophes on an unprecedented scale. We are living witnesses to—and the cause of—the sixth great extinction event in earth's history. We are extracting so many fish from the oceans that they are predicted to be fished out by mid-century. Ocean acidification from rising carbon dioxide levels is already killing off coral reefs and mollusks. The Arctic icecap is melting much faster than predicted just a few years ago. And we are creating an American Sahara right here on our home turf, while the nation's attention is attuned to pizza, beer, and football. Yes, people will wake up to the issues eventually, but we are already losing hundreds, if not thousands of species to extinction every day. Will there be anything left to save by the time humanity figures it out?

The great irony of our cultural disconnect with nature is that most people don't know enough about their immediate environment to see it changing. If you don't know what lives outside your window, then how will you notice if it disappears? In fact, you can take a lush and forested ecosystem and completely denude it, and if it happens slowly enough, than nobody will notice any difference. For example, we all know the Middle East as desert, that's "normal." But much of the region was once a rich cedar forest, until people cut down the trees and ultimately created the desert. Pay attention to the bare ground between the plants, and you can watch the desertification advance right here in the Mountain West.

Harvesting camas bulbs. Foraging helps build first-hand awareness of the local environment.

And that's where foraging comes in. In the process of foraging, you learn to identify the plants and animals in your area, and you start to notice details like soil health. You will see shifting populations of plants and animals that other people are totally oblivious to. You will be on the front lines of consciousness, becoming aware of the biosphere, aware of your intimate connection to the biosphere, and therefore aware of yourself, or self-aware. Bring awareness to yourself, and you can share that awareness with others, and together we can make a difference.

Caretaker Guidelines

Different authors offer different rules for calculating how much of a wild food crop can be sustainably harvested, and how much should be left alone. For example, "Don't gather more than one-tenth of the available roots," or "Leave a quarter of the berries for the birds." However, rigid rules don't fit particularly well in nature. We don't go by any specific rules ourselves, and we won't pretend to have any magic numbers for you. The best we can do is to offer general guidelines.

Introduced/Invasive Species: Many plant and animal species have been introduced from distant lands. Some species integrate cohesively into the ecosystem and enhance biodiversity, while other species, such as knapweed or carp, become invasive, much like cats and rats introduced to tropical islands. A new species can become invasive when there are no natural checks-and-balances in the new environment, but also because the ecosystem itself is out of whack enough to favor invasive species. Knapweed, for example, is often blamed for displacing native species, which is true, but it typically thrives in landscapes that are desperately in need of the hoof impact of a thundering herd of bison or cows to restore balance. Eating invasive species is great, except that many are tough or more medicinal than edible.

Carp are an invasive species. Hunting them helps balance the ecosystem.

Burdock is one species that is mildly invasive and highly edible. The burrs can be a nuisance, so it is helpful to harvest and eat as many of the roots as possible. Carp are considered highly invasive and sometimes wildly abundant. Encouraging people to dine on carp is perhaps the best way to restore balance in the ecosystem. Teaching bears when and where to find carp could also help. Some species of crayfish are also introduced and invasive.

Introduced/Noninvasive Species: From broadleaf plaintain to pheasants, introduced species often contribute to biodiversity without becoming invasive, and many are highly edible. About half the salads and greens covered in this book are not native to this continent, including watercress, purslane, tumble mustard, and some species of goosefoot amaranth, dandelion, salsify, and clover. Siberian elms are invasive in some parts of the country, but can be a welcome addition to biodiversity in much of the Mountain West. Most introduced species can tolerate high levels of foraging and still maintain sustainable populations.

Annuals: Annuals are plants that typically complete their life cycle within a single growing season, like common sunflowers. They sprout, grow, flower, produce seed, and die before winter. Annuals include some introduced species discussed above, including goosefoot, amaranth, purslane, and most mustards. Being seed-dependent for survival, annuals typically produce a great number of seeds and thrive in disturbed soils where there is little competition from other plants. These plants are often highly prolific and can be grazed on to any extent.

Burdock is a biennial plant that produces a rosette of leaves the first year, then sends up a flowerstalk the following year.

Biennials: Biennials are plants that take two years to complete their life cycle. Most biennials are taprooted plants like carrots. The plants typically produce a basal rosette of leaves the first year and utilize solar energy to produce a big, starchy, sometimes edible root. The following year the plants utilize that stored energy to grow a flowering stalk and produce seeds. Biennials with edible leaves, stalks, or roots include salsify, burdock, and some species of thistles and dock. Most biennials can tolerate significant foraging, and they can easily be sustained through soil disturbance and by leaving a flowering stalk behind to go to seed. Be a gardener and caretaker. Do you want more or less of these species in the neighborhood? Manage them accordingly.

Milkweeds are perennial. Harvesting too many shoots can sap the root of energy needed for regrowth.

Perennials: Perennial plants are those that die back above ground, then sprout up from stored energy in the roots year after year. Some perennial plants with edible greens include asparagus, milkweed, stinging nettles, and most violets. Harvesting the leaves or tops, such as with stinging nettles, is highly sustainable unless repeated too frequently. Harvesting whole shoots, such as asparagus or milkweed, can adversely impact the plants by sapping energy needed for regrowth. Leave some shoots to grow, produce leaves, and re-energize the roots.

Consider spreading the seeds or transplanting the roots of desirable perennial plants to other suitable habitats. Milkweeds, for example, are critical to the survival of monarch butterflies, yet often sprayed as a weed along public roads. Observe the habitat characteristics, and watch for similar habitats to start new milkweed colonies.

Harvesting sego lily bulbs. Some bulbs can take years to mature, and dozens of bulbs to make a single meal.

Harvesting the roots of perennial plants is a bigger concern. Many species can take years to mature, including glacier lilies, spring beauties, camas, yellowbells, brodiaea, and bitterroots. Harvesting kills the entire plant, and it may take dozens or hundreds of specimens to make a single meal. Caution is advised here. Fortunately, many species benefit from the soil disturbance, and harvesting can counter intuitively increase the population. There are no good rules to go by. Observe and try to make constructive choices that will sustain or grow the population.

Fruits, Nuts, and other Seeds: Most plants reproduce primarily through seeds in some form or another. In many cases, plants co-evolved with animals to develop novel dispersal methods. For example, fleshy fruits entice animals to eat the fruits. The seeds are then dispersed and fertilized through their manure. The fruits are often produced in mass quantities and intended to be eaten. Being a caretaker can be as simple as eating wild fruits and crapping in the woods like a bear. Observe and use your own judgement to determine what to take and what to leave behind for the birds.

Cooking kills the seeds, of course, but in most cases the plants produce so many fruits, nuts, or seeds, that there is no harm in harvesting them in quantity. And except for invasive species, there is no harm in planting them in habitats where they might grow and thrive.

Caretaking is especially important as global warming changes the climate and alters habitat niches. In the Rocky Mountains, for example, wildflower season is more than a month longer than it was in the 1970s. Shifting conditions makes old habitat niches unsuitable and necessitates migration into new locations where plants might grow and thrive. As foragers and caretakers, it is our responsibility to help our plant friends find their way to new and suitable homes.

Distributed and fertilized in bear scat, young chokecherry seedlings offer the promise of bountiful harvests for another generation of foragers.

This salad includes goosefoot greens, mallow leaves, prickly lettuce, tumble mustard, and aster blossoms. It is good to know the individual plants covered in this book, yet even better to learn family patterns so that you can safely experiment with new plants and find delicious edibles wherever you go.

Salads and Greens

There are hundreds of wonderful edible plants throughout the Rocky Mountains and across the West. Some are great for salads, others good as cooked greens, and many are crossover plants, useful either way. It would be easy to fill an entire book like this with various salads and greens, listing, describing, and photographing each species. Speaking from the stomach, however, we prefer to allocate precious space to more substantial food that can actually fill the belly.

Besides, it isn't always necessary to know the species name for every edible plant. Sometimes just being able to recognize simple family patterns is enough to reveal hundreds

There are thousands of plants that are not really food, but are not poisonous either. I wouldn't sit down to a whole bowl of aster blossoms, but they make a nice garnish on a salad.

39

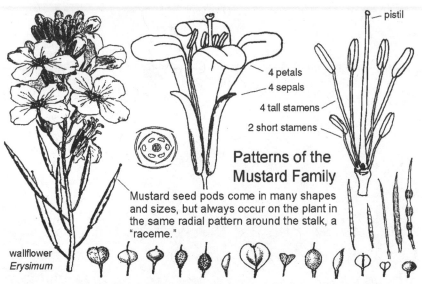

pistil

4 petals
4 sepals
4 tall stamens
2 short stamens

Patterns of the Mustard Family

Mustard seed pods come in many shapes and sizes, but always occur on the plant in the same radial pattern around the stalk, a "raceme."

wallflower
Erysimum

There are about 3,500 different species in the Mustard family, and all are more-or-less edible. Learn the patterns for identifying the mustard family, and you can recognize and use them anywhere in the world.

of edible plants all around you. For example, all 3,500 species in the Mustard family are more-or-less edible, although some taste better than others. If you can remember that the Mustard family has 4 petals and 6 stamens (with 4 tall and 2 short) then you have all the information you need to identify Mustard family plants anywhere in the world. This pattern is illustrated above and detailed in my book *Botany in a Day*.

All Mustard family plants are edible, although some taste better than others.

For this book, we've only included a couple of our favorite Mustard family plants: tumble mustard (*Sisymbrium altissimum*) and watercress (*Nasturtium officinale*). But learn a few such family patterns, especially the Mustard, Mint, Mallow, Violet, and Amaranth/Goosefoot families, plus the Chicory or Dandelion subfamily of the

Aster family, and you can build some amazing salads wherever you go. A few key plants from these families are included in this text. Refer to *Botany in a Day* and *Shanleya's Quest* to learn the rest.

In addition, many plant families are rich with species that are not really used as salad plants or greens, but are not poisonous either. For example, the Aster family includes a few plants to avoid, such as the many species of groundsels (*Senecio*) and *Arnica*, plus a few plants that are excessively aromatic, but about 19,000 other species that are either edible or at least nonpoisonous. Like aster blossoms, many of these plants are not suitable to build a salad, but they make a great garnish in modest amounts, contributing a unique color, texture, and flavor.

Harvesting Tips

Proper harvesting techniques can go a long way towards keeping your enthusiasm high and your salad bowl full. Nobody wants a salad of tough old leaves, or fare that is gritty, too bitter, or too astringent. A few quick tips will ensure that your wild salads are gourmet dining rather than survival roughage.

• Smaller, young leaves are more tender and tasty than larger, old leaves. Older leaves fill the collecting bag faster, but taste some before you start gathering. If the leaves are too tough or too strong tasting, then look for smaller, younger leaves.

• Greens taste best in spring when soil moisture is abundant, al-

We want prime wild salad greens, not survival roughage!

lowing for rapid growth. Leaves become tougher and stronger tasting through the summer, as the rains decline and the sun swings higher into the sky, blasting the plants with heat. Leaves grow slower, and become darker green, concentrating bitter or astringent properties until the plants are unpalatable.

• Extend the foraging season by searching out moist and shady growth spots, finding plants with large foliage as a probable indicator of good palatability. Tasty salad greens can be found mid-summer in cool, moist woods or even on the shady north side of a building.

• Plants that grow flat on the ground, like a dandelion, are often gritty around the outside. Pick from the center of the rosette to get the youngest, most tender, tastiest leaves with the least possible grit. Wash carefully to remove any remaining grit.

• As a plant matures, its stem has no need to expand anymore and so it strengthens itself by becoming woody and inedible. When gathering anything with a stem, harvest early in the season, before the stalk stiffens. If collecting later in the season, bend the stem to see where it is flexible and where it is rigid, and then cut the stem above the stiff part.

• Avoid gathering greens close to busy roads, where toxins may accumulate in the vegetation. Also avoid herbs that may have been sprayed by herbicides. The chemical smell is hard to miss while fresh. Curled over leaves and stems are also a sign that the vegetation has been sprayed.

• Avoid over-harvesting. Be reasonable. Don't pick so many leaves from one plant that it cannot recover quickly. Also leave enough plants to quickly regenerate the crop. However, many "weedy" plants, like dandelions, can be harvested en masse without ever endangering the population.

• Start timidly and expand from there. Don't try gorging on wild greens right off the bat, as it may kill your desire to become a forager at all. Try adding a few wild greens to a regular salad or sandwich for starters. Gradually add more greens until you reach your comfort level with wild flavors, then add more as you adapt to the new taste sensations over time.

• Try bringing a bottle of salad dressing (any favorite flavor) on foraging hikes and camping trips. A little dressing goes a long ways towards taming a bowl of wild greens. We find that our salad consumption goes way up whenever we bring salad dressing on a camping trip. It is also a great way to introduce wild greens to finicky kids. Add a familiar taste, such as ranch dressing, and maybe some cheese and garlic croutons, and they will dig right in as if it's their favorite fast food.

Water hemlock (*Cicuta* spp.) is the deadliest plant in North America.

Edible or Poisonous?

There are many "poisonous" plants, but only a few that could easily kill a person, especially water hemlock and poison hemlock. Learn to recognize these plants, and be cautious with anything that resembles them. Both plants belong to the Parsley family, easily recognized by the distinctive compound umbels (see page 12). To be on the safe side, avoid eating any Parsley family plants until you are highly confident with your identification skills.

Water hemlock (*Cicuta maculata, C. douglasii*) is the most poisonous plant in North America. Notice that the leaf above is divided into many smaller leaflets. In other Parsley family plants, the leaf veins end at the tip of the serration, but in water hemlock, some of the veins end at the cut, as shown in the detail photo.

Water hemlock leaflet. Notice how some veins end at the cut in the serration.

43

A dime-sized slice of water hemlock root, sometimes mistaken for a wild carrot, is potent enough to kill a healthy adult. The greens are highly toxic, too. Cows have enough body mass to be able to handle eating a few plants, but too much will kill them. People have much less body mass, so the lethal dose is lower, too. Water hemlock contains a neurotoxin that can cause convulsions. Victims can shred their own tongues before they die. Bottom line: leave it alone!

Poison hemlock (*Conium maculatum*) also has compound umbels with little white flowers, however, the leaf is much more fern-like. The plant often has reddish-purple spots on the hollow stalks. Poison hemlock can be prolific in neglected lots, such as woodsy city parks.

Poison hemlock is a nerve paralyzer. It basically puts the body to sleep, permanently. Poison hemlock juice was used to execute prisoners in ancient Greece, including Socrates in 399 B.C. He was instructed to walk around the room until his legs felt numb. Then he laid down and the numbness gradually moved up his body until it reached his heart and killed him. Bottom line: for anyone looking for a way out, this is the way to go. Otherwise, leave it alone!

Other poisonous plants of concern are introduced in the "Edible or Poisonous?" section of each chapter. Be sure to study these plants carefully. Otherwise, there are relatively few poisonous plants overall, and most of them are relatively harmless in modest doses. Be sensible when foraging, but not paranoid.

Poison hemlock (*Conium maculatum*) was used to execute Socrates.

Trees of the Elm family typically have slightly asymmetrical leaves.

Ulmus pumila
Elm Family

Siberian Elm: Invasive or Inviting?

Siberian elms were originally introduced and promoted for use in shelterbelts after the Dustbowl of the 1930s. I learned about the trees from an elderly man who planted a Siberian elm in his yard fifty years earlier and watered it until it grew into a great tree. What caught my attention was that seedlings were sprouting up all over his property, surviving without irrigation in a dry and dusty landscape with only 11.5 inches of annual precipitation. The new trees took root in the shade of his extensive collection of antique mining equipment. The old equipment served as a rainwater catchment system, concentrating runoff into small pockets throughout his property.

I transplanted some of these young Siberian elms from a clump growing under the dripline of his garage roof. I had grand visions of being able to transform eroding, arid grasslands into green forests. However, I found that the trees do require water in an arid environment—even if only a scrap of plywood to funnel rainwater to the roots.

Siberian elms are now considered invasive species in many parts of the country. While I believe that Siberian elms will continue to spread here in Montana, the natural niches are fairly limited, and I do not foresee the tree displacing other species in this environment. It remains, however, a tasty springtime treat.

Description, Habitat, and Range

Siberian elms, like most members of the Elm family, have simple, alternate, serrated leaves that are noticeably asymmetrical. The trees grow 50 to 60 feet tall, with rough, grey bark. They are wind-pollinated, with inconspicuous, bisexual flowers that bloom early in spring, releasing pollen to the wind before the leaves can obstruct it. The fruit matures as a

The trees fruit shortly before the leaves emerge in the spiring.

flat, oval-shaped winged seed called a *samara*. Siberian elms are resistant to Dutch elm disease that wiped out most of our native elms.

Siberian elms can be found along streets in towns from coast to coast, as well as naturalized in the countryside. The trees do not grow in permanently damp soil like cottonwoods, but often in drier soil just beyond the cottonwood zone.

Siberian elms may be confused with the Chinese elm (*U. parvifolia*), which isn't as cold hardy, but may be used similarly. Worldwide, there are about 20 species of *Ulmus*, including 7 species in North America. Any are worth experimenting with.

Immature samaras, ready to eat.

Grazing on Trees

Immature elm fruits are edible and delicious early in the spring, before the leaves pop out. Strip the samaras off by the handful; it takes only minutes to gather more than one can reasonably eat. The samaras are surprisingly sweet, and I find myself grazing while picking, grabbing handfuls and stuffing them in my mouth!

Samaras can be added to a salad or any other dish. Gather them as they first appear in spring. In two or three weeks, the samaras begin to dry out as a hard seed with a papery wing.

It is always fun mucking around in a swamp harvesting cattails.

Typha latifolia, T. angustifolia
Cattail Family

Cattails: Food from Swamp Muck

No other wild plant receives more praise for its dynamic usefulness than the cattail. The rhizomes are rich with starch and can be harvested as an abundant, life-sustaining food crop throughout the fall, winter, and spring, as long as the marsh isn't frozen solid. The young shoots and stalks are delicious on the spot, or added to any stir-fry. Spring and early summer give rise to cattail pollen flour and cattail-on-the-cob. The mature seedheads can be used as a fire starter and serve as great insulation for your moccasins. The leaves serve as excellent shingles for waterproofing a shelter. And if the sun gets to you in the cattail swamp, pluck a few leaves and weave a hat!

A nice pile of cattail stalks and rhizomes.

Description, Habitat, and Range

Cattails are easily identified by their long, slender, flat leaves and a seedhead that looks like a hot dog on a stick. The flowers start out as two hot dogs on a stick, with male flowers above and female flowers below. Male flowers produce pollen for about two weeks. This upper hot dog withers away and eventually drops off. The lower hot-dog-on-a-stick is comprised of thousands of female flowers, each producing a single seed. The little seeds and fluffy cattail down are carried away by the wind.

Sprouts emerge from a water-logged seedhead.

Worldwide there is 1 genus with 15 species, 4 of which are found spanning most of North America. The common cattail (*T. latifolia*) and narrowleaf cattail (*T. angustifolia*) are most frequently encountered, typically growing in murky, smelly, and possibly leech-infested swamps, or along the edges of slow-moving streams. All species can be used similarly.

Stalking the Wild Cattail Stalk

Cattails may be edible in a dozen different ways, but the premium food item is the tender, young stalks, served up in a salad or stir-fry, or eaten on the spot. Naturally, these tender stalks are best harvested in the spring, but a few young stalks can usually be found throughout the summer.

Green stalks can be harvested by reaching down, grabbing, and yanking upward. As long as you are in the swamp already, it usually makes sense to gather rhizomes and young shoots as well. To do that, follow the green stalk down with your hands into the swampy water and muck, then feel around for one or more rhizomes extending out horizontally from the main stem. Cattails spread by these rhizomes, and sometimes you can pull up a run a few feet long, with several green stalks attached.

To process, plunge the stalks and attached rhizomes in the swamp to wash off as much of the mud as possible. Next, cut the rhizomes off at the base of the stalk and set them aside for later. Peel off one or two

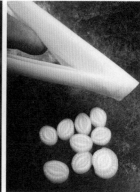

Peel off the outer layers of the cattail stalk to get to the tender and clean core. Then cut off the dirty base. Slice the tender portion of the stalk, then peel back additional layers to expose more of the tender core.

of the outer leaves to expose the leaf heart. Trim off the base of the stalk to ensure a clean, swamp-free surface on the end of the stalk. Then take a bite from the bottom. If it is tough, then pull off another leaf from each side and try again.

Eat your way up the tender stalk until it starts to get tough again, then pull off a leaf from both sides and continue eating. Repeat this process until you've pulled away all the outer leaves, exposing tender young leaves from inside the stalk. I usually eat several on the spot, then process and slice the rest for use in a salad or stir-fry. Cattail stalks are bland, slightly starchy with a hint of sweetness, and almost crisp — all exceptional qualities in a wild food. Strangely, Kris insists that the stalks are "spicy" and actually too spicy for him to enjoy, but he is an odd duck.

Harvesting cattail stalks is a rite of spring to me. Every year we take the local junior high kids out for three or four days of primitive living, survival, and nature aware-ness skills in mid-May, just as the leaves are popping open on the cottonwood trees. We wade into the swamps to gather cattails and then make a big salad on a slab of cottonwood bark. Cattail stalks serve as the bulk ingredient, mixed with dandelion leaves and flowers, a few tree mush-

Chopped cattail stalks, ready for a salad.

rooms, sometimes a few goosefoot greens, and usually some wild mustards.

I add croutons and ranch dressing to tame the flavor a bit for the kids, and everyone digs in and eats salad by the fistful. Yes, these are actual American teenagers, eating wild greens and liking it!

This spring salad on a slab of cottonwood bark includes cattail stalks, dandelion leaves and blossoms, garlic croutons, and ranch dressing.

The tender stalks are also delicious in a stir-fry. We often find quantities of morel mushrooms and tree mushrooms and add them all to our stir-fry on our junior high camping trip.

Rooting for Rhizomes

Cattails grow starchy horizontal underground stems called rhizomes that extend outward from a parent plant. Starch is stored in the rhizomes over winter and used to grow new plants in spring. Consequently, cattail rhizomes are packed with starch from fall until spring, but are largely depleted in summer, although worth trying on a survival outing any time. As described previously, let your fingers slide down the stalk to the base, then feel around underneath until you find the horizontal rhizome. Support it from underneath, and wiggle it out of the mud. You may not get the entire rhizome on your first few attempts, but keep working at it and

This delightful salad includes cattail stalks, mustard greens, dandelions, and blue camas flowers.

Cattail rhizomes are abundant and packed with starch. The young shoots are the best eating.

you'll be feasting in no time. Give the rhizome a quick wash right where you are standing and then heave it towards shore and move on to your next cattail. One person can gather four gallons or more of rhizomes per hour of effort, and that is more than most people would know what to do with.

For simplicity, roast the rhizomes on hot coals, then strip off the spongy outer skin and eat the slightly sweet, starchy core. Chew the starch out of the core and spit out the fibers. This is the most economical way to process the rhizomes, especially in primitive circumstances, even if not very elegant. When berries are available in the summer or fall, try eating berries and starchy cores together to add an interesting flavor.

Extracting Cattail Flour

A more refined product can be obtained by extracting cattail starch for flour. The work is pleasant enough, but not highly efficient. Expect about an hour of labor per cup of starch flour. First, peel the spongy outer layer off the fresh (uncooked) rhizomes to expose the starchy cores. Then, separate the starch from the fibers using one of the following three methods.

To extract starch with the **wet method**, shred and mash the cores in water, and discard the fibers. Allow the starch to settle to the bottom, and pour off the water. This method works well if you have a pot and warm water. Ideally, the starch should be allowed to settle overnight before pouring the water off. The wet starch can be blended with wheat flour to dry it out for immediate use. Note that the discarded water contains quite a bit of carbohydrates, which can be utilized as water for cooking stew or hot cereal.

To extract starch with the **dry method**, strip out and dry the starchy, fibrous cores, then pound and rub out the starch between two rocks, or with a rock on a flat log. Sam Thayer removes the starchy cores, cuts them into sections a quarter to a third of an inch long, then dries them, grinds them in a flourmill, and sifts out any remaining short fibers. Read *The Forager's Harvest* for details.

The **knife method**, as shown here, was developed by John Kallas, author of *Edible Wild Plants: Wild Foods from Dirt to Plate*. Remove the outer layer, then stroke the starchy core with the back of a knife. The starch gradually loosens and squeezes out of the fibers. This method is slightly faster than the other methods, and the starch can be used immediately. However, it appears to be more efficient to make a quick pass, dry the starch, then rub it between the hands to remove any remaining fibers. Cattail flour can be used on its own, except that it contains no gluten to hold it together. It works best mixed with an equal amount of wheat flour.

While it is pretty nifty to make cattail starch flour, it is hard to jus-

Squeeze the starch out of the fibrous core with the dull edge of a knife.

tify the labor cost. If you abandon the notion of bread as a staple food, then you'll enjoy the simple primitive past-time of "chewing the cud" with friends around the fire, swallowing the starch and spitting out the wads of fiber as you go.

Stir-Fried Shoots

Best found in late fall or early spring, but available in limited quantity any time of year, the young shoots or buds at the end of the rhizomes are starchy without the stringiness. Left alone, these shoots grow up to form new cattail stalks. To the forager, they are the premium cut off the rhizomes, delicious sliced and stir-fried. It is possible to gather a half-gallon or more of these starchy tips per hour of effort, typically a side-benefit to gathering the rhizomes.

Cattail on the Cob

In spring or early summer, depending on your latitude, green flowerheads from the cattails are steamed or boiled and eaten like corn on the cob. Male or female flowerheads are prepared this way, as long as they are still young and tender. They are especially delicious when slathered in butter. The male flowers

Roasting green cattail heads and wild veggie wraps on a hot rock. A sprinkling of male flowers on the rock helped prevent sticking and burning.

dry up and fall off shortly after pollination, while the female flowers quickly become fibrous and ultimately fuzzy as they mature into seed-heads. Therefore, the best time to gather the flower spikes is just before or during pollination. Fortunately, cattails do not flower all at the same time, so it is possible to find a few ripe cattails on the cob before and after most of the others bloom.

Pilfering the Pollen

Cattail pollen may be gathered and used as a flour additive or sprinkled into a stew for nutrition. Cattails are wind-pollinated and produce prodigious amounts of pollen. The pollen accumulates on the male flowers at the top of the stalk, then waits for a windy day to cast

Stripping male flowers off the cattail stalk. From our video, *Canoe Camping: On a Song and a Paddle.*

out to the neighboring female flowers. The primary challenge to gathering cattail pollen is 1) the season is very short, and 2) the wind often gets it first, especially when there are few trees around to shelter the swamps.

Shake or tap the flower stalks over the edge of a can or bucket to catch the pollen. Or make a specialized pollen-gathering bucket by cutting a hole in the side of a milk jug about half way up, then put the flower spike inside and shake it vigorously.

Rather than collecting just the pollen, a more practical alternative is to strip the male flowers off the stalk for use as pollen-rich meal. It can be mixed with flour for baking or added to stews and stir-fry.

As seen on the previous page, the male flowers can also be sprinkled on a hot rock or hot pan to prevent your food from sticking or burning.

Cattail Hats

If you are hanging out in the cattail swamp, why not also make a sun hat? Gather twenty to thirty long, green leaves. Learn how to weave a cattail hat or visor through the instructions in our video, volume four of *The Art of Nothing Wilderness Survival Video Series*, titled *Canoe Camping: On a Song and a Paddle*, available from **www.hopspress.com**.

It is easy to weave a visor-style hat from cattail leaves, so that you can be as stylish as me!

Wild asparagus is identical to cultivated asparagus, only free!

Asparagus officinalis
Asparagus Family (formerly in the Lily family)

Wild Asparagus: Defend your Territory

The greatest challenge to finding and harvesting wild asparagus is to get it before somebody else does! This is the same plant cultivated as a vegetable and sold in the stores. Asparagus has escaped cultivation in many places, growing wild along ditch banks and roadside fences throughout the West. It prefers soil that is moist, but not too wet, in protected places where it isn't likely to be trampled by livestock.

Description, Habitat, and Range

Asparagus is a perennial plant that, once established, sends up a fresh crop of delicious new spears every spring. It is harvested by scores of people who otherwise know nothing about real wild foods. These people heed the call of the foraging instinct to go find free food, but haven't always taken it to the next level to learn about other wild edibles. Ironically, milkweed (covered on the follow-

Asparagus can be identified by its tall, dead flower-stalks.

55

ing pages) tastes almost identical and colonizes similar habitat.

Wild asparagus is easily identified by the tall, almost fern-like flower stalks, which turn vibrant yellow in the fall and then light brown through the winter, often remaining erect to flag the location of fresh crop in the spring. Look at the base early in the spring, when daytime temperatures are regularly reaching the high 60s or low 70s, and you will likely find fresh new spears, or at least the stumps, where some other forager has already broken them off. Break the spears near the base just above the tough fibrous part. It will break naturally as you work your way up the stem. Be sure to leave at least one spear to mature into a flower stalk to produce the seeds that will help spread this wonderful plant.

Raw or Cooked?

Most people cook asparagus, simmering the spears in water until limp. That makes sense with asparagus that has been picked in a field, processed, rubber-banded, and shipped a thousand miles to a grocery store. But there is nothing quite as good as nibbling on fresh asparagus, eaten right on the spot. Cooking it seems like a tragic waste of perfectly good asparagus!

Taxonomic Note

Originally included in the Lily family, asparagus and its kin have been split out into their own family by modern taxonomists. See the latest edition of *Botany in a Day* for more information.

Asparagus is a treasure hunt. Sometimes you come home empty-handed, but sometimes with a nice bunch!

Milkweed shoots sprout up early in spring then bloom in mid-summer.

Asclepias speciosa, A. syriaca
Dogbane Family / Milkweed Subfamily

Milkweed: The Other Asparagus

Milkweed is a delightful find at any time of year. Like asparagus, tender green milkweed shoots are one of the first greens available in the spring. They also taste similar.

By midsummer, milkweed grows into a stout plant sporting a crown of astonishingly majestic, sweet-scented flowers. Monarch caterpillars can sometimes be found on the plants.

After pollination, the flowers begin to produce alien-looking pods, which can be cooked up as a delicious vegetable while still young. The older pods are full of seeds and fluff that is fun to scatter in the wind. In winter the dried, white stalks are useful for making cordage.

Pick milkweed shoots early in spring, ideally before the leaves spread out. This one is a little bit too mature.

Showy milkweed (*A. speciosa*) is common in the western states (shown here), while common milkweed (*A. syriaca*) is widespread in the eastern states.

Description, Habitat, and Range

Milkweeds are perennial, often growing in patches along rivers, roadside ditches, and meadows with a high water table. It has a slightly fuzzy greenish-red stalk with gray-tinged, opposite leaves. The stalks typically grow two to three feet tall. Break the stem and you will see the milky juice that gives the plant its name.

The flowers are bisexual and regular, typically grouped in clusters. There are 5 separate sepals and 5 united petals, plus a corona (different from the corolla) that looks like an extra set of petals. The corona consists of 5 hood-like forms facing towards the center of the flower. In the middle, there are 5 stamens fused to the ovary. The ovary is positioned superior. It consists of 2 mostly-separate carpels. Each carpel matures as a separate follicle, a pod-like dry fruit with a seam down one side. The pods are filled with numerous seeds with silky tufts.

Worldwide there are about 140 species of milkweed, including about 75 species in North America. Common milkweed (*A. syriaca*) is found in the eastern two-thirds of the continent, while the showy milkweed (*A. speciosa*) is the distinctive and common milkweed of the West. Other milkweeds should be approached with caution, as they may or may not be edible.

Watch Out for Dogbane

Dogbane (*Apocynum cannabinum*) is a poisonous plant that resembles milkweed, but the two can be easily distinguished from each other. Milkweed has a thick, hollow stalk that remains thick all the way up, while dogbane has a thinner, solid stalk that tapers more. Both have milky sap, but milkweed is much more sappy.

In addition, milkweed has slightly thicker, fuzzy leaves, that decrease in size up the stalk, while dogbane has thin, smooth leaves that are typically all the same size. Dogbane leaves also have less of a stem.

The fruit and flowers of these two plants bear no resemblance. They are easily distinguished when they conveniently grow next to each other for easy comparison. The possibility of confusion arises when dogbane is found alone, but as long as you check for hollow stalks, you'll never be tricked into eating the wrong one. These are the key differences in my mind, but you'll notice more ways to tell these two apart as you gain foraging experience.

Dogbane has deeper red stems and thinner leaves than milkweed.

Taxonomically, the Dogbane and Milkweed families were always known to be closely related, and now genetic evidence revealed that Milkweeds emerged from within the Dogbane family. Therefore, the former Milkweed family has been reclassified as a subfamily of the Dogbane family.

Tastes Like Asparagus

Milkweed stalks can be gathered early in the spring. In Montana the season starts in May and continues well into June. The stalks are best gathered when no more than a foot high, generally while the young leaves are more upright than horizontal. The stalks can be cooked like asparagus. Put them in a pan of water and simmer for fifteen or twenty minutes, then drain off the water. Coincidentally, the taste is very similar to asparagus. If the milkweed is bitter, then it may be the wrong species, or you may have mistakenly picked dogbane—in any case, do not eat it! If it isn't bitter, then go ahead and chow down.

In his popular 1962 book *Stalking the Wild Asparagus*, author Euell Gibbons wrote that the common milkweed (*A. syriaca*) "has an extremely bitter principle that seems to permeate every part of the plant." Putting the plant in cold water and bringing to a boil somehow set the bitterness and rendered it inedible. Gibbons established a method for removing the bitterness and rendering the milkweed edible, by covering it with boiling water for one minute, draining, and repeating the process at least three times. His cautions and instructions were subsequently copied by other authors into nearly every wild food book after that, but ap-

Milkweed is often found along rivers.

A handful of milkweed shoots, ready for the cooking pot.

parently nobody ever questioned Gibbons' claim that milkweeds were bitter and toxic. And who would want to mess with such a scary plant as that anyway? Many foragers, myself included, never got past the text to bother with the plant in the first place.

But fortunately, Sam Thayer, author of *The Forager's Harvest*, overcame his fears of milkweed enough to try Gibbons' method and found that milkweed was delicious. Eventually, he tried fewer changes of boiling water and even brought the milkweed to a boil starting in cold water, yet never found the bitter taste Gibbons described. He later fed milkweed to hundreds of people and never found even one person who described them as bitter. Thayer speculated that Gibbons must have either mistaken dogbane for milkweed, or possibly cooked a toxic milkweed, such as *A. amplexicaulis*.

In fact, milkweed shoots are a wonderful edible. Just place the milkweed in cold water and bring it to a boil for a few minutes until tender and then drain. The cooking water should not be consumed. We've eaten giant portions this way without ever feeling ill effect, except possibly too much satisfaction!

The next edible portion to emerge is the flower buds, which can be cooked just like the stalks. Snap off the buds and check to make sure there are no monarch butterfly caterpillars nesting in them. The buds

61

have a short season, blooming when summer really begins to heat up, and I'll often pass them by, preferring to wait until the young pods emerge.

Aliens for Dinner

Milkweed pods look like something out of a science fiction movie. It is easy to imagine that aliens might burst out of them and take over the world. But you can help defend the planet. These aliens are delicious! The season starts in mid-summer, and the pods are best gathered when they are shorter than your middle finger. Pods that are an inch or two long can be cooked as a potherb and eaten whole. Optionally, strip the husk and eat the tender silk raw as a trail nibble.

Venison steaks and milkweed pods. The pods are edible and delicious while still young and tender.

The pods snap off easily at the base. However, as with all milkweed gathering, be prepared to get plenty of sticky white sap on your fingers.

If a pod is too large and tough to eat, try peeling it open and cooking the immature silk. In a few weeks the season is over, and the pods become hard husks full of dry fluff. With practice, you will know when a pod or stalk has become too tough to gather and will float your fingers on past them.

Tie it Up

Milkweed, particularly *A. speciosa*, is an excellent fiber plant like its second cousin, the dogbane. It produces beautiful, white cordage or string. Instructions for making cordage are included in my book *Participating in Nature: Wilderness Survival and Primitive Living Skills.*

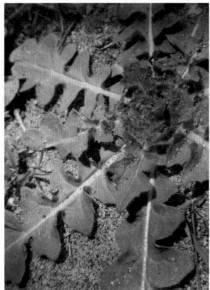

Tumble mustard appears as a green snowflake in early spring, maturing as a full-size plant in early summer.

Sisymbrium altissimum

Mustard Family

Tumble Mustard: Wild Broccoli

If you live in the West, then you've probably seen dried tumble-weeds rolling across the prairie in the wind, piling up along fences, or leaping out in front of your car on a windy day. There are several unrelated species of tumbleweeds, but the most common is tumble mustard. Tumble mustard is one of my favorite summer greens. The tops are delicious just before or during the bloom. They taste a lot like broccoli, but with a spicy mustard bite.

Description, Habitat, and Range

Tumbleweeds characterize the West, including the Old West that we see in Hollywood movies. However, tumbleweeds are not native to this country and didn't grow here back then. But once introduced, tumbleweeds found suitable habitat, and are continuing to spread with climate change and desertification across the West.

Look for a basal rosette of deeply indented, fuzzy leaves very early in the spring, followed by a flower stalk early in summer. Like all Mustard family plants, tumble mustard flowers have four petals with 6 stamens, 4 tall and 2 short. It grows on barren ground and disturbed soils throughout the West. Worldwide there are about 40 species, including

10 species in North America. Eared hedge mustard (*S. auriculatum*) of Texas is the only species native to this continent. All species of tumbleweed are edible, as are other plants of the Mustard family.

The immature flowerheads taste like broccoli, but with a mustard-like bite.

Broccoli with a Bite

Tumble mustard is in the same family as broccoli (*Brassica oleracea*), and shares a similar flavor, but with a peppery bite to the flavor. The effect could be described as a blend of broccoli and watercress. I love to nibble on the tender young flower stalks before the individual flowers spread apart and bloom. I eat only the tender tops off the tumble mustards, often adding a few tops to a salad to give it some zing. The leaves are also edible, especially early in the spring as a salad or potherb, but my favorite part is definitely the flower stalk.

Make your own Mustard!

Tumble mustard seeds are easy to collect and can be used to make mustard. Gather dry tumble mustards before they blow away and scatter their seeds to the wind. Smash and thrash the dried plants in a five-gallon bucket to beat out the seeds. Separate the larger debris by hand and winnow out the rest (see page 253), saving the seeds. Try sprouting the seeds like alfalfa sprouts, or grind the seeds to make mustard.

Grind the seeds with a flour grinder, spice grinder, or mortar and pestle. Add enough cold water and vinegar to make mustard paste. Let the mix stand overnight for the mustard chemicals to react with the water and vinegar, and it is ready to use.

Related Species

All Mustard family plants are edible, although palatability varies significantly from plant to plant. Every species smells and tastes different, yet there is a distinct underlying mustard-like smell common to most species. If I see a plant that might be a mustard, I often crush and smell the leaf for verification, without even looking at the flowers.

American wintercress (*Barbarea orthoceras*) typically grows in damp soil.

Wild mustards are usually too strong-tasting to form the bulk of a meal by themselves. However, they add great flavor to any salad, sandwich or stew. And while any part of the plant is edible, the root and stalk quickly turn woody, so we normally use only the leaves, flowers, and seeds.

All mustards have unique tastes and properties. We collected some pepperweed seeds (below) and tried sprouting them, but the seed coats swelled with water to become a mucilaginous mass like plantain (see page 98) or chia seeds. The slimy mass clogged the screen on the sprout jar and made it impossible to drain the seeds! However, the seeds worked fine for making mustard.

Clasping pepperweed (*Lepidium perfoliatum*). The seeds are easily gathered.

Dandelions are as easy to find as the lawn in your yard.

Taraxacum spp.
Aster Family / Chicory Subfamily

Dandelion: Supermarket of the Lawn

What do dandelions and cattails have in common? Cattails are sometimes referred to as the "supermarket of the swamp," since so

many different foods come from a single plant. Similarly, dandelions are like the "supermarket of the lawn," since so many unique foods come from this unassuming little plant.

When collecting dandelions, I sometimes put out separate dishes for the roots, root crowns, leaves, stems, flower buds, and flowers, each destined to become a different delectable dish. With a bit of culinary practice, dandelions can become everything from salad greens or cooked greens to fritters, garnishes, hors d'oeuvres, or even a substitute for coffee!

Dandelion lettuce.

Description, Habitat, and Range

Dandelions are as easy to recognize as weeds in the lawn. If you are unfamiliar with the leaves, then wait for the plants to bloom. The dandelion flowerhead is not a single flower, but a composite of many flowers. Each so-called "petal" is an individual flower with its own stamens and pistil!

While most Aster family plants, like sunflowers, have disk flowers in the middle and ray flowers around the perimeter, dandelions have only ray flowers, overlapping all the way to the center of the flowerhead. Dandelions are perennials with a slender, carrot-like taproot. Older dandelions may have multiple taproots.

Worldwide there are about 60 species of dandelions, including about 9

A—Two dandelion flowerstalks, one open and one closed. B—A single flower. C—One seed. D—The pitted disk or receptacle with a single seed and parachute.

native and introduced species in North America. Foragers are most likely to encounter *T. officinale* and *T. laevigatum*. Subspecies of the latter are listed in some books as a separate species, *T. erythrospermum*. All dandelions are equally edible.

Dandelion leaves can vary considerably, even on one plant.

Poisonous? Ha!

Dandelions are a great plant to begin a foraging career because almost everyone recognizes them already and they are insanely abundant. More than that, they are delicious when properly prepared.

Strangely, this was the first "poisonous" plant Kris learned. He was told, after being caught sucking on a dandelion stem in kindergarten, that the milky sap was deadly poisonous!

The only thing poisonous about dandelions is the chemicals applied to kill them. But in the attempt to create the perfect lawn, homeowners unwittingly create a yard as natural as Astroturf. As attitudes slowly evolve, people are beginning to perceive the perfect lawn as an artificial and chemical-laden concoction. It is a sign of poisoned groundwater and irresponsible use of fossil fuel resources, with likely consequences to insects, pets, and children.

Dandelions do not grow in the lawn by accident. Like any species, they only inhabit the specific ecological niches for which they are adapted. Rather than marring the perfect lawn, perhaps they are arguably balancing an impaired ecosystem. If your dandelions are out of control, then it might be sensible to pick up a book on organic lawn care. Or better yet, save money on groceries and lawn maintenance by harvesting the dandelions to feed your family!

Great on a Sandwich or in a Salad

The dandelion is often the first plant hopeful foragers try. It is rich in vitamins A, B, C, and E and the minerals iron, phosphorus, potassium and calcium. It has fiber content double and triple that of domestic greens. It is good for stimulating digestion, cleansing the liver, and purifying the blood. Its cure-all status is only matched by hydrogen gas or fusion power. You'll hear shouts from rooftops about its ability to replace coffee, be a hit garnish for salads, and end your dependency on store-bought salad. The cooked root will feed your family after the apocalypse, and daisy-chain necklaces of the flower stems will cure your mind from wishful thinking.

Dandelions are one of the first salad greens of spring and among the last available in fall. This October salad includes dandelions, spearmint, parsley, sage, and homegrown tomatoes.

You may rush to your lawn with great excitement, ripping up handfuls of leaves and stuffing them in your mouth, only to spit out the bitter greens in disgust. Many people give up on wild edibles at this point, dejectedly turning back to tasteless domestic foods, but it doesn't have to end that way.

All dandelions are bitter to some degree. This bitterness stimulates saliva and digestive fluids, useful to aid digestion and cleanse the liver. The trick is knowing when and where to gather dandelions to minimize the bitterness to palatable levels. With a little culinary know-how, you will soon include them among your favorite wild edibles.

Dandelions can be found growing anywhere, from cracks in a sun-baked sidewalk to the moist and shady sides of buildings; but when and where you gather them can make the difference between delight versus disdain. As John Kallas observed in *Wild Edible Plants*, bitterness among dandelions is largely a factor of sunlight and growth rate.

Dandelions exposed to intense heat and sunlight, such as an open field in the height of summer, are typically smaller and darker green, thus concentrating the bitters. Dandelions tend to develop larger, lighter, and less bitter leaves early in the spring when moisture is abundant. The season can be extended by searching out moist and shady growth spots, with large foliage as a probable indicator of good palatability. Large-leafed dandelions are often grown in greenhouses and sold at many health food stores.

That being said, don't imagine that dandelions will ever be as bland as domestic lettuce. It is a real plant with real flavor. Start by adding a few leaves to your sandwich at lunch. The bread and meat and cheese, or whatever you have, will tame the bitterness to a suitable level. Soon you will find your sandwich incomplete without them. As your

Gathering dandelion flowerheads.

palate adjusts to the flavor, you may eventually wonder why you ever thought them bitter in the first place! You will add them in greater and greater quantity to your sandwiches and salads, even enjoying straight dandelion leaves with a bit of salad dressing.

Although I prefer dandelions as a salad green, they can also be served as a potherb. Simmer in a large volume of water to cook out the bitterness, and leave the lid off to allow the bitter compounds to evaporate out.

Flowerheads Raw or Batter-Fried

Dandelion flowers are edible and pleasantly sweet. They're a joy to pick while milling around outside and tasty when popped straight in your mouth. The green bracts surrounding the flowerheads are edible but bitter, so you may want to avoid eating that part raw. The "petals"

Dipped dandelion flowerheads, into the frying pan.

can be pulled out and sprinkled as a decorative topping over salads, soup, or just about any other dish.

Try the batter-fried flowerheads as a fun way to introduce some nutrition into your kids' morning pancakes. Simply dip the blossoms, bracts and all, into the batter and fry them like little pancakes. They are delicious!

Dandelion Crowns

One delightful appetizer or side dish is the fried root crown. The crown is the tender, blanched portion above the root, but below the green leaves. Crowns vary from white to pink, and a

Dandelion fritter fun. Its a great way to introduce kids to wild foods.

little green is okay, too. If you dig up the whole dandelion, then the root crown is right in the middle. But it is a shame to waste the rest, so try making separate piles for roots, crowns, leaves, and flowers.

Trim away the brown root bark from the base of the crown and peel off the outer leaf stems, then rinse the root crowns to remove any lingering grit. Next, fry the crowns with a little salt and pepper in olive oil, bacon, or burger grease to make a tasty, mildly bitter treat. Dandelion crowns are best served hot.

Roots, Boiled or Roasted

Cleaned, chopped, and boiled dandelion roots make a passable meal, especially by survival standards, and it can be one of the more efficient root crops to gather. The roots are rich in inulin polysaccarides, which sweeten the longer they are cooked.

I like to dig dandelion roots out of the lawn for use as a coffee substitute. The roots should be washed, dried, and then slow roasted in the oven until dark in color and rich in aroma, but not

Dandelion crowns, ready for frying.

burned. Turn the oven to its lowest setting and leave the door open. The roasted roots can be ground into powder in a grinder, as shown, or ground on a stone metate. Steeped in hot water, roasted dandelion roots make a flavorful and healthy drink.

Roots, cleaned and ready to dry and roast.

Related Species

All plants from the Chicory or Dandelion subfamily of the Aster family have dandelion-like flowers, which are usually yellow. All have milky juice in the stems, all are bitter-tasting to some degree, and all are edible. Lettuce, endive, and chicory are included in this subfamily. Leave your garden lettuce to mature and bloom to see the flowers.

Grinding roasted dandelion roots for use as a coffee substitute.

71

Field sow thistle (*Sonchus arvensis*). Note the dandelion-like leaves and flowers.

Sonchus spp.
Aster Family / Chicory Subfamily

Sow Thistle: The Bigger Dandelion

Although the common name implies a relationship to thistles, sow thistles are better thought of as oversize dandelions, rather than true thistles, which are more closely related to artichokes.

Sow thistles are possibly the most prolific producer of white milky sap of all the dandelion kin. The plants were supposedly fed to lactating pigs in the hope that the milky plants would somehow stimulate greater milk production, but the relationship is suggestive only. The milky sap of the sow thistle is a type of latex, not remotely like milk. In spite of

The flowers mature into a dandelion-like seedhead, but with much more silky hair.

the abundant sap, the plants are less bitter than many dandelion-type greens and make an excellent wild food.

Description, Habitat, and Range

As with many other plants of the Aster family / Chicory subfamily, sow thistles have dandelion-like leaves, flowers, and milky sap. But in this case, the leaves have pointy, almost spine-like edges, and the stout flower stalks can grow to several feet high, with alternating leaves up the stem.

Field sow thistle (*S. arvensis*) is a perennial plant with spreading horizontal roots that help the plant spread to become a colony. Once established, this species can successfully compete with other perennial plants. Common sow thistle (*S. oleraceus*), spiny sow thistle (*S. asper*) and other sow thistle species are annuals that favor disturbed soils such as gardens, farm fields, construction sites, roadsides, and trails. All species prefer ample exposure, found up to the edge of a dense forest, but usually not in the forest itself.

Worldwide there are 50 to 60 species of *Sonchus*, with 5 species in North America, none of them Native. All may be used similarly.

Common sow thistle (*Sonchus oleraceus*).

Great in Stir-Fry

At first glance, sow thistles do not seem overly inviting as food, and since they are uncommon near my home, I saw no reason to seek them out. I tried my first sow thistle on a camping trip where there wasn't much else available for edible greenery. We had some nice cattail shoots chopped up in our stir-fry pan and needed a complimentary plant to add to the dish. Knowing that all plants of the Chicory subfamily are edible, I decided to chop the prickly leaves into the pan. It was delicious, and sow thistle quickly became one of my favorite wild greens. The flavor is very mildly bitter, entirely palatable, but with a unique sow thistle flavor that is difficult to describe. The young leaves can also be eaten raw or steamed, but stir-fry remains my personal favorite. Both John Kallas and Sam Thayer consider the steamed or boiled young stalks to be the best part of this plant, which we have not yet tried.

Related Species

Sow thistles are most easily confused with prickly lettuce (*Lactuca*). The key difference is that the bottom side of prickly lettuce leaves have spiny hairs along the midrib while sow thistle does not. Prickly lettuce is also edible, but I prefer sow thistles.

Canada prickly lettuce (*Lactuca canadensis*).

Salsify flowers burst forth from a tight wrapping of pointy bracts, then fold up after pollination to protect developing seeds. At maturity, the dandelion-like seedhead emerges, and the seeds blow away with the wind.

Tragopogon dubius
Aster Family / Chicory Subfamily

Salsify: A Forgotten Delicacy

The radiant flowers of the salsify invoke the image of the sun itself, borne in ephemeral form here on earth. Bursting forth from a tight wrapping of pointy bracts (modified leaves), the flowers light up vacant lots and undergrazed pastures like a thousand little suns. They seem to last forever, yet slowly wink out of existence and collapse back within their wrapping of bracts, only to burst forth again in a supernova of oversize dandelion-like seedheads, casting their essence to the winds. Harvest a piece of the sun to discover a stellar delicacy to light up your summer cuisine.

The blossom radiates like the sun.

It is challenging to find young salsify plants in a grassy field.

Description, Habitat, and Range

Salsify belongs to the Chicory or Dandelion subfamily of the Aster family and shares some similar characteristics, such as a (more-or-less) dandelion-like flower, milky sap, and an oversized version of the dandelion seedhead. However, salsify is distinct from other dandelions with its slender, grass-like leaves and the narrow, pointy bracts that radiate out beneath the flowerhead. Salsify typically thrives in disturbed soils and open fields with sufficient bare ground for the plant to take root.

Worldwide there are 100 to 150 species, including 9 species introduced to North America. Only 3 species are widespread here. All species are edible. *T. dubius* can be distinguished from others by its extra long bracts that extend beyond the flowerhead. Purple salsify (*T. porrifolius)* is cultivated as a root vegetable.

Steamed Flowerheads

Gather the unopened flowerheads along with an inch or so of the fast-growing peduncle, or tip of the flowerstem. You may not think of it until the salsify is in full bloom, but look around, you can usually find some stragglers that are still in the bud stage. Do not confuse them with old flowerheads, which close up while their seeds mature, then open up again to reveal a big, dandelion-like seedhead.

The cut or broken ends will ooze milky latex sap,

Steamed salsify flowerheads are delicious with a little butter and salt.

but it is harmless and easily washes off your hands. Try the flowerheads steamed or stir-fried. With a sprinkling of salt and a little butter, the flowerheads are a delectable treat!

For additional substance, try gathering the tender flower stalks before they bloom and serve as a side dish cooked like asparagus.

Mountain Oysters

Like carrots and other biennial, tap-rooted plants, salsify roots are tender and edible during the first year of growth, turning woody the second year. They are typically harvested in late summer, fall, or early in spring the following year, before they become too tough. Without a flower stalk, however, the rosette of grass-like leaves can be nearly impossible to spot. Look for the dead standing stalks as a clue, then crawl around on the ground looking for young plants to harvest.

Salsify has a carrot-like taproot which is edible before becoming too woody.

Here in the West, the roots are seldom much bigger than a pencil, but still add up quickly. It is often said that the cooked roots taste like oysters. In my opinion, the roots are flavorful, almost meaty, but with a slightly bitter aftertaste. At the very least, they are good forage for survival.

Goosefoots often have "goosefoot-shaped" leaves and a coat of waxy powder, mostly underneath, that may give the leaves a greenish-gray appearance.

Chenopodium album
Amaranth Family / Goosefoot Subfamily

Goosefoots: Better than Garden Greens

Growing a garden takes a dedicated effort to till the soil, add compost, plant seeds, keep it watered, and yank up all those pesky weeds that compete with your treasured garden greens. The funny thing is that the vast majority of those pesky weeds are edible, often delicious, and typically ready to eat long before the crop plants!

Many common garden weeds long ago adapted to the nitrogen-rich, disturbed soils associated with human-habitation and have traveled with humans ever since. The king of all garden weeds is goosefoot, also known as "lambs quarters," for its tendency to grow in sheep manure. I prefer to go by the name goosefoot, since that is a direct translation of the botanical name, *Cheno* (goose) *podium* (foot). The name comes from the shape of the leaves, which are often, but not always, goosefoot-shaped.

Description, Habitat, and Range

Goosefoots have alternate, slightly fleshy leaves covered with waxy powder that gives them a slightly grayish appearance. This natural wax helps prevent moisture loss, enabling the plants to survive in bare ground where rainwater may be quickly lost to runoff and evaporation.

The flowers are wind pollinated and therefore lack showy petals to attract insects. Basically, the flowers are small, obscure, green globs forming close to the main stem.

Goosefoot typically grows in disturbed, nitrogen-rich soils in barnyards, gardens, plowed fields, and construction sites across the continent—pretty much any place that has been colonized by our species.

Worldwide, there are about 150 species of *Chenopodium*, including about 50 species scattered across North America. *C. album*, long ago introduced from Eurasia, is now widespread. Many species of *Chenopodium* are edible, but palatability can vary considerably from one species to another. Epazote (*C. ambrosioides*, now reclassified as *Dysphania ambrosioides*) is highly aromatic, medicinal, and definitely not edible. Fortunately, it is not easily confused with *C. album*.

Easy to gather by the handful.

WEED: Wild Edible Enticing Dinner

Goosefoot is a classic WEED – a Wild Edible Enticing Dinner – often found growing in the garden and ready to eat before anything else. Goosefoots are related to spinach and taste somewhat similar. The greens can be substituted in any recipe that calls for spinach.

The leaves and tender young stalks are delicious eaten fresh in salads or on sandwiches. The greens can be cooked as a potherb, and Popeye would surely gain as much or more strength from goosefoot

Goosefoots are delicious added to a quiche like spinach.

79

greens than spinach. Unlike Popeye, however, I don't get too excited about a glob of cooked greens of any kind. It seems like a poor use for such a fine WEED.

But I do like goosefoot greens cooked in any other way that spinach might be used, such as in an omelet, quiche, or lasagna. Use any standard spinache recipe and substitute an equal amount of goosefoot greens for spinach.

Wild Quinoa?

Goosefoot is closely related to quinoa (*C. quinoa*), which was domesticated in South America more than 3,000 years ago. It has been grown ever

The seeds can be stripped off with a gloved hand or the whole plant can be picked and rattled around in a bucket to shake the seeds out.

since for its nutritious seeds that are typically cooked as hot cereal. It also appears as an ingredient in many food products. However, quinoa has a bitter, saponin-rich outer coating that is removed before the product is sold for food. Native peoples apparently first roasted the seeds to loosen the bitter seed coat, then placed the seeds in a stone basin and worked them with the soles of their feet to separate and pulverize the seed coat. The resulting dust was winnowed out of the grain on windy days.

Archaeologists in southwest Montana discovered that Paleo Indians were making extensive use of local goosefoot seeds some 9,400 years ago. However, that was before the introduction of *C. album*.

We sifted out the biggest junk with the aid of a nylon window screen.

They used a narrowleaf goosefoot instead (probably *C. leptophyllum*), which has a remarkably bitter seed. It is unclear whether the natives somehow processed away the seedcoat like quinoa, or just adapted to the bitter taste. A local archaeologist made a loaf of bread that included goosefoot seed flour, and it tasted awful. I also collected some narrowleaf goosefoot seeds, but later threw them out. They were just too overpowering for me!

The seeds of *C. album* are slightly less bitter, at least when eaten whole, and they are easy to harvest in quantity. Break the stalks and whack the whole plant upside down inside a bucket to shake the

We ran a batch of goosefoot seeds through the flour mill.

seeds loose. It doesn't take long to gather a gallon or two of seeds and fluff. Screen out the junk with a scrap of nylon window screen. Use a bungee cord to secure it tightly over a bucket or pot, then rub your harvest through the screen. The result is a fluffy pile of seeds and plant matter. Unfortunately, the seeds are too small and lightweight to effectively winnow them out from the surrounding "chaff." Fortunately, it isn't necessary, since the "chaff" is basically dried goosefoot greens,

Our goosefoot seed bread cooked well (left), but came out distinctly bitter tasting.

and not an indigestible cellulose associated with grass seeds.

These seedheads can be boiled like hot cereal, which is edible in the survival sense, but not remotely appealing in taste or texture. I have also added the seedheads, both dry and pre-cooked, into pancake batter, mixed 50/50 with Bisquick. It makes a decent pancake, but I'm not sure there is realistically much nutritional benefit, since the seeds largely pass through the digestive tract intact. It does facilitate a good bowel movement.

Breaking through the seed coat to facilitate digestion can be a bit of a challenge, especially with primitive means, but we ran a bunch of seedheads through the finest setting on a flour grinder. Then we made bread, substituting goosefoot "flour" for half of the whole wheat flour in the recipe. The loaf rose nearly as well as the control loaf made without goosefoot flour, but unfortunately, the bread was distinctly bitter tasting. Grinding made the seeds more digestible, but less edible! Kris slathered the bread in butter and honey and managed to eat a fair bit, but it ultimately made him vomit. Kallas suggests that the bitterness comes from saponins. Thayer, on the other hand, describes using cracked or ground goosefoot for hot cereal or flour substitute, and mentions nothing of bitterness. It is possible that plants grown in moister climates produce less bitter seeds. More research is needed!

Orache (*Atriplex hortensis*) is similar in appearance and just as tasty as goosefoot.

Edible Look Alike

The plant most likely to be confused with goosefoot is orache (*Atriplex hortensis*), an imported weed and garden green from Europe. Overall, the leaf shape, color, and texture of orache are quite similar to goosefoot, right down to the waxy powder on the leaves. Fortunately, orache is just as delicious as goosefoot, and maybe even better!

Like many other plants of the Goosefoot subfamily of the Amaranth family, orache is adapted to alkaline soils and has a mildy salty flavor. The plant is often grown as a garden green. Some cultivated varieties have reddish-purple leaves.

Non-edible Look Alikes

Ragweed (*Ambrosia*) and false ragweed (*Iva*) of the Aster family could potentially be mistaken for goosefoots, especially because they often grow in similar habitats. However, these plants tend to have fuzzy leaves, not waxy leaves like goosefoot.

This spring salad includes orache, goosefoot, dandelions, sowthistle, a touch of peppermint, parsley from our greenhouse, and a smattering of lilac blossoms for color.

Strawberry goosefoot (*C. capitatum*) has fleshy, bland-tasting berries.

Related Species

Strawberry goosefoot (*C. capitatum*) is unique among goosefoots because it develops a fleshy bright red berry around its seeds. The berries are bland and uninteresting compared to other berries, but easy to gather and highly nutritious. I gathered 3 1/2 quarts of berries in one hour.

Stinging nettles often grow in dense, well-defended patches.

Urtica dioica
Stinging Nettle Family

Stinging Nettles: Food that Bites Back

Stinging nettles have a memorable way of identifying themselves for you. Hairs underneath the leaves function as hypodermic needles to inject a mix of formic acid, serotonin, and histamine into the skin

as you brush against them. The reaction is typically mild—a few little white bumps or a pink rash. A little mud, cold water, or time is usually sufficient to take away the sting. Some individuals may experience an allergic reaction.

Stinging nettle is a crossover wild edible. No longer the exclusive domain of wild food-eating bush hippies, stinging nettle is widely known and very popular among health fanatics. Many people use stinging nettle like a dietary supplement, eating it on a regular basis to get their vitamins and minerals.

Nettles emerge in early spring.

Description, Habitat, and Range

Stinging nettles have simple, opposite, serrated leaves and typically hairy, square stems, reaching 3 to 7 feet tall. The tiny green or brownish flowers hang down in panicles from the leaf axils, with male and female flowers appearing on separate plants.

Stinging nettles typically grow in rich or damp soils, often along woodland trails and sometimes around a yard faucet. They are found throughout the U.S. and Canada. Once established, nettles spread via horizontal rhizomes, often forming dense patches.

Worldwide there are about 35 species of *Urtica*, with four species found in North America. Only *U. dioica* is widespread across the continent, with three subspecies that may vary signficantly in appearance. All species and subspecies are equally edible.

Careful Collecting

Ideally, nettles should be collected with gloves. Snip or break off the tender top of the plant, and put it in a bag or pot. Don't have gloves? Improvise with a plastic bag or a shirtsleeve for a glove. Optionally, nettles can be picked carefully by hand. The stingers are on the underside of the leaves. The stem hairs have no sting. Grab each stalk carefully by the stem and break it off. It is hard to avoid all of the stingers, but most can be avoided. This technique works well for picking a few stalks, but too many stings can make the fingers go numb for days or weeks. Gloves are highly recommended!

Cook like Spinach

Stinging nettles are often cooked and eaten like spinach. Cooking wilts the stinging hairs and neutralizes the chemicals, rendering the plants safe to eat. Collect only the tender young tops. Trim off any stiff stems and rinse off any dirt.

Cook whole leaves or chop the nettles before or after cooking. Simmer the nettles in a little bit of water in a pot for a few minutes until the leaves are wilted completely. For additional flavor, sauté like spinach

Nettle leaves trimmed off the stems.

with garlic, oil, and red pepper flakes and a sprinkle of lemon juice. If you like cooked spinach, then you will probably really enjoy stinging nettles.

Unfortunately, I really don't like cooked spinach; I prefer to eat it raw in salads and on sandwiches. Ditto for chard and goosefoot greens. Therefore, I am not a big fan of nettles cooked like spinach, but I do appreciate nettles for their nutritious qualities, and I

Stir-frying stinging nettles and porcupine meat with hot rocks on a slab of cottonwood bark. From our video, *Three Days at the River* in *The Art of Nothing Wilderness Survival Video Series.*

enjoy a few nettles chopped and added to an omelet.

In addition, nettles can easily be dried and crumbled for use as nutritive nettle flakes or to make a healthy tea. Nettles are high in vitamins A, C and D, the minerals calcium, iron, phosphorus, potassium, sodium, silica and albuminoids, and relatively high in protein. The

Dried nettle leaves can be used for a healthy tea, or crushed into flakes and added to meals.

plants should be harvested when young, before blooming, as they may accumulate nitrates or form calcium carbonate cystoliths as they continue to age.

Cut and dry the whole plants, then run a hand along the stems to strip off the dried leaves. Crush the leaves with your hands if you want smaller flakes.

I like to take nettle flakes along on winter camping trips when other greens are scarce. A spoonful of flakes contributes some essential vitamins and minerals to any meal.

Look online to find recipes for nettle soups, nettle pasta, nettle pesto, nettle smoothies, nettle tea, and more. Try some, and you too may get caught up in nettle mania!

Raw Nettles?

Yes, you can eat nettles raw. The trick is to fold the leaf in half, with the stinging hairs folded inside to reduce the chance of being stung in the mouth. A sting or two is usually tolerable. For additional insurance, fold the leaf and then roll and mash it really good between your fingers to crush the stingers. While this process is generally considered safe, there is always a remote chance of a severe allergic reaction that will cause your throat to swell shut. Caution is advised.

Alternative Uses

Medicinally, stinging nettles have been used as a rubifacient to irritate rheumatic joints by whipping the afflicted joints with the plant, or by applying crushed leaves as a poultice to stimulate healing activity in the area.

Stinging nettle stalks have strong fibers for making cordage. For instructions, please see *Participating in Nature: Wilderness Survival and Primitive Living Skills*.

Related Species

Three closely related genera in North America also have stinging hairs: *Hesperocnide*, *Laportea*, and *Urera*. These plants may be confused with stinging nettles, and fortunately, all are considered edible.

Participating in Nature. Learn how to make cordage from nettles, as well as dozens of other essential survival skills.

White clover (and other species) are widespread, found from the lawn in your yard up to high mountain meadows.

Trifolium repens, etc.
Pea Family / Pea Subfamily / Clover Tribe

White Clover: Always a Lucky Find

Have you ever spent a lazy afternoon searching the lawn for a four-leaf clover? These lucky clovers are as elusive as one's own lost childhood. Unfortunately, many people "mature" from looking for four-leafed clovers as kids to trying to poison them in the lawn as adults. Herbicides poison the clover, poison the groundwater, and poison our kids. Fortunately, clover never gives up, and it always comes back. It belongs in our lawns and parks, complementing the grasses and adding nitrogen to the soil.

Making friends with clovers is a good way to let go of some of the stresses of the adult world and recapture a bit of lost childhood. Even if you don't happen to find a four-leaf clover, at least you can make a salad. Get to know this delightful little friend, and you might start casually spreading clover seeds to lawns around the neighborhood.

Red clover, *Trifolium pratense.*

Description, Habitat, and Range

Clover is widely recognized but seldom noticed. You may be able to identify one in your yard, but have you ever stopped to look at it? Clovers have the familiar three-parted leaves that give the plant its botanical name, *Trifolium*. The flowerhead is not a single flower, but dozens of individual flowers, each with a banner, wings, and keel typical of Pea family flowers (see *Botany in a Day*). Wait until the flowers wilt away after pollination, and notice how each flower develops its own little pea pod. Various species of white clover can be found growing in backyard lawns, livestock pastures, and mountain meadows across the continent. Worldwide there are about 300 species of *Trifolium*, including about 90 species scattered across North America. This text applies primarily to *T. repens* and to white clovers in general, but all clovers can be experimented with.

Grazing on the Lawn

Clover gets surprisingly little press as an edible plant. In his 1970 book, *Wild Edible Plants of the Western United States*, Donald Kirk suggested soaking clover in saltwater to make it more digestible, which somehow didn't inspire me to try it. However, Linda Runyon turned me onto clover with her *Essential Wild Food Survival Guide*. Runyon lived semi-primitively without plumbing or electricity for thirteen years and foraged for the majority of her food. As a vegetarian, she was wholly dependent on wild edible plants for survival and sustenance, and clover was a major part of her diet.

Just as beans and grains can be combined to make a complete protein, so can clovers and grasses. Runyon mowed her clover patch with scissors and turned the harvest into numerous wondrous recipes. She even dried and ground clovers and grasses into flour. We often enjoy white clovers in wild salads, especially on wilderness walkabouts.

This summer salad includes clover leaves and blossoms, dandelion leaves, strawberry leaves, and yampa flowers.

Sheep sorrel (*Rumex acetosella*) often grows in patches, easily recognized by it's red tops and arrowhead-shaped leaves.

Rumex spp.
Buckwheat Family

Sorrel and Dock: Sour or Astringent?

If you like the lemony-sour taste of rhubarb (*Rheum*), then you will enjoy getting to know its relatives, the sorrels and docks (*Rumex*), all members of the Buckwheat family.

Sorrels and docks are all classified as species of *Rumex*, but to the forager, these are two different groups of plants. Sorrels have a lemony-sour taste, somewhat like rhubarb, while docks are typically more astringent, which is often described as a bitter flavor.

Get to know the different species of *Rumex* in your area and you will discover that some taste good in salad, some are useful as rhubarb substitutes, some are passable as cooked greens, and some don't quite taste like food at all. Your own taste buds are the best judge of palatability.

Veiny dock (*R. venosus*). The three-winged seeds are conspicuous and beautiful.

Description, Habitat, and Range

Sorrels and docks are highly variable in size and form, however many species somewhat resemble scaled-down rhubarb plants, but typically with much more narrow leaves.

Like all members of the Buckwheat family, sorrels and docks have distinctive nodes or joints where leaves attach to the flower stem. However, *Rumex* species typically have mostly basal leaves, and only a few leaves are attached to the flower stems.

The flowers are small lack any true petals. Instead, there are typically 5 or 6 petal-like sepals, of which the inner three sepals expand around the developing seed to create what looks like a three-winged seed, very similar to that produced by rhubarb. This three-winged seed may be the most distinctive trait of the genus.

Canaigre dock (*R. hymenosepalus*) leaf stems make a passable substitute for rhubarb.

Sorrels and docks are often found in disturbed, often gravelly soils, such as along roadsides and pathways, but also in pastures where there are sufficient patches of bare ground to take root.

Worldwide there are about 200 species of *Rumex*, with about 50 native and introduced species in North America, including a dozen or so species found in the Mountain West.

Almost Rhubarb

True rhubarb leaves are considered potentially toxic due to significant quantities of oxalic acid and anthraquinone glycosides, but the leaf stems are prized for use in pies and jams. Any species of *Rumex* with large, sour-tasting stems can be utilized as a passable substitute for rhubarb. I made a "rhubarb" pie on an extended walkabout along the Verde River in Arizona, using leaf stems from canaigre dock (*R. hymenosepalus*). I chopped the stems and cooked them with sugar in a pot, then added the filling to a pie shell of ashcake dough, and cooked the pie directly in the hot coals, as described in my book, *Participating in Nature*.

Salad Green or Potherb?

My grandmother grew French sorrel (*R. scutatus*) in her garden. It was a perennial plant that grew a never-ending crop of wonderful, lemony-sour leaves for our salads. In the wilds I have enjoyed the equally flavorful sheep sorrel (*R. acetosella*), pictured on page 90. My only complaint about this delightful wild sorrel is that it's little arrowhead-shaped leaves are so small, at least here in the arid Rocky Mountains, that it takes awhile to harvest enough to make a decent contribution to a salad.

The emerging leaves of the introduced patience dock (*R. patientia*) are wrapped in a mucilaginous sheath until they unfurl.

Most docks taste too bitter-astringent to be used in salads, beyond a few of the very youngest, most tender leaves. Best of all are the emerging leaves of the patience dock (*R. patienta*), which are wrapped in a mucilaginous (slimy) sheath until they unfurl. These emergent leaves are a tasty treat on the spot, or delicious added to a salad.

Otherwise, the docks are best known as potherbs. I am not overly fond of dock greens—or potherbs in general—but some people really love them.

Just don't expect to fill a pot with mature dock leaves and produce a palatable dish, or you may never try dock greens—or any other wild edible plant again. Boil or steam the tender young leaves for a flavorful mess of greens. If need be, consider diluting the flavor with other, comparatively bland greens.

Experiment with any species of *Rumex* in your area to discover your own favorite salad greens and potherbs.

Photo by Rosalee de la Forêt

Curly dock (*R. crispus*) has wavy leaf-edges. The plant turns rich orange-brown in the fall, due to the presence of tannic acid in the vegetation.

Tan your Tummy

Some species, especially curly dock (*Rumex crispus*), produce great quantities of little three-winged seeds that look temptingly like food. However, the orange-brown color of the stalk and winged seeds indicates a high tannic acid content, useful for tanning hides, but a little harsh on the stomach lining.

Tannins are common in plants and we consume them without ill effect, but usually in moderate amounts. Plants with excessive tannins typically taste bitter-astringent. The acids close off secretions, such as saliva, making the mouth feel dry.

Dock seeds can be used whole or ground in a flour mill and blended into recipes, but it is more for flavor than substance. Add salt to help tame the flavor. Encouraged by my friend Ronda, I made some tasty and addictive curly dock crackers. Optionally, try curly dock sprouts (page 118).

Fiber-rich curly dock crackers, made with equal parts flour and curly dock fluff, plus salt, baking powder, oil, and sour cream.

Viola adunca (left) and *V. canadensis* (right). Violets come in many colors, but always have 5 petals, with 2 petals up and 3 down. The bottom petal is usually larger and often decorated with stripes to guide in prospective pollinators.

Viola spp.
Violet Family

Violets: They're not all Purple

If you've seen a pansy in a flowerbed, then you can recognize a violet. Pansies, Johnny-jump-ups, and violets are all species of *Viola*. Wild violets are generally smaller than the ones you find in a flower bed, but similar, and of varying colors from white to yellow to blue and violet.

Description, Habitat, and Range

Violets are perennial plants with simple, basal leaves. The flowers are distinctive and slightly irregular with 5 petals (2 up and 3 down, with the lowest, center petal being the biggest). The fruit is a capsule, packed with little seeds, that splits open along three sides.

Violets are found in either moist or dry soil, in sun or shade, but typically only where there is little com-

Yellow prairie violet (*V. nuttallii*).

petition from other ground-level plants. Worldwide there are 400 to 500 species, including more than 100 species and hybrids found in North America. About 30 species are found in the West, with less than 10 widespread over the whole region.

In a Cup or a Bowl

I get a warm, fuzzy feeling when I find blue violets, such as *Viola adunca*, hidden in the grass, mostly because it was one of Grandma Josie's favorite herbs. She was ecstatic every time she found them, and she often collected and dried the leaves and flowers for tea. I pick violets once in awhile, but never harvest the quantities my grandmother did. While she used them for tea, I typically prefer to add a few leaves and flowers to a salad.

The introduced sweet violet (*V. odorata*) is widely naturalized.

North American violets are edible as salad greens or potherbs, although some species, notably yellow violets, tend to be laxative in excess. Most species in the Mountain West are too small enough to gather in quantity anyway. I often enjoy them as a trail nibble while hiking, or mix them into a salad with numerous other wild greens. My favorite violet is the Canadian violet (*V. canadensis*), which is substantially bigger and grows in thick patches, making it easy to gather.

Small white violet (*V. macloskeyi*). Violet leaves and flowers are a nice addition to any salad and also make a delicious, mild tea.

Violets are sometimes used in cancer cases as "blood purifiers" to aid the liver in eliminating waste from the blood, so there is no junk to feed to cancer cells. That's not a bad bonus in an artificial world where everything is a carcinogenic. They are also high in vitamins A and C.

Brook saxifrage grows in clumps along babbling mountain streams. It is easily identified by its rounded, scalloped leaves.

Saxifraga odontoloma
Saxifrage Family

Brook Saxifrage: Mountain Lettuce

Brook saxifrage is a soul of the mountains. The plants cling to thin soil and bare rocks along babbling mountain streams. Climb high in the mountains, where snowbanks persist until mid-summer, and you are sure to find some. It is one of the most abundant edible wild greens of the high country, and it tastes good, too. It is our favorite salad green in the mountains.

Description, Habitat, and Range

Brook saxifrage is easily recognized by its basal, rounded, scalloped leaves. The flowers are small, typically no more than a ¼ inch in diameter, with 5 separate petals.

Like most members of the Saxifrage family, the flower has an oblong-shaped ovary, consisting of 2 united carpels, with two styles. But all you really need are the leaves and habitat to confidently identify the plant.

Brook saxifrage flower.

Worldwide there are about 440 species of *Saxifraga*, including about 70 species in North America, mostly inhabiting alpine or sub-alpine habitats. Other species are also edible, but not necessarily as abundant or palatable as the brook saxifrage described here.

A simple wild salad featuring brook saxifrage leaves and wild aster blossoms.

Delightfully Tasteless

Brook saxifrage has several essential characteristics that make it an ideal wild salad green. First, it is often very abundant in an environment where there may be few good alternatives. Second, it is easy to identify. Third, it has a good texture for tearing, chewing, and swallowing. And fourth, the plant is nearly tasteless.

Being nearly tasteless may not seem like a great marketing pitch for an edible wild plant, but in foraging, a lack of flavor is often the most desirable flavor of all. Brook saxifrage can be very prolific and easy to gather in large quantities. That's the beauty of it. Gather a big bowl of nearly tasteless salad, then toss in anything else for flavor: a few wild onions, some dandelion leaves, blue violets, aster blossoms, and maybe some clover or strawberry leaves. If you spend much time in the high country, you will quickly become a big fan of this little plant!

Broadleaf plantain has a habit of showing up underfoot. Note the stringy veins.

Plantago major

Plantain Family

Plantain: White Man's Footsteps

It is always a thrill to find broadleaf plantain (*Plantago major*), especially in the Mountain West where good greens are often scarce or scrawny. Imported from Eurasia, Native Americans called the plant "white man's foot print," because it appeared wherever Europeans traveled.

Description, Habitat, and Range

Broadleaf plantain is a low-growing plant with deep, straight veins in the leaves and small, greenish flowers on a short stalk, forming seed capsules with a lid like a pot. It is the most widespread and easily recognized member of the genus. Learn this one, and you will recognize other species, too.

Plantain likes moist soil, yet does not compete well with taller plants. It is often found underfoot in moist, grazed pastures, and occasionally in the lawn or along a sidewalk. Worldwide there are 260 species of *Plantago* with 29 species across North America.

Narrowleaf plantain (*Plantago lanceolata*).

Plantain Leaves Raw, Cooked, or Batter-fried

Tender, young plantain leaves are edible raw—a nice addition to a salad or a sandwich—or cooked as a potherb. Older, larger leaves are less appealing due to the stringy veins, but plantain leaves of any age or size are delicious batter-fried. At home or on the trail, I like to mix

up a batter of flour, water, and a pinch of baking soda, then dip the leaves in the batter and fry them in oil. Salt and pepper are optional. As with most things fried in oil, batter-fried plantain leaves are a hit with both kids and adults. It is a nice way to introduce skeptics to the delights of wild foods.

Plantain leaves are delicious dipped in batter and fried in butter.

Psyllium Cereal

Plantain seeds are highly mucilaginous and swell up like slimy, translucent fish eggs when cooked. They are also quite nutritious, if you can find them in quantity. Using two fingers to strip the seed capsules and catch them in my hand, I harvested six cups of rough material in a one-hour study. It took twenty minutes to winnow out the chaff for a final yield of 1-3/4 cups. It might be more efficient to harvest the whole stalks, then rub them between your palms to loosen the seeds.

Psyllium (*Plantago psyllium*) is raised commercially for its seeds. The seeds are utilized as a bulk laxative in products like Metamucil®. The seed husks swell in water, resulting in softer, larger stools that are easier to pass. Unlike other laxatives, consuming plantain seeds in quantity doesn't lead to diarrhea. However, it is important to allow the seeds sufficient water and time to swell when cooking to make the seeds more digestible and less likely to take water from your body.

Medicinal Uses

Plantain leaves are commonly mashed and used as a poultice on bee stings. The leaves contain allantoin, useful for soothing skin sores, and fresh leaf can be secured over a wound like a bandage. A salve of plantain leaf tea, olive oil, and beeswax is greatly helpful for healing wounds and blisters.

Nodding thistle (*Carduus nutans*) and Canada thistle (*Cirsium arvense*).

Cirsium and *Carduus* spp.

Aster Family / Thistle Subfamily

Thistles: Food with a Security System

Plants have evolved many different strategies to survive in a world overrun by animals with insatiable appetites. Some plants are tough and woody. Others taste bad. Grasses grow from the base instead of the tip to recover more quickly from grazing. Thistles are armed with thousands of hair-like spines for defense. But did you ever stop to wonder why thistles require such armament to protect themselves?

Is it possible that all that armament might protect something tender and delicious? Thistles are often overlooked and underrated. Try some, and you might be surprised!

Bull thistle (*Cirsium vulgare*) has a similar flowerhead as nodding thistle, but a thinner, tougher stem.

Description, Habitat, and Range

Thistles belong to the Thistle Subfamily of the Aster Family, along with artichokes. Compare an artichoke and a thistle, and notice that they are very similar, except in size. Like other members of the Aster Family, these are composite flowers, with many very small flowers clustered together on a disk, which is typically protected by overlapping layers of bracts. In other words, those are not sepals surrounding the flowerhead, but modified leaves called bracts. With a cooked artichoke, you can peel the bracts off one at a time, dip them in butter and eat the tender base of each one. You could do the same thing with thistles, except that the bracts are too small to bother with.

The Thistle Subfamily includes several genera of plants that are commonly known as thistles. Worldwide there are about 100 species of *Carduus*, 250 species of *Cirsium* and a few species each of milk thistle (*Silybyum*) and Scotch thistle (*Onopordum*). Any species of thistle is worth experimentation, but this text focuses primarily on a handful of species of *Carduus* and *Cirsium*. Identify your local thistles and try out any of the processing methods described here to see what you can do with what you have.

Canada Thistle: Just Eat It! (*Cirsium arvense*)

Canada thistle or Canadian thistle (pictured on the opposite page) is native to Eurasia, where it is known as creeping thistle, due to its ability to spread via roots into dense patches. It is also known as cursed thistle, probably due to the fact that chopping the roots with a plow effectively spreads the thistle across a field. Thus, it is considered an invasive species across much of the globe, including in its native lands.

The name Canada thistle is an American misnomer. I would rather call it creeping thistle, but it is so well known by the erroneous name that it would just confuse the issue to change it now.

Canada thistle leaves are surprisingly good in a sandwhich or a salad... although it is better to crush the leaves first.

Canada thistle is widespread and locally abundant in plowed fields and pastures, as well as riparian areas and woodlands near places of human habitation. Wherever we go, it goes. Learn to recognize the plant in its adult form, and you may soon realize that smaller versions of it are everywhere, possibly including the spiny greens underfoot in your lawn.

Due to the comparatively small size of the leaves, stem, and flowerheads, it is impractical to peel away the spiny exterior to get at any part of the Canada thistle. Therefore, I say, "Just eat it!" Look for the youngest, most tender leaves, and try eating some plain. The leaves prickle the mouth a bit, but to a tolerable degree. Even better, fold and crush the leaf in your fingers to break down its spiny defenses before you eat it. Best of all, throw a few leaves on a sandwich or chop them in a salad, diluting the prickles with your other food, and you can easily forget the little spines are there!

The leaves are the primary food from the Canada thistle, a decent green in times and places when other greens may be wholly absent. In addition, the young flowerheads can be cooked like miniature artichokes, then eaten whole. I wouldn't call it a great wild food, but it is decent survival fare. Just be sure to gather them before flowering, since the heads quickly fill with fuzz after pollination.

Nodding Thistle: Wild Celery Delight (*Carduus nutans*)

It's like peeling a spiny banana.

The nodding thistle, pictured with the swallowtail butterfly on page 100, is also a native of Eurasia, as are all species of *Carduus*. It, too, is adapted to human ecology, favoring disturbed soils along roads, fields, building sites, and pastures where livestock have grazed too long in one spot, tramping out the competition. As the name implies, the flowerhead is often bent over.

Nodding thistles are a favorite trailside snack. The growing flower stalks are succulent and tasty before stiffening with age. Grasp the tip of a budding flower and bend the stalk over to see how much of the plant is still flexible and where it has al-

Tasty and tender inside.

ready become too woody. Give a quick chop with a knife to cut through the stalk, but not quite through the outer skin on the other side. The thistle top will flop over, hanging by one side. Carefully grab the exposed stem and gently pull it away from the main stem, effectively peeling the outer skin off one entire side of the thistle top. This peeled side of the stem provides a safe, spineless place for your fingers. The rest of the process is like peeling a spiny banana. Start at the cut end and peel the spiny skin off each side of the stem. Enjoy the crisp and

juicy stem as a delectable treat. It is a bit like eating a stalk of celery, but better.

Young flowerheads can be cooked like artichokes, but they are too big and spiny to eat them whole and too small to eat the individual bracts. However, thistle hearts taste just like artichoke hearts, just not quite as big. Break open the cooked heads and eat the heart out for a delicious survival dish. Just be sure to watch for beetle larvae, since several species of beetle have been introduced from the Old World to help control thistles and the related knapweeds (*Centaurea*) in the New World.

A gigantic tender thistle stalk.

Elk Thistle: Angel in the Sunlight (*Cirsium scariosum*)

Much like a glowing angel, elk thistles often glow in the sunlight reflected off their abundant silvery hairs and spines. These lovely thistles are native to the Rocky Mountains and typically found at higher elevations. The juicy stalks can be peeled and eaten similar to nodding thistles, but take care to avoid over harvesting.

Elk thistle is native here.

On one survival outing it occurred to me that the densely packed, immature clusters of flowerheads might have some potential as a food source as well. I found a flowerstalk where the buds were not yet fully differentiated and carved away the hairy spines on the outside to reveal a carbohydrate-rich core the size of a small pear. We sliced it up raw and passed it around. It was pretty dang good. The next one we put right on the fire to reduce the labor by burning off the hairs

and spines. The blackened flowerhead that came out of the fire was not only ready for eating, it was amazingly delicious!

Elk thistle roots are also edible and pretty good, chopped and added to a stew.

Roasted immature elk thistle heads make a delicious, black, starchy treat.

Photo by Matt Lavin

Plains prickly pear (*Opuntia polyacantha*) is common in the Rocky Mountains.

Opuntia spp.
Cactus Family

Prickly Pear Cactus: Good Green Slime

If you ever want a cool treat on a hot hike, consider trying prickly pear cactus. If you can get past the spines on the flower buds and pads, you will find a cool, succulent, slimy treat inside. Even the petals have a thick, succulent, slightly mucilaginous texture to them, once you safely separate them from the prickles. Prickly pears have a long history of use, especially in Mexico where the pads are known as "nopales" or "tunas." But make no mistake, the plants are not closely related to tuna fish, since the most recent common ancestor between the two lived about 1.6 billion years ago.

Description, Habitat, and Range

Big or small, prickly pear cacti have distinctive, pear-shaped pads dotted with a few big spines, each of which is surrounded by a cluster of much smaller, hair-like spines called glochids. Technically, the pads are swollen stems and the spines are modified leaves. The pads swell in wet weather then slowly dehydrate and shrivel in hot, dry weather. The pads snap off easily at the joints and can put down roots wherever they land.

Prickly pear cacti have showy flowers with numerous (more than ten) sepals, petals, and stamens. The ovary matures as a pulpy "berry"

with numerous seeds. The fruit is usually also covered with spines.

Prickly pear cacti inhabit arid landscapes and dry, south-facing slopes from Argentina to southern Canada. Worldwide there are about 200 species of *Opuntia*, and like all cacti, they are native to the New World. About 50 species occur north of Mexico, of which only 4 are found in

Prickly pear pads swell with moisture in wet weather. Compare the pad above to the shriveled pad on the previous page.

colder climates. Readers are most likely to encounter *O. polyacantha*, followed by *O. fragilis*, *O. macrorhiza*, and to the east, *O. humifusa*. All can be used similarly.

Penetrating the Pads

The Indian fig (*O. ficus-indica*) is widely cultivated for food and often sold in Mexican markets and sometimes grocery stores. Like a lot of wild plants, our local prickly pears are smaller and more challenging to process than their cousins from warmer climates. But if you practice on our native prickly pears, you will be better prepared to feast on larger species you might encounter in your travels.

I struggled for years to figure out how to safely get at the cactus flesh. Burning effectively removes the big spines, but not the clusters of hair-like glochids that surround the base of each spine. I also tried

Split the pad while still attached at the base, then scrape out the flesh.

many times to skin prickly pears with a knife, but typically ended up with little more than prickled fingers for my efforts. Interestingly, archaeological studies in the Southwest revealed that Native Americans ate many of the prickly hairs with their cacti. It is not as bad of an experience as you might imagine. Remove as many hairs as you can, and the few that are left will stick to your lips and the roof of your mouth. The irritation will go away after a few days and you might even grow used to it if you're eating cacti every day!

Alas, such desperate measures are not required. The easiest way to get the flesh is to slice a pad in half while it is still attached to the plant on the ground. Then scrape out the flesh from inside with a knife or spoon. There isn't a lot of meat inside our native prickly pear pads, but you will get something to work with. Amputate the pad when you are done operating on it, to reduce the amount of wounded flesh exposed to the sun, wind, insects, or disease.

The green slime from the pads is edible raw and acceptable when cooked, and very good with just a little sugar added. Also, prickly pear flesh helps thicken other recipes. For example, you can make a primitive "jelly" without pectin by adding prickly pear flesh to a pot of berries and sugar. The end product is slimy more than jelled, but thick enough to function as jelly.

Pads from larger prickly pears found in the southwest (and cultivated in many cities) are far easier to process. Most of the spines are

Have a heart... with prickles. Photographed near the Verde River in Arizona.

clustered around the perimeter of the pad, so I often trim away the edge first, then carve out each remaining cluster of spines and glochids. The remaining pad can be cut into slices, like slimy green beans, and added to a stew, stir-fry or other dish.

Buds and Flowers

Prickly pear buds and flowers are edible, tasty, and typically more tender and succulent than the pads. But like the pads, the challenge is to get past the defenses to the tasty treat inside. Again, it is easier to trim away the spines and glochids on the larger southern and cultivated varieties than on Rocky Mountain species. Preparing any quantity of buds or flowers from our little prickly pears may be impractical, but I often like to process one or two for a moist trailside nibble on a hot summer day.

Soothing for Sunburns

Have you ever used *Aloe vera* on a burn or sunburn? Like Aloe vera, cactus flesh osmotically draws out waste material from bruised, burned, or other injured tissues, while also soothing those tissues with its mucilaginous property. This mucilage is a complex sugar called a mucopolysaccharide. A similar mucopolysaccharide forms a "hydrogel" between your body's cells. This gel can dry out or break down after an injury, especially from a burn or sunburn. Your skin absorbs mucilage from the cactus pad to strengthen your own mucopolysaccharide gel.

Smear cactus slime over a burn and you will feel the mucilage quickly absorb into the skin. Add more each time your skin dries out, and you can quickly recover from even a pretty serious burn. Recovering from embarrassment may take longer, however, since cactus slime is a bit green and clumpy, and the sunburn remedy looks suspiciously like green snot wiped on your skin!

Slimy cactus pulp is just as effective at treating sunburn as *Aloe vera*.

Purslane is a low-growing plant with fat, succulent leaves and stems.

Portulaca oleracea

Purslane Family

Purslane: A Delicacy Underfoot

Purslane isn't found everywhere, but if you find any, you will likely find a bunch. Imported from the Old World, it largely follows human habitation, and is often found as a garden weed. But don't discard it! Purslane is a delicious and unusual wild plant with fat leaves and stems and a texture all its own. Purslane remains tender and tasty even into the fall season, when many other greens have become woody and tough.

Description, Habitat, and Range

Purslane is a low-growing plant with fat, succulent stems that typically lay flat on the ground. It has alternate leaves, which are fleshy and oval- to teardrop-shaped, varying from green to red, depending on water availability and exposure to heat and sunlight. The flowers are small and yellow, with 2 sepals and 5 petals, opening for only a few hours on sunny mornings. The ovary matures as a lidded capsule filled with little black seeds.

Originally native to marginal habitats from northern Africa to India, purslane likes bare ground and sandy-grainy soils. It is sometimes prolific as a garden weed, but also found along the edge of gravely driveways and sandy river beaches.

Worldwide there are 40 to 100 species of *Portulaca*, none of which are known to be poisonous. Most species bear little resemblance to purslane, such as moss rose (*P. grandiflora*), which is commonly cultivated as an ornamental flower. Moss rose is edible raw or cooked.

Purslane is rich in omega-3 fatty acids.

Grit-Free

Harvest purslane by pulling up whole plants or trimming off individual stems. On sandy beaches, it can be difficult to separate sand from vegetation, even with extensive washing. Chop off the base, where most of the grit clings, and clean the rest well, or look for grit-free purslane to begin with, and you have an amazing, highly nutritious new vegetable to expand your culinary repertoire. Purslane contains more omega-3 fatty acids, especially alpha-linolenic and eicosapentaenoic acids, than any other leafy vegetable.

Purslane is delicious fried in a little butter.

Salads, Sautee, or Stir-Fry

Purslane is widely prized as a leafy vegetable in the Old World. Raw purslane leaves, flowers, and small stems add a mildly sour taste and slightly crunchy texture to any salad. The whole plant, including larger stems, can be softened with cooking, which brings out a mildly mucilaginous texture. The plant can be cooked like spinach or chopped and added to soups and stews. Try sautéing purslane in butter for the full purslane experience or blend the chopped leaves and stems into a stir-fry. For a gourmet purslane dish, try it Greek-style, frying leaves and the stems with tomato, onion, garlic, oregano, and olive oil. Then add some feta cheese.

Adapted to desert environments, purslane alters its metabolism when stressed due to lack of water. It absorbs carbon dioxide during the cool of night, rather than the heat of the day. The CO_2 is converted to malic acid (the taste of sour apples) for the night and then converted to glucose through photosynthesis the following day. Thus, the leaves can contain ten times as much malic acid when harvested in early morning rather than late afternoon, resulting in a more tangy flavor.

Purslane Pickles

Purslane pickles are easy to make. Add purslane to a leftover jar of pickle juice and let it sit for a couple days. The salt and vinegar in the brine do the work. Just don't recycle the same pickle juice over and over, as it loses potency and could allow spoilage. Optionally, look up pickling recipes online and try anything that suits your fancy.

Purslane pickles are best eaten sooner, rather than later. Fresh purslane pickles have a nice, crisp texture. Left in the brine too long, the pickles become increasingly soggy.

Purslane pickles!

Watercress thrives in freshwater springs.

Nasturtium officinale
Mustard Family

Watercress: Available in Any Season

If you find watercress then you may be near a source of good drinking water. Watercress lives in the water and grows all year long. It can grow up to two feet tall in summer and then dies back to water level in winter. It cannot survive in any creek that freezes over in winter, but it does quite well close to a spring, where the water is still somewhat warm as it emerges from the ground. Follow the watercress upstream, and you will likely find the water source.

Description, Habitat, and Range

Watercress is an aquatic plant with pinnately divided leaves and typical mustard-type flowers with 4 petals and 6 stamens (4 tall + 2 short). Pull the plants up out of the water and you will see white, stringy roots.

Worldwide there are 5 species of *Nasturtium*, including 4 in North America, but most

The plants freeze off above water in winter, but emerge early in spring.

people will only encounter *N. offici-nale*. The plant was native to Europe and Asia, but has spread to waterways across North America.

In the botanical name-changing game, the plant has also been known as *N. microphyllum, Rorippa nasturtium-aquaticum, R. microphylla*, and *Sisymbrium nasturtium-aquaticum*. Unfortunately the current name *Nasturtium* remains confusing, because it is identical to the common name nasturtium, which refers to the popular, sprawling garden plant *Tropaeolum* from an entirely unrelated family!

Watercress has four-petaled flowers.

Soup or Salad?

Watercress is best picked above the water to reduce the labor of cleaning mud or grit out of the submerged stems and roots, but that is a worthwhile necessity in winter or early spring, before any other greens are available. If the water source is clean, or the plants are growing above water level, then it is safe to eat watercress raw. I like to nibble away as I collect some to take home. Watercress has a hot, peppery flavor, which is not usually overpowering, unless you eat the fresh, green seedpods. I usually eat watercress in a salad, but it also makes a really good soup with lots of watercress, some rice, and a little chicken bullion. Experiment to see what recipes you can come up with.

Tropical Fishing

One local warmspring has bathwater warm water, lots of watercress, and thousands of tropical fish. Originally household pets, the fish were long ago released into the warm water of this secret, natural garden, where they thrive even through Montana's frigid winters. It is a fun outing to catch fish to restock our aquarium.

A local warmsprings grows lots of watercress and thousands of tropical fish.

Watercress and other greens can be found in limited quantity in winter.

Greens in Winter: Foraging for Hope

Foraging begins as a hobby but often grows into a lifestyle. Buying groceries at the store becomes increasingly unsatisfying. Why pay good money for pesticide-laden, vitamin-deficient greens imported from thousands of miles away, when you can go out and pick fresh, healthy greens for free? By the end of a season of feastful foraging, you may feel a natural high that comes with self-sufficiency. But then winter comes, and what other choice do you have? You might resist, going as long as you can without greens at all, but ultimately you succumb to consumerism in debilitating defeat out of sheer hunger. Meekly, you push the shopping cart down the produce aisle at the grocery store looking for something green to eat.

Brooklime (Veronica americana) often grows intermingled with watercress.

Learn to identify brooklime in summer so that you can recognize it by its leaves under water in winter.

But all hope is not lost beneath that wintry blanket of snow. In addition to watercress (previous pages), there are a handful of additional wild and domestic greens that can be harvested all winter long—if you know where to look.

You can also plan ahead and blanch and freeze your summer's harvest, or even dry some greens. Best of all, you can grow your own winter greens with the aid of sprouting jars, cold frames, or an attached greenhouse. For the determined forager, here are a few tidbits for harvesting any time of year:

Brooklime (*Veronica americana*)

Like watercress, brooklime can be found growing beneath the surface of the water in winter. It is often found intermingled with watercress, but also grows more widespread, surviving in small streams where watercress does not. Brooklime is often bitter, so it is best mixed with other greens to tame it. In winter, it may be the only green available, but it can be tamed by adding a few leaves to a sandwich. Originally a member of the Figwort family, brooklime has been reclassified as part of the Plantain family.

Monkey Flower (*Mimulus spp.*)

Monkey flowers also grow in and under the water, usually in small mountain streams, and sometimes intermingled with brooklime. It is also bitter-tasting, but can be used sparingly in a salad or on a sandwich. Monkey flowers were traditionally considered part of the Figwort family, but genetic analysis reveals that the plants more properly belong in the Lopseed family.

Monkey flower (*Mimulus guttatus*).

Chickweed is small, but grows thickly.

Chickweed (*Stellaria media*)

Chickweed is another European species naturalized across North America. Patches of green chickweed can sometimes be found in otherwise mostly barren ground beneath conifers in winter, a nice accent to add to a sandwich or a salad. Chickweed is a member of the Pink family.

Ornamental Kale (*Brassica oleracea*-varieties)

Wild cabbage (*Brassica oleracea*) is a member of the Mustard family, native to the coasts of southern and western Europe. Through selective breeding of specialized starch storage organs on the plant, this one species was bred to become kohlrabi, kale, broccoli, cauliflower, collard greens, and brussels sprouts.

Kale is easy to grow as a garden vegetable, while multi-colored varieties are often grown in flowerbeds. All are edible. Some gardeners blanche and freeze kale at the end of the summer season. But kale often remains green beneath the snow, a tasty edible that can be scavenged from gardens and downtown flowerbeds through much of the winter. Use the leaves as a salad or sandwich green or cook as a potherb.

Preserving Wild Greens

After a season or two of gathering wild greens, you may find that winter brings a deep, craving hunger for a real meal of wild greens. But with a little forethought and effort, you can preserve your favorite greens for winter.

Blanche and Freeze: Blanching is a fancy word for boiling with the intent to freeze. Plunge the greens into boiling water for a few seconds, then remove and chill in ice water, drain, bag, and freeze. Blanching sets the color, but does not cook the greens all the way through, thus preserving the crisp texture. You can store as many greens as your freezer will hold! To keep your greens truly "green," recycle old bread bags for storage and avoid buying any new plastic baggies. Thaw your savory greens as needed through the winter, and use them as potherbs, steamed, or in a stir-fry.

Dandelion flakes can be added to any dish for a nutritious dash of summer.

Drying Greens: Drying is a great way to store herbs for tea, and it can be a good way to store greens for winter use. Dried greens can be added to stews or crumbled and spread as flakes over a variety of dishes. Dry greens in a food dehydrator or in racks and trays in warm shade. Allow air circulation to avoid spoilage, and avoid direct sunlight, which breaks down nutrients.

I often dry dandelion leaves as a by-product of root harvesting. Digging up a large pile of roots results in an even larger pile of leftover leaves, far more than I can use fresh. Therefore, I dry the leaves, crumble them, and store them for later. The crumbles are much like parsley flakes in size and appearance. For a small dose of dandelion flavor and a big dose of essential vitamins and minerals, add a sprinkle of dandelion flakes over any soup, stew, salad, stir-fry, or your mashed potatoes.

Sprouts: Garden in a Bottle

Growing sprouts is amazingly easy. To make a sprouting jar, cut a square of nylon window screen big enough to fit over a wide-mouth jar, and screw a metal ring on over the screen. Nylon screen can be salvaged from old windows, or purchased new from the hardware store. Make three or four sprouting jars to have sufficient capacity to grow nutrient packed greens all winter long.

You may have sprouting seeds in your cabinet already, such as lentils or other small legumes. Otherwise, purchase alfalfa seeds, radish seeds, mung beans, wheat, arugula seeds and more from your local organic food store, as well as through many garden catalogs. For the hardcore forager, harvest radish seeds from the garden, alfalfa seeds from a farm field, or wild seeds,

Sprouting jars are an easy way to keep low-cost organic greens on the menu all winter.

117

Sprouting wild curly dock seeds (*Rumex crispus*).

such as watercress or other types of mustard. I have also sprouted curly dock seeds.

Add a quarter cup of seeds to a sprouting jar, fill the jar with water and allow it to soak overnight. Then drain off the water, rinse and drain again. Rinse and drain twice a day to keep the sprouts moist and fresh. The seeds will sprout in two or three days, and they are immediately edible, although it is usually preferable to let them grow a little bigger.

A few sprouts are a great addition to sandwiches, salads, burritos, and even pancakes. Just be sure to eat some every day or the sprouts will quickly grow so thick in the jar that you won't be able to get them out without a knife! Most importantly, remember to keep the sprouts well-watered and well-drained to avoid spoilage.

Cold Frames

A cold frame is a low-budget greenhouse, consisting of an old window placed over a sturdy wooden or insulated box on the ground, preferably angled to face the sun. This mini-greenhouse keeps the temperature inside from 5 to 20 degrees warmer than the surrounding environment. Cold frames can be used to start seedlings earlier in the spring, or to extend the growing season for garden vegetables (and delicious weeds) into the fall.

For winter use, do a fall planting of winter-hardy greens like kale and chard, planting early enough to allow the plants to gain some size before cold weather hits.

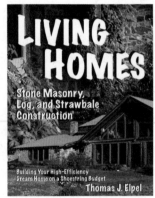

Living Homes. Our house features a large built-in greenhouse, which collects heat on sunny winter days and provides a limited amount of greens all winter long.

Attached Greenhouses

Many houses can be retrofitted with a greenhouse along a south wall. An attached greenhouse can serve as a great source of free food and free heat all winter long.

See my book *Living Homes: Stone Masonry, Log, and Strawbale Construction* for more information about building energy-efficient homes with attached greenhouses.

Sego lily bulbs (*Calochortus nuttallii*), harvested with a weeding tool.

Rooting Around

Salads and greens are wonderful, yet a person cannot live on mere lettuce. A real meal requires food with substance, such as some nice starchy potatoes and onions. Wouldn't it be great to trek into the wilds and dig up a satisfying meal?

There are a many wonderful edible root crops, including cattails, dandelions, and salsify, which were covered within the previous section. The plants covered in this section are harvested especially for their roots. In most cases, it is fairly labor intensive to forage enough of a root crop to make a meal, but it can be a worthwhile endeavor to try. The big issue is that digging up a plant for its starchy root usually kills the plant. Digging up enough roots to make an entire meal can require killing dozens of plants just to satisfy one's palate. Ultimately, we must face the question:

To Dig or Not to Dig?

Pick an apple and you leave behind the unharmed tree to produce a whole new crop. But harvest the root of a plant, and the plant is gone. Killing the plant eliminates it as a source of seed to propagate more of its kind. Moreover, each individual plant is as genetically unique as you or I, and harvesting it permanently removes it from the gene pool. In many cases, starchy bulbs take several years to reach maturity, and it may be necessary to harvest a hundred or more bulbs to make a single meal. By any reasonable standard, it is ethically wrong to play God with a digging stick, making decisions that permanently impact the gene pool.

On the other hand, native peoples sustainably harvested wild root crops for millennia without wiping them out. And while there are vastly more people alive today than in the past, few will ever forage for roots. Those who do are likely to harvest only enough for an occasional meal, rather than depending on wild roots as daily fodder. Harvesting roots can be a good deal of work. Anyone who unearths enough starchy roots for one meal is likely to be impressed that our ancestors had the diligence to follow through and harvest them en masse. Fora-

Calochortus elegans. Digging for root crops can loosen the soil and improve habitat to increase the population.

gering is a minor threat to wild plants, especially compared to habitat loss due to suburban sprawl, new roads, agriculture, and poor grazing practices.

Interestingly, foraging can actually improve habitat and expand the wild food supply. In at least some cases, digging up wild root crops helps break up hard soil or tightly thatched ground cover, making it possible for new seedlings to germinate and thrive. We are accustomed to believing that everything we do has a negative impact on the environment, and that the best we can hope for is to be less bad. But Larry Olsen, author of the 1969 classic, *Outdoor Survival Skills*, discovered otherwise. As told in an interview:

> "I used to take my classes out to a place called West Mountain and there was a hillside out there that was just lush with biscuit root and sego lilies and fritillary bulbs. There were seven or eight different bulbs you could dig out there. And I would take a class of thirty to forty people at a time, and sometimes three or four sections of those and have a hundred people out there, all with their digging sticks, digging on that hillside. I pretty well let them randomly go through but always with the caution that if you are digging a little patch here, always leave two or three. Don't dig all of them; leave some of them. They were pretty respectful for that. Then I began to notice after the third year of doing this using this same area that every year they'd come up

just as thick or thicker. And by the third year we began to notice that the bulbs were bigger and better. And after eight years of working that same ground every spring, we were getting that little thing they call the Indian potato that was usually about as big around as the joint in your little finger, they were now as big as onion bulbs."

Without controlled tests, it is hard to know which crops would benefit and increase in number from the act of harvesting, versus which crops might be susceptible to overharvesting. There are many variables to consider, such as different species, climates, soil types, and different levels of harvesting pressure. The bottom line is, be a caretaker of the land. Avoid over-harvesting, and observe your foraging grounds for trends toward lesser or greater numbers of plants.

Tools for Digging

There are many good tools available for digging root crops, each with its own advantages and disadvantages, including:

Digging Stick: It is nice to be prepared for anything, but also highly unrealistic, especially when it comes to foraging. As a forager, you are gauranteed to encounter unexpected root crops without a proper digging tool. No worry. There is no need to scrape at the ground with your fingernails or ruin a perfectly good knife. Look around for a sturdy stick instead. Just breaking a stick will often produce a nice, tapered point for digging. The taper-

This beveled digging stick was used to dig up a nice mess of bistort roots.

can be refined if you happen to have a knife. I prefer a stick that is 16 to 24 inches long and 1 to 1-1/2 inches in diameter, but in a pinch, I'll use anything.

Ideally, the tip should be angled to one side, rather than beveled to a central point. The one-sided bevel makes a sharp tip and leaves the circular growth rings intact on the unbeveled side. When using the stick as a lever, pry against the unbeveled side. The force against the stick compresses the circular growth rings and strengthens the tip.

A digging stick with a side brach can be pushed into the ground like a shovel.

The digging stick is handled differently for different tasks. For digging up a root, push the stick in beside the plant, force it downward, and work it back and forth into the ground. Work the stick under the root and then lift the root out of the ground. However, if the root is too deep, then it may be necessary to dig a trench beside the plant, then thrust the stick into the soil and leverage the root towards the trench. If there are additional roots nearby then try leveraging them towards the hole left by the first root. The soil will give way into the existing hole and makes digging easier.

Working with a digging stick in hard, dry soil can be much more challenging. Sometimes it is advantageous to use a short, tough stick and a rock or mallet to drive the stick into the ground. Sometimes it is best to look for a better place to dig. Using a digging stick raises your awareness of soil composition. Notice that roots grow larger and are easier to dig in different types of soil. Part of the art of using a digging stick is finding the best place and time to use it.

Dandelion Weeder: I have tried a number of digging tools generally known as dandelion weeders, which are basically glorified digging sticks. The tools typically have a wooden handle with a two-lobed metal digging tip, like the one shown on page 119. These tools are sharper and more durable than a regular stick, making it easier to dig in hard, dry ground. However, the fork-like tip frequently cuts through the sought-after root. And the wood handles are not very durable; I have broken several dandelion diggers.

Digging yampa roots in hard soil with a short digging stick and a bone mallet.

Hori Hori: Thrusting a knife blade into the ground is typically a good way to break, chip, or dull the blade. However, a hori hori is a Japanese digging knife intended to take exactly that kind of abuse. The hori hori comes with a sheath that fits on the belt, a convenient tool to have whenever you need to dig up a root.

Shovel: A shovel is a logical, but usually not very efficient tool for harvesting most root crops. A shovel typically brings up a whole clod of dirt that must be broken apart to retrieve little bulbs. By comparison, a digging stick brings up a bulb without much dirt. However, a shovel can be the most efficient tool for digging long taprooted plants such as burdock (page 148).

I traded books for this home-made hori hori, and I have found it to be a wonderful digging tool.

Types of Root Crops

We naturally tend to label any underground part of a plant as a "root," but botanically speaking, most root crops are not roots at all. This glossary will help you navigate the various terms encountered in this and other texts. Don't sweat it if you can't remember what's what. Being botanically illiterate won't diminish the taste of your next great meal!

Taproots: A taproot is a vertical, carrot-like root that tapers as it descends. Most taproot crops are biennial. Biennial plants grow a rosette of basal leaves without a stalk the first year, storing energy in the root. The next year the plant draws on that stored energy to send up a flower stalk and produce seeds. Taproots are typically tender the first year and woody the second year. Biennial plants typically die after producing seeds.

Bulbs: We typically think of onions as root crops, but technically, the bulb isn't a root at all. A bulb is a bud in which the

taproot

bulb

leaves are enlarged and thickened to store energy. Bulbs, such as camas (page 136) are usually layered like an onion. These are typically perennial plants, and the stored energy in the bulb is utilized to build leaves and stems in the spring, giving the plant a boost on the growing season. In many species the bulbs grow deeper into the ground with age. A bigger plant is a good indicator of a bigger bulb, but also suggests that the bulb may be deeper in the soil.

Corms: A corm is the base of an upright stem enlarged to store energy, such as found in spring beauties (page 131), glacier lilies (page 143), yellowbells (page 146), and brodiaea (page 155). A corm doesn't have layers like a bulb. It is typically a solid

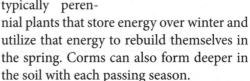

corm

tubers

mass of starch. However, as with bulbs, these are typically perennial plants that store energy over winter and utilize that energy to rebuild themselves in the spring. Corms can also form deeper in the soil with each passing season.

Tubers: Tubers are starchy swellings that typically form on underground stems or rhizomes. The potato, for example, seems like a root crop, but it is actually a starchy swelling of an underground stem. Tubers store starch which is then utilized to grow a new plant the following season. Arrowhead (page 167) has tubers.

Rhizomes: A rhizome looks like a horizontal root, but it is technically a horizontal stem utilized by a plant to spread and send up new shoots, basically establishing clones of itself as it creeps along. These are perennial plants, such as cattails (page 47), hairbells (page 163), or lawn grass.

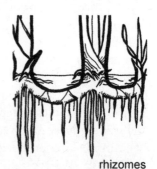

rhizomes

Leaves of mountain death camas (*Anticlea elegans*, a.k.a. *Zigadenus elagans*) resemble common camas leaves, but the flowers are smaller and greenish-white.

Edible or Poisonous?

Have you spent much time looking at plants from the bottom up? Most plant roots are stringy or woody. Relatively few plants have tempting, starchy roots, and not many are poisonous. However, the percentage of poisonous starchy roots is relatively high, only because the total number of starchy roots is so low. In addition, the toxins are typically more concentrated in the starchy roots than in the vegetation, and therefore, consuming the wrong root could have serious consequences. Fortunately, there are only a few deadly roots to worry about, notably death camas, poison hemlock, and water hemlock. Learn to identify these plants with confidence.

Meadow death camas flowers (*Toxicoscordion venenosum*, formerly *Zigadenus venenosus*).

Death camas is the plant of greatest concern, especially given its close resemblance to common camas. It could also be mistaken for sego lilies, onions, or other edible bulbs, and death camas often grows intermingled with any of these root crops. One concern is that it is easy to break the stems while digging for bulbs, such that a person could identify the proper plants, but dig up the wrong bulb. For insurance, avoid collecting bulbs after breaking off the tops, at least until you are comfortable identifying plants from the bottom up. See page 138 for more details on death camas.

Poison hemlock and water hemlock are typically more toxic than death camas, and could be mistaken for wild carrots (page 166), since all belong to the Parsley family and have similar flowers. See pages 43-44 for more details on the hemlocks, and avoid foraging for Parsley family plants until confident with your plant identification skills.

Another plant that warrants discussion is the yellow pond lily (*Nuphar polysepalum*), which is said to have starchy, edible roots, according to many different plant books. The roots are big enough that it would be a major root crop if edible. However, edibility is apparently something that authors have copied from book to book without testing it. Few people actually muck around in swamps and dig up the roots to try them, but we did. A friend threw up after eating the roots. I should have thrown up, but instead felt sick and nauseated for a whole day.

Yellow pond lilies (*Nuphar polysepalum*) are said to have edible roots, according to many books, but we've experienced otherwise.

Bitterroots often grow on windswept ridges, free of competition from other species. The leaves appear like green snowflakes on the ground very early in spring, often whithering away before the plants bloom in mid-summer.

Lewisia rediviva
Miner's Lettuce Family (formerly in the Purslane Family)

Bitterroot: Spirit of Montana

Bitterroot is the official state flower of Montana. Most other state flowers are abundant and widely visible along roads and fields, but not the bitterroot. Bitterroots are common enough, but finding them requires a) getting out of the car, b) hiking, and c) a bit of luck. In some respects, it seems like an odd choice for a state flower, since many increasingly urbanized Montanans will never see or recognize it in their lifetime.

On the other hand, when you find a bitterroot, you will realize that it is the perfect flower to represent Montana. After all, this is a land of extremes—often cold, sometimes blazingly hot, and frequently windy and dry. Winter can persist into May or June, where summer is a flash in the pan, sometimes roasting hot, before winter starts all over again.

Walking along a windblown ridge or parched sagebrush field in June or July, you will likely not see a bitterroot until you are right on top of it. Yet, suddenly you see this amazing, tropical-looking flower blooming from the most hostile looking soil, often without any apparent leaves. Bitterroot honors the spirit of Montana pioneers who tenaciously struggled to survive and thrive in a less-than-accommodating landscape. The species name, "*rediviva*" comes from the plant's ability to spring back to life, even after being dried and stored for a long period of time.

Description, Habitat, and Range

Bitterroots leaf out very early in spring, tapping into the energy reserves of their starchy, branched roots to generate new growth. The plants form a rosette of fleshy little leaves, clinging close to the ground where the soil's thermal mass moderates temperature extremes. The leaves typically wither away before the flowers bloom, and thus bitterroots are most often discovered as a big flower on a short stem with no apparent vegetation.

Most other plants of the Miner's Lettuce family (formerly included within the Purslane family) have 2 sepals and 5 petals, but *L. rediviva* typically has 5 or 6 linear bracts midway up the stem, plus 6 to 9 oval-shaped, green or reddish sepals, and 12 to 18 slightly fleshy petals, varying in color from magenta to pink to white.

Flowers emerge from the soil after the leaves are gone.

Bitterroot grows in rocky soils, from sagebrush plains to windblown ridges of lower mountains. It ranges from British Columbia and Alberta all the way to southern California and Arizona. It is common throughout the Rockies, except for New Mexico. Bitterroots are perhaps most prolific in northwest Montana, giving name to the Bitterroot Mountains, Bitterroot Valley, and Bitterroot River. And yes, harvesting bitterroots is perfectly legal, even though it is the Montana state flower, just be concientious in collecting.

Edible... but Well-Named

Bitterroots have a white, starchy root encased in very bitter, brown or reddish bark. The root is edible and good after all traces of the bark are removed, including any pinkish color that may remain after most of the bark has been stripped away. As with many plants, the bark slips off easily early in the spring when the plant is very moist. The bark adheres firmly to the starchy core as the soil dries out later in the season. Since the roots are slender and branching, cleaning them can be a challenge under the best of circumstances. Therefore, plan on harvesting bitterroots in spring, long before they bloom.

In a timed experiment, I collected more than a gallon of whole plants in a one-hour harvest in May. Trimming away the vegetation left about 1.5 quarts of roots. Peeling off the bitter bark took another eight hours! In my wanderings, I have stumbled across a few bitterroots in which the bark slid off easily. I would like to do another timed study someday when I happen to be in the right place at the right time to harvest them in quantity.

The nutritious, starchy roots are encased in bitter red bark.

The peeled roots should be boiled; they are starchy, gelatinous and filling. However, it is important to remove all of the red bark. Even a little bit will make the whole stew bitter beyond edibility. It may be an acquired taste.

A one hour harvest of bitterroots with a digging stick.

Lewis and Clark acquired a bag of dried bitterroots that was abandoned by Shoshone Indians after a scuffle over a gun. The roots were mostly clean, but still had small bits of bark attached. Lewis experimented, boiling some roots until soft, but they were still nauseatingly bitter. Having made peace with the Shoshone, Lewis returned the roots, and they "ate them heartily." Perhaps it is more palatable if one grows up with the flavor.

Bitterroots remain an important food to the Salish, Kootenai and Pend d'Oreille tribes of the Flathead Nation.

Native peoples monitor the bitterroot crop each spring to see when the bark slips most easily off the root, usually late April or early May. Then they have a big harvest day to collect roots for a feast. The roots are boiled and then included in a variety of dishes, frequently mixed with salmon or added to huckleberries and sugar.

Please harvest bitterroots only in areas of extreme abundance. It would be easy to over harvest the plant in many localities. However, disturbing the soil can create favorable conditions to expand the populations of many root crops. I do not know if that is the case with bitterroots. For most aspiring foragers, bitterroot is an interesting food worth experimenting with, but probably not a regular addition to the diet.

Pygmy bitterroot (*Lewisia pygmaea*) is typically found high in the mountains, above timberline.

Related Species

There are at least 15 species of *Lewisia* in the western states and provinces, mostly with white flowers. The number of sepals and petals varies from species to species, but if you know *L. rediviva*, you will likely recognize its cousins.

Photo by Glen Lee

Spring beauty is a perennial plant with a tuberous, potato-like root. Unlike potatoes, however, spring beauties can take years to reach maturity.

Claytonia lanceolata
Miner's Lettuce Family (formerly in the Purslane Family)

Spring Beauty: Potato of the Rockies

It is often challenging to describe the taste of one food by comparing it to another. For example, how do you explain the taste of a pineapple or coconut to someone who has never tried either one? But spring beauty is an easy one to describe. The cooked, starchy root has a taste and texture reminiscent of fresh, garden-grown baby red potatoes with a hint of butter.

Softer than a regular potato, spring beauties melt in my mouth, taking me back to my childhood, when Grandma Josie would cook up the first, fresh red potatoes from the garden. Spring beauties are worth the effort to harvest—even if more calories might be expended in the digging effort than gained from the meal.

Description, Habitat, and Range

Spring beauties are aptly named. Western spring beauty (*Claytonia lanceolata*) grows high in the mountains and blooms in early spring, shortly after snow melts. In the Mountain West, that could be May, June, or July, depending on elevation.

Western spring beauty typically has a single pair of fleshy leaves, and the whole plants are seldom more than a few inches tall. Basal leaves are possible, but seldom seen. The white or pinkish (rarely yellow) blossoms have 5 petals, but only 2 sepals—an easy way to identify the plant.

One-to-several flower stalks grow from a single tuberous root, providing a good indicator of root size. A single stem suggests a pretty small tuber, one-fourth to one-third of an inch in diameter, and possibly only a year old. Multiple stems indicate bigger, older tubers, with some more than an inch in diameter. Given that a single tuber may be several years old, and it can take dozens of them to make a meal, conservation is a critical concern. Be careful to avoid excessive harvesting.

A one-hour harvest of spring beauty tubers and greens.

Western spring beauty is found throughout the Rockies, as well as the Sierra Nevada and Cascade ranges, typically growing in exposed soils with ample moisture and sunlight.

Size Makes a Difference

Spring beauties are one of many wild edible plants I experimented with in my "backyard" of the Tobacco Root Mountains. As a teenager and young adult, I was constantly out practicing survival skills, trying to learn how to live off the land. Spring beauties were mentioned in my field guides as a favored crop of Montana Indians, and quite prolific in the mountains here, so I often harvested them on my survival treks.

The problem was that the starchy roots were disappointingly small. In a timed study I harvested only about one cup of tubers per hour of digging. Cleaning took another ten minutes or so. While it made a gourmet meal, it was hard to justify

Spring beauties in better soils have bigger tubers.

the labor expense. A person could easily starve to death faster than they could sustain themselves in an unlimited patch of spring beauties!

As I eventually figured out, other root crops like yampa were also disappointingly small, as were our dwarf huckleberries. It didn't seem to matter what I harvested; I was always lucky to get about one cup of food per hour of effort.

Cooked spring beauty tubers taste much like baby red potatoes with butter.

Venturing out beyond the Tobacco Root Mountains, however, I soon realized that soil quality was the critical factor. The grainy, decomposing granite of the local mountains failed to grow anything very well. Roots and berries tend to be about one-third the size of those from the same species in many other mountain ranges.

I have sporadically encountered spring beauties with larger roots in other mountains, although not always in quantities big enough to justify harvesting an entire meal. But in a timed study in rich brown soils west of Yellowstone National Park, I harvested nearly three cups of tubers in one hour of digging. Much of that time was spent wandering around looking for clusters of stems, which indicate larger roots.

The tubers can be substituted for potatoes in any dish, or boiled in plain water to get the full flavor and experience of spring beauties themselves. Some authors suggest peeling the dark skin off before or after cooking them, but I found that unnecessary and inefficient. Spring beauties make delicious and gourmet survival fare; I only wish they were much more abundant and consistently of the larger sizes.

When harvesting spring beauties, I am reminded that potatoes were similarly small at one time, and that modern potatoes were created through hybridization, breeding, and manual selection to enlarge the size of the tubers. I sometimes wonder if a similar miracle could be achieved by crossbreeding and cultivating the various species of *Claytonia*. Perhaps one day someone will take on that challenge, making it possible to grow a worthwhile crop of spring beauties in the garden.

Don't Waste the Greens!

Digging up spring beauties results in greater quantity of greens than tubers. Don't waste them. The greens are edible and delicious

raw or cooked. I like to graze on the greens while digging, but save most of them to add to a salad or stir-fry. The greens have a very mild sour taste, suggestive of oxalic acid, which is common among plants of the Miner's Lettuce family. Fried by themselves in oil, the taste and texture is reminiscent of bean sprouts.

The whole plant is edible, so be sure to save the greens for use as a salad or potherb.

Related Species

Worldwide, there are 26 species of *Claytonia*, primarily native to North America, with a few species extending as far south as Central America and west all the way to Siberia and Mongolia. Several species have starchy, potato-like tubers. *Claytonia virginica* is abundant from east Texas to Minnesota and all the way to the east coast, typically found growing on the forest floor. *Claytonia caroliniana* is found over much of the same range. Sam Thayer reports in *The Foragers' Harvest* that there are millions of acres of spring beauties in Wisconsin alone. These species can likely

Miner's lettuce (C. perfoliata) is a good salad green, but doesn't have a fleshy root.

withstand greater harvesting pressure than our western spring beauty.

In the Sierra Nevada, also look for *C. nevadensis*. Farther north,

C. tuberosa grows from British Columbia to Alaska. Several species were previously included in the genus *Montia*, but were shuffled into the *Claytonia*, although they lack tuberous roots. All species of *Claytonia* can be eaten for their greens, including *C. perfoliata*. Also known as miner's lettuce, the plant was eaten as a salad green by miners during the 1849 California Gold Rush.

One unusual species is alpine spring beauty (*C. megarhiza*). Growing above timberline throughout the West, alpine spring beauty has a large starchy taproot up to one inch in diameter and a foot long, but is relatively uncommon… and I have yet to find one myself.

Alpine spring beauty (*C. megarhiza*).

Spring beauty is a member of the Miner's Lettuce family, formerly included within the Purslane family.

Common camas is typically found in moist soil and often grows abundantly.

Camassia quamash
Asparagus Family / Agave Subfamily (formerly in the Lily Family)

Common Camas: Slow Cooking

Many root crops are so scattered in distribution that the ambitious forager will seldom find enough in one spot to efficiently or ethically make a meal. But not so with common camas. Find one camas and you will likely find hundreds, if not thousands, nearby. Camas is so prolific in its habitat that a field of flowers often looks like a lake or stream, as noted by William Clark of the Lewis and Clark expedition on June 12, 1806: *"The quawmash is now in blume at a Short distance it resemhles a lake of fine clear water, So complete is this deseption that on first Sight I could have Sworn it was water."*

Camas flowers.

Finding camas can be like finding a lake of food. Being abundant, easy to gather, and very nutritious, it was a major food source for tribes lucky enough to share its territory. But it isn't a food you can just dig up and eat. Camas requires an extensive cooking process, preferably a day or two, to convert the carbohydrates into a digestible form.

Description, Habitat, and Range

As with other lilies and lily-like plants, common camas (*Camassia quamash*) has flower parts in multiples of three. Starting from the outside layer and working inward, there are 3 sepals and 3 petals (identical in size and color), plus 6 stamens, and a 3-parted pistil. For the less botanically-oriented, it looks like a six-petaled flower. Flowers form along a flower stalk or raceme typically 1 or 2 feet tall. Color varies from deep purple or blue violet to pale lilac or white. It blooms between April and June, depending on elevation.

Camas is a perennial plant with basal linear leaves and a layered, onion-like, but odorless bulb that stores energy over the summer to rebuild itself quickly in the early spring. It varies from marble-size to about golfball size, with most bulbs about midway in between. Camas favors moist soils and full sun. While most prolific in the Columbia Basin and Great Basin Desert, common camas can be found from British Columbia and Alberta south into parts of California and east as far as Montana

Ease of harvesting depends on soil quality.

and Wyoming.

Three other species of camas (*C. leichtlinii, C. cusickii,* and *C. howellii*) look similar to common camas and grow within the same or lesser range. Farther east, prairie camas (*C. angusta*) grows from Texas east to Mississippi and north to Iowa and Indiana. Atlantic camas (*C. scilloides*), with pale blue or whitish flowers, covers a similar territory, but continues east to the Atlantic Coast and north to Quebec. All species are edible.

Death by Camas

Would-be foragers are often dissuaded from feasting on common camas for one reason more than any other: death camas. Death camas is a group of plants with similar leaves and bulbs as common camas. Death camas contains a toxic alkaloid that may be twice as potent as strychnine. Ingestion can cause vomiting, diarrhea, and death. According to some reports, entire Indian families were killed when a single bulb was mistakenly added to the stew. However, other reports suggest a person would have to ingest several bulbs to get a lethal dose. The potency probably varies between species and locations.

It would be helpful to do a side-by-side comparison be-

Meadow deathcamas (*Toxicoscordion venenosum,* formerly *Zigadenus venenosus*). The many species of death camas have similar leaves and bulbs to common camas, but smaller, white or greenish-white flowers.

tween true camas and death camas, except that there are six species of the former and twenty species of the latter. Complicating matters, botanists have recently reclassified death camas from one genus (*Zigadenus*) into five genera (*Zigadenus, Toxicoscordion, Stenanthium, Anticlea,* and *Amianthium*), which makes it confusing to lump them together in discussion.

The principle concern is that you might learn to confidently distinguish one species of death camas from one species of edible camas, only to be fooled by a different species. For example, the leaves of meadow death camas (*Toxicoscordion venenosum,* a.k.a. *Zigadenus venenosum*) are brighter green and more sharply V-shaped than the leaves of *Camassia quamash,* but mountain death camas (*Anticlea elegans,* a.k.a. *Zigadenus elegans*) has leaves that are very similar to common camas. The bottom line is that, to ensure safety, dig camas bulbs while the flower is in bloom. Common camas is blue. Death camas is white or greenish-white. You may see some pale common camas, but you will never see a blue death camas.

Details for Digging

In 1806, Meriwether Lewis wrote that Indians harvested it starting in mid-July, when the bulbs were big and the plants began to wither away. They continued harvesting camas until the leaves grew to substantial size in the spring. That makes sense, because the plant extracts energy from the bulb to grow in the spring then replenishes it after flowering to prepare for winter dormancy.

However, camas bulbs are edible at any time of year, and some tribes harvested it while in bloom. With practice, you can learn to identify camas from seed capsules and withered leaves, but for starters look for it in bloom. It is the safest way to avoid accidentally harvesting death camas.

Camas bulbs are often deep in the soil, as indicated by the long white stem.

As with any root crop, digging camas bulbs quickly increases a person's awareness of soil properties. Camas bulbs tend to be smaller and challenging to dig in dense damp sod, where competition with other plants is greatest. Bulbs grow bigger where fluctuating water levels drown out the competition.

An average size bulb.

Similarly, intermittent flooding in northern desert canyons can wash out competing plants, leaving sand and gravel beds where camas thrives. However, the bulbs may be so thoroughly wedged between rocks that they are nearly impossible to retrieve.

Conditions may vary tremendously over a small distance, so it is worthwhile to dig a bulb here and there until finding an optimal location.

Almost too pretty to harvest!

I did timed studies harvesting camas roots in washes in south central Idaho, using a metal-tipped digging stick to pry the roots out of the ground. In the first study, I worked in a very rocky creek bed, breaking off more stems without recovering the bulbs than I care to admit. In one hour I gathered a nice bag of whole plants, resulting in about one quart of actual roots. I did the second study in a similar wash, and harvested a similar quantity of bulbs, but spent more of my time walking and testing soil conditions, rather than digging. Looking for bulbs in sandy pockets, I significantly reduced the number of harvesting casualties.

When harvesting most root crops, it is necessary to push the digging stick below the bulb and pry upward. With camas, however, prying upward can mash the soft bulb. Instead, remove any obstructions above or beside the bulb, since the onion-like rootlets below the bulb don't have much holding power. Then grasp the base of the stalk and gently pull upward. The bulb may move very slightly at first, sometimes as slow as one millimeter per second, moving faster as your force slowly overtakes suction holding the bulb in place. Just don't pull too hard, since the stems break off quite easily.

Sometimes it is possible to pull camas right out of the sand or muck without using a digging stick at all, especially when the bulbs are clustered together. With optimal conditions, I can harvest an hour's worth of bulbs in fifteen or twenty minutes of searching and pulling.

Fabulous Food or Fantastic Flatulence?

Raw camas bulbs are starchy, nearly tasteless, and packed with a carbohydrate called inulin, plus a dietary fiber called hemicellulose. Neither are digestible raw, so they ferment in the gut and produce prodigious flatulence. However, the inulin can be converted to fructose, a type of sugar, through extended cooking.

Lewis wrote that the Indians gathered twenty to thirty bushels of camas bulbs then dug a steam pit 2 ½ feet deep and 10 feet wide.

They covered the pit a foot deep with firewood, and covered that with rocks, then lit the wood to heat the stones. When the rocks were red hot, the Indians leveled the stones, then sprinkled a thin covering of earth over the rocks. To this, they added an inch-thick layer of green grass, and then the cleaned, white camas bulbs in a big pile and covered them with a few more inches of grass. Water was added to generate steam, and the pile was covered with four inches of earth and a new fire was built on top of that, cooking the bulbs from above as well as from below. The bulbs cooked this way overnight, after which the dirt and grass covering was removed and the bulbs allowed to cool. According to Lewis, the bulbs were soft and sweetish, much like the consistency of a roasted onion.

Cleaned and peeled bulbs, ready for cooking.

The cooked bulbs could be dried in the sun until black, or processed into more refined loaves of "bread" by pounding the cooked bulbs between two rocks to obtain the consistency of dough. This dough was rolled in grass, forming eight to ten pound cakes and cooked in the steam pit again, mixed with more cooked camas, and then remade into thin cakes to dry in the sun. Lewis concluded, *"The bread this prepared if kept free from moisture will keep sound for a great length of time. this bread or the dryed roots are frequently eaten alone by the natives without further preparation, and when they have them in abundance they form an ingredient in almost every dish they prepared. this root is palateable but disagrees with me in every shape I have ever used it."*

You won't need twenty or thirty bushels of camas bulbs to do a steam pit. To make a small steam pit, dig out a regular fire pit, line it with rocks, then burn a fire for several hours to heat the stones. Sweep out the ashes and put down a layer of greens. Earth and grass can impart a flavor that might be less appetizing for the modern palate, so try a layer of edible greens, such as goosefoots or thistles. The camas bulbs can be put in a clean, untreated canvas bag or pillow case to help protect them from dirt sifting through from above. Cover the bag with a layer of grass or other nonpoisonous greenery, sprinkle some water for steam, then add a layer of bark (optional), and cap it with earth. Camas bulbs need to steam bake for 10 to 72 hours, the more the better. An additional fire on top will help ensure adequate cooking.

The steam pit also works great for other foods. Try a dinner of chicken, potatoes, carrots, and onions. It only takes a few hours to cook and may not require a fire above the ground, depending on the weather.

If cooking in the ground sounds like too much trouble, try cooking camas bulbs for one to several days in your kitchen. According to one study, boiling camas for twenty-four hours converts all the inulin into digestible forms. Simmering them in a crockpot for a day or two (or more) is also effective. The liquid slowly turns into a rich, caramel-like syrup. Just be sure to add water to keep them from drying out and burning.

A pressure cooker can be used to speed up the process. John Kallas reported in *The Wild Food Adventurer* newsletter that pressure-cooking the roots at 257°F for nine hours produced the sweetest tasting roots. Go to www.wildfoodadventures.com for more information about Kallas' newsletter and book.

Cooked bulbs can be dried and ground into a powder and used as a thickener in soups or as an additive to cereal flours when making bread. The bulbs can reportedly be boiled down to make something like molasses.

Taxonomic Note

Cross-referencing *Camassia* through various plant books, you may find it listed as a member of up to five different families. Originally lumped in with the Lily family or split out into the Hyacinth family or the Scilla family, taxonomists more recently shuffled *Camassia* and other related plants into the Asparagus family / Agave subfamily, based on biochemical evidence.

Glacier lilies are a beautiful flower. The corms grow deep in the ground.

Erythronium grandiflorum
Lily Family

Glacier Lilies: Too Pretty to Eat?

I love watching spring advance from the valley floor to the foothills and up into the mountains each year. Spring begins with the hunt for buttercups, yellowbells, and shooting stars in April, then advances into the foothills by the end of May, bursting into bloom with carpets of glacier lilies and spring beauties in the mountains. Week by week, spring advances up the mountains all the way into July, as these same flowers follow the melting snow all the way to the high country. Glacier lilies generate their own heat to help melt away the snow, bringing spring just a little bit sooner. Glacier lilies are edible, too, although sometimes I wonder if they might be too pretty to eat!

On top of a mountain.

Glacier lilies often grow in dense patches.

Description, Habitat, and Range

Glacier lilies regenerate each year from a deeply buried, starchy corm (similar to a bulb), repurposing stored energy to send up leaves and flowers in the wake of the melting snow. The leaves are basal, and generally look like monocot leaves, although the veins are not as straight as in other monocot flowers.

As with other lilies, glacier lilies have flower parts in multiples of three. Starting from the outside layer and working inward, there are 3 sepals and 3 petals, identical in size and color, plus 6 stamens and a 3-parted pistil. The stamens typically have large reddish-brown anthers.

Glacier lilies are common in cool, moist mountain meadows, typically partly shaded by aspens and Douglas firs. They don't compete well with tall grasses. *E. grandiflorum* is found in the high country throughout the West from Alberta to New Mexico and throughout the Pacific coast states.

Worldwide, there are about 30 species of *Erythronium*, primarily in North America. They are variously known as glacier lilies, avalanche lilies, fawn lilies, and dog-tooth violets, ranging in color from white to yellow to pink, red, or purple. Any species would be worth trying for food, although most do not grow in dense patches like ours.

Digging up glacier lilies.

Crispy Sweet

There are acres and acres of glacier lilies in my area, carpeting the ground in yellow below aspens and Douglas fir trees each spring. The slender corm, or swollen stem base, is crisp and sweet. The leaves and flowers may be added to salads in moderation. The leaves are tasty, but with a slight after-bite that may be unpleasant in excess. The corm is the real prize, but I also save the crisp underground stems.

Unfortunately, glacier lilies are difficult to dig because mature roots are about 4 to 6 inches deep in the ground. Immature plants are not so deep, but the corms are not as big either. One plant can take as long as seven years to mature, the corms getting bigger and deeper each year. Fortunately, glacier lilies often grow close together so that you can dig up one then pry surrounding corms into the hole left behind. Grizzly bears sometimes feed on them as well, raking their massive claws through the lilies to extract the roots en masse. Plowing up the soil like a bear may actually create favorable conditions to grow more lilies.

A one-hour harvest of glacier lily corms.

The roots vary greatly in size, so take samples to find the best patch before doing an extensive harvest. A good patch, by Rocky Mountain standards, can yield one to two cups of roots per hour of digging. They can be eaten raw or cooked. The starchy corms are likely bigger in moister, richer climates, such as the Pacific Northwest. Given the slow rate of growth it may be unsustainable to harvest glacier lilies if they are not overly abundant.

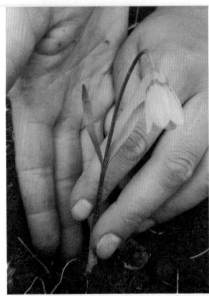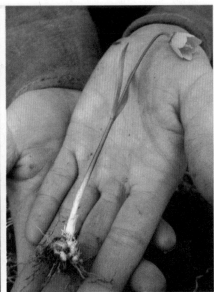

Yellowbells bloom very early in spring, often before the grass turns green.

Fritillaria pudica
Lily Family

Yellowbells: Chiming in Springtime

Winters are not usually too cold or too stormy in the sunny Rocky Mountains, but they can be really, really long. We often get our biggest snows of the season in March and April, while the rest of the country is thawing out and enjoying spring flowers. And here in Montana, those intermittent snowstorms can linger into June. These long winters make springtime that much more important when it finally arrives.

Every spring my grandmother and I eagerly searched for early bloomers - the yellowbells, buttercups, and shooting stars that signaled the coming spring. They often bloom even before the grass turns green, bringing a splash of color to a dormant, desolate landscape. Yellowbells are edible, but often too few in number to justify digging.

Description, Habitat, and Range

Yellowbells are monocot plants with slender leaves and parallel veins. These are true lilies with 3 sepals and 3 petals that are identical in size and color, producing what looks like a six-petaled flower. The flowers droop downward. Inside there are six stamens and a pistil with a 3-parted stigma. Dig up the plant, and you will find a starchy corm surrounded by little starchy scales and roots.

Yellowbells do not compete well with taller vegetation. Look for them on open slopes with short grass or mossy soils in the hills and mountains, from Alberta to New Mexico, west to the Pacific coast.

Buttery Good

Yellowbells are edible from top to bottom. The flower, greens, and corm are edible and delicious, just not very economical to harvest. In the Rocky Mountains expect to harvest a cup or less of starchy corms per hour of work. Unfortunately, yellowbells seldom grow in sufficient abundance to justify harvesting.

Larger yellowbells can be found in the Cascades and Sierra Nevada, with starchy corms up to one inch in diameter. These are delicious raw, cooked, or dried and later added to stews. Native Americans sometimes mixed yellowbell corms with bitterroots, which might arguably improve the latter.

Pocket gophers, ground squirrels, and bears also dig for yellowbell corms, and are presumably more efficient at harvesting, or at least less particular about eating a lot of dirt in the process.

Related Species

Worldwide there are about 100 species of *Fritillaria*, greatly varying in size and appearance. There are about 20 species in North America, found only in the western half of the continent, mostly in the Pacific states. Only yellowbells and spotted fritillary (*F. atropurpurea*) are widespread across the region. The latter is seldom found in abundance. All native species are considered edible, while some cultivated species imported from Europe and Asia may contain toxic alkaloids.

Spotted fritillary (F. atropurpurea).

Burdock has thistle-like flowers that turn into Velcro®-like burrs.

Arctium lappa, A. minus
Aster Family / Thistle Subfamily

Burdock: Eating an Invasive

Some invasive species are better than others. For example, broad-leaf plantain (*Plantago major*) integrates well into an ecosystem, adding biodiversity without becoming a nuisance, while spotted knapweed (*Centaurea maculosa*) or kudzu (*Pueraria lobata*) have a reputation for taking over ecosystems. Burdock is not nearly as invasive as these latter species, but not as benign as plantain either. In some environments the plant can form large patches, becoming a significant nuisance, especially due to its trademark burrs, which provided inspiration for the invention of Velcro®.

Although burdock can become a problem weed, it is also an excellent edible plant, favored for its big taproot. I don't recommend introducing it or helping it along. But if you know of a burdock patch, you can help control it through selective grazing. Dig it up, bring it home, cook it, and enjoy!

Description, Habitat, and Range

Burdock is a biennial plant with a big taproot. The first-year plant has basal leaves and stores starch in the root. The following year the plant utilizes the stored energy to send up a flower stalk with thistle-like flowers, set seed, and die. Burdock could be mistaken for rhubarb due to its big leaves. But the stems are not red like rhubarb, and the flowers look more like its close cousins, the thistles. Worldwide, there are four species of *Arctium*, all native to the Old World, but widely naturalized in North America. *Arctium minus* and *A. lappa* are most common, but any species would be worth trying.

The basal leaves resemble rhubarb.

Passable Survival Grub

Burdock grows quickly, so the roots can be harvested by the beginning of summer and throughout the growing season. But only the first-year plant is edible. The roots become too woody to eat by the second year.

Using a simple digging stick, I dug up a quart of roots in one hour. Washing added another ten minutes. Digging the roots with a shovel is much easier. The roots are so deep that you will likely break most part

A nice mess of burdock roots.

way down, no matter what you dig with. At home you can use a hose and bristle brush to wash the roots, holding onto the hose and the end of the root with one hand, while scrubbing with the other.

Burdock roots make passable survival fare, and they are easy to obtain in bulk. The texture seems woody, and yet they are readily chewable. The bark of the root can be eaten but is better removed. Al-

Cleaning burdock roots with a bristle brush and a hose.

though not too exciting when cooked alone, chopped burdock root imparts an interesting flavor and texture to a stew.

Taste of the Orient

Burdock is a traditional Asian food, and the plant is grown as a crop. Under cultivation, the taproots can grow up to one inch in diameter and three feet long. In Japan it is known as "gobo."

To appreciate the texture and flavor of burdock, it is best eaten in Asian cuisine, such as in a stir-fry. Given the almost woody texture, the roots are best sliced thin, and either added directly to the stir-fry

or boiled first on their own. With the burdock ready to go, look around the kitchen for anything else that might taste good in a stir-fry.

In the photo here I added grated carrots, bell peppers, ginger, rice noodles, sesame seeds, lemon pepper, soy sauce, and balsamic vinaigrette. It was delicious!

Burdock root tastes great in a stir-fry.

Additional Uses

Young burdock leaves are eaten in Japan, although I don't care for the flavor. However, the big leaves are ideal for covering a steam pit to keep dirt out of the food. The immature flower stalks are also said to be edible early in the season, before the flowers appear. Peel off the outer rind and eat the flower stalk raw or try boiling it in saltwater. I have not yet tried them.

Pokey bristles (bracts) on the outside of the flowerheads have hooked tips that cling to your clothes or hair when you walk by. They even cling to bare skin, as you will notice when trying to remove them from clothing. They are tenacious in their ability to hang on and catch a ride to some new place to germinate and grow a new plant. In a pinch, you can use the burrs as survival Velcro®, such as to button up a shirt, at the cost that you may not be able to extract all of the bits and pieces later.

Calochortus nuttallii. Sego lilies grow a single, U-shaped leaf prior to blooming.

Calochortus spp.

Lily Family

Sego Lilies: Food with Fashion

Before flowering, a field of sego lilies could easily be dismissed as mere blades of grass, but come back during the bloom and it is impossible to miss the showy flowers. The sego lily, also known as the mariposa lily, was a staple food crop for many western tribes. Collectively, Native Americans must have harvested tens of thousands of sego lily bulbs every year. Still, I find it difficult to shrug off pangs of guilt when digging up even one beautiful flower for its little bulb, let alone enough for an entire meal. It is part of our cultural conditioning. We can blindly bulldoze entire fields of sego lilies for a subdivision, shopping mall, or highway, but when faced with a single, beautiful blossom, the act of killing becomes a crime.

Fortunately, evidence suggests sustainable harvesting can expand sego lily habitat and increase the population (see page 120) The best way I know to deal with the guilt factor is to work blindly: Dig them up before they bloom!

Calochortus macrocarpus.

Calochortus apiculatus (left) and *Calochortus lyallii* (right). Sego lilies vary tremendously in shape, color, decoration, and texture.

Description, Habitat, and Range

For something that looks more-or-less like a blade of grass, sego lilies are actually very easy to recognize. Tapping into energy reserves from its starchy bulb, the sego lily sends up a single, long, U-shaped leaf first thing in the spring. The dull green leaf grows straight up, and if long enough, it arches over, U-shape upward. Soon afterwards, the flower stem and additional, smaller leaves emerge.

The flowers are unique. Most Lily-type flowers have sepals and petals that are identical size and color, but in sego lilies they are distinctly different from each other. Depending on the species, the sepals are sometimes greenish or sometimes petal-like, but always narrow compared to the petals. Petals vary in color from white to pink to lavender to purple… or yellow, orange, or red. Moreover, sego lilies are uniquely unique in that very few species have monochrome petals. Most have a splash of color at the center, such as white petals with yellow and/or purple center, or inverted with purple petals and a white center. In addition, many species of sego lilies have fuzzy petals, sometimes downright furry. Like other Lily-type flowers, there are six stamens surrounding a pistil with a three-parted stigma.

Worldwide there are about 70 species of *Calochortus*, native to western North America from British Columbia as far south as Guatemala. Sego lilies are common in desert environments, plus some species are found in lower elevation mountain meadows. A few species are widespread across the American West, while many have a limited range and some may be endangered.

Almost half of all species are found solely in California. Do not harvest any sego lilies that are not widely abundant, and consider breaking up the soil around them so they can expand.

Dig a trench beside a sego lily. Then push the digging stick on the opposite side of the plant and leverage it out towards the trench.

Roots Enough for One Meal

Dig up one sego lily bulb and you have a tasty treat to try on the spot. Dig up enough bulbs to make an entire meal and you will begin to understand the challenges faced by hunter-gatherers. Try digging with a sharpened stick, and you will doubly appreciate what our ancestors did to stay alive. Lucky for us, they didn't give up and drop out of the gene pool!

Nowadays, harvesting sego lilies is a curiosity rather than a necessity. Try a sego lily dish as alternative cuisine. Learn about the people who inhabited this land before us by harvesting and eating as they did. Or test your abilities on a survival trip: Can you harvest enough calories to sustain yourself?

Sego lily bulbs grow deep in the soil. It isn't practical to dig when the soil is dry and hard. Wait until the ground is moist and soft. Dig a trench alongside the plant, then push the digging stick into the ground on the other side of the plant and pry it towards the trench. If you lose a root, don't bother looking for it. Don't risk blindly digging for a missing bulb. You might dig up death camas by mistake. Instead, nibble off the white base of the sego lily stem, discard the greens, and move onto the next plant. Move around, harvesting a few bulbs here and there, leaving the rest to recolonize the disturbed ground. Gather a nice mess, wash them, and rub off the outer skins to expose the white starchy bulbs. A pressurized hose and spray nozzle helps clean and skin the bulbs in one quick shot.

Calochortus nuttallii.

A nice harvest of sego lily bulbs.

Fresh bulbs are good raw and better cooked. Cooked alone, the bulbs are mildly sweet and creamy textured, but not overly flavorful. The longer they cook, the sweeter they become. Best of all, add sego lilies to a stew. Let the other ingredients provide flavor, and enjoy the bulbs for their creamy texture.

Two types of brodiaea: *Triteleia grandiflora* and *Dichelostemma capitatum*.

Brodiaea spp., *Triteleia* spp., and *Dichelostemma* spp.
Asparagus Family / Brodiaea Subfamily (Previously in the Lily and Amaryllis Families)

Brodiaea: What to Call It?

I first identified *Brodiaea grandiflora* as a teenager. I learned about its starchy, edible corm, although it wasn't common enough in my area to harvest en masse. My sources didn't have a common name other than brodiaea, so that's what I called it. Taxonomists later split *Brodiaea* apart into several closely related genera, including *Dichelostemma* and *Triteleia*. The plant I knew as brodiaea became *Triteleia grandiflora*, so it wasn't a brodiaea at all. I have struggled to find an acceptable common name ever since.

Generally speaking, flowers of the *Brodiaea* are known as cluster lilies. The various species of *Triteleia* are known as triplet lilies, while those of *Dichelostemma* are known as blue dicks, papago lilies, or firecracker lilies. Most of these flowers are greatly similar in appearance, so it is not always evident which genera is which.

Given that all three genera belong to the Brodiaea subfamily of the Asparagus family (having been previously kicked out of the Lily family and the Amaryllis family), it may be sensible to retain brodiaea as a common name for all of them.

Fortunately, they are all edible, so it doesn't matter what you call them. The text and photos here apply just as well to one genera and species as another!

Description, Habitat, and Range

The Brodiaea are monocot plants with slender, U-shaped basal leaves that are similar to sego lilies, but unlike sego lilies, there are usually multiple leaves. The plants typically grow in bare ground where there is little competition from other plants.

D. capitatum corms.

The lily-like flowers have 3 sepals and 3 petals that are identical in size and color, producing what looks like a six-petaled flower. There are six stamens and a pistil with a 3-parted stigma. Dig up the plant, and you will find a modest, two-tiered starchy bulb-like corm. If it doesn't have a two-tiered corm then it isn't a brodiaea. It could be death camas (page 138) or sego lily (page 151) instead.

Plants of the Brodiaea subfamily are native to western North America, south to Central America. There are about 15 species each of *Brodiaea* and *Triteleia* and 6 of *Dichelostemma*, mostly restricted to California or up the Pacific coast. Only *T. grandiflora* is widespread throughout the West.

Peeled corms, ready for a final wash and cooking.

Easy to Harvest, Good to Eat

Brodiaea is common in the mountain country, yet I seldom see patches large enough to justify harvesting any. However, some species are very abundant in the desert, which is where we typically harvest it. The starchy corms are edible raw and delicious cooked in a stew or roasted in hot coals. The flowers can be added to a salad.

Native Americans widely utilized brodiaea wherever the plants grew in abundance. The Miwok Indians of northern California, for example, harvested large quantities of brodiaea corms and held great feasts.

Allium geyeri. Wild onions vary in color and habits, but all smell like onions.

Allium spp.
Amaryllis Family / Onion Subfamily
(Previously in the Lily Family)

Wild Onions: Diverse and Delicious

One doesn't normally sit down to a dinner of onions, yet onions are one of the most commonly used vegetables, adding zesty flavor to hundreds of favorite recipes. Most cultivated onions are varieties bred from *Allium cepa*, which is closely related to wild onions in Central Asia. Onions vary in flavor from mild to hot to spicy. Garlic (*A. sativum*) and chives (*A. schoenoprasum*) are also included in this genus.

Wild onions vary as much as cultivated onions, with an estimated 750 species of *Allium* around the world, mostly in the northern hemisphere. Wandering around marshy lakes high in the Rocky Mountains, you may even find something that looks and tastes like chives, which is exactly what they are. Chives are native to both North America and Europe. Wild onions are vastly smaller than their domestic kin, but they make a wonderful addition to just about any cooked dish or wild salad.

Chives (*Allium schoenoprasum*).

157

Description, Habitat, and Range

Onions have superficially grass-like leaves, which are *usually* hollow rather than flat. The flowers are borne in umbels, typically varying from white to pink, red, or purple. Flower parts form in multiples of three, with 3 sepals and 3 petals that are identical in size and color. Wild onions have a bulb that typically varies from small to smaller. The nodding onion (*A. cernuum*), which grows throughout the continent, may be the largest wild onion found in the West.

Avoid confusing wild onions and

Allium brevistylum.

death camas (*Toxicoscordion venenosum* – a.k.a. *Zigadenus venenosus*). Crush and smell the leaf to verify that it has an onion smell. Keep in mind that the smell on your fingers can carry over to the next plant you smell.

Wild onions can be found in just about any habitat, from scorching hot deserts to moist forests, from the plains to mountaintops, and from Florida to Alaska. There are hundreds of different species found across the continent, but comparatively few in core Rocky Mountain states. Colorado, for example, has only about ten species of wild onions.

Allium cernum.

Great Flavor for the Wild Gourmet

Like domestic onions, wild onions are a great addition to salads and cooked dishes, but not usually a meal by themselves. Wild onions can be harvested, dried, and stored for later use. I prefer to eat them fresh. I add the chopped bulbs, leaves, and flowers in salads, soups, stews, and stir-fries. On wilderness camping trips, we often catch and clean our trout, then fill the cavity with wild onions and cook the whole fish on hot coals.

Allium geyeri bulbs.

Yampa can be very prolific in mountain meadows, often with thousands of plants.

Perideridia gairdneri
Parsley Family

Yampa: Twins are Normal

Yampa can be enormously prolific in mountain meadows, yet somehow easily overlooked as just another pretty flower. But dig up the starchy little nut-like root and you will find a treat that is good raw and delicious cooked. Each season the plants extract energy from these roots to build new vegetation, then grow one or more new roots to replace the old one. Twin roots are common, but the actual number varies from plant to plant.

Description, Habitat, and Range

Yampa has slender, grasslike leaves, that although pinnately divided, blend in with the grass so well that yampa can be virtually invisible until the flowers pop open. The flowers are classic Parsley family compound umbels, although less substantive than many other parsleys. Do not confuse it with poison hemlock or water hemlock (pages 43-44).

You may need to dig up one or more plants and look for the twin roots to

Digging yampa roots.

ascertain your identification of this plant. Yampa typically grows among the grasses of sunny mountain meadows. *P. gairdneri* is widespread from British Columbia to Saskatchewan, and south as far as California and Colorado.

Worldwide there are about a dozen species of *Perideridia*, all native to North America, mostly restricted to the Pacific states, with the exception of the eastern yampa, *P. american*a, found throughout much of the Mississippi watershed.

Twin roots are common, although the actual number varies from plant to plant.

Nutty Tasting

Yampa roots are one of my favorite wild edibles. The raw roots are sweet and nutty-tasting, and absolutely delicious cooked. As with many wild foods, the challenge is in harvesting them efficiently. With a simple digging stick in dry soil, I harvested one cup of roots in one hour. In better soil, the roots can be three times as large, so it may be possible to dig up to three cups of roots per hour of work. The leaves and flowerheads or seeds also make a tasty trail nibble or a good addition to a wild salad.

A nice harvest of yampa roots.

Two species of biscuitroot: *Lomatium cous* (left) and *L. dissectum* (right).

Lomatium and Cymopterus spp.
Parsley Family

Biscuitroots: Facts versus Reality

Sometimes facts don't match reality. Consider *Lomatium cous*, known as the biscuitroot or breadroot. Biscuitroots were a significant food source for western tribes. The root was peeled and eaten raw or boiled, sun-dried, or pulverized into starchy goo and molded into cakes to dry. Some cakes were reportedly one foot wide, three feet long and one-fourth to one-half inch thick. Those are the facts.

The reality is that *Lomatium cous* tastes more like medicine than food. I've harvested a significant quantity of this little plant and never found it palatable. Did I misidentify the species? I've rechecked it a hundred times. Did I harvest it at the wrong time? I don't know. Are some patches better tasting than others? Maybe. Or is it simply an acquired taste? Definitely maybe. Maybe it is a food that tastes good if you've eaten it your whole life. I still don't know what the answer is.

Overall, my experience with biscuitroots is that the most abundant species in the Mountain West tend to be powerfully aromatic and unpalatable, while the mild and sweet-tasting species tend to grow too few in number to warrant harvesting. My best experience with biscuitroots was in the Pryor Mountains of south-central Montana where I harvested nearly a quart of delicious starchy roots in about an hour. Unfortunately, I don't know what species it was.

Description, Habitat, and Range

Biscuitroot species vary from a few inches to a few feet tall, with fernlike leaves of different shapes and patterns. Flowers are mostly yellow, but sometimes cream-colored or rarely purplish, grouped in classic Parsley family compound umbels. Biscuitroots grow mostly in dry soils and thrive in the plains and high deserts. All biscuitroots have starchy taproots of various sizes. Some are edible while others are highly medicinal. Medicinal biscuitroots have a strong smell; the edible species do not.

Lomatium triternatum.

Worldwide, there are at least 70 species of *Lomatium* and 35 species of *Cymopterus*, mostly native to western North America. Biscuitroots are easy to recognize, yet not always easy to identify to the correct genus or species. In addition to *L. cous*, mentioned above, a few other notable species are emphasized as follows.

Nineleaf Biscuitroot (*Lomatium triternatum*)

Nineleaf biscuitroot may be the easiest species to recognize. The species name, "triternatum" means "three times ternate." The leaves are usually split three times and then again three times and then again – which adds up to more leaves than the common name, nineleaf, implies. It is widespread at low elevations in mountain country, and has a good-tasting starchy taproot. The root is deep, just not usually numerous enough to gather in quantity, but it is a good one to sample.

Lomatium dissectum.

Fernleaf Biscuitroot (*Lomatium dissectum*)

Due to its size, widespread distribution, and tendency to grow in patches, fernleaf biscuitroot is easy to identify. It has a sizeable starchy root, but the root has a strong odor and taste due to the presence of balsamic resins. It is popular as an antiviral and antibacterial plant, used primarily for upper respiratory infections. Nevertheless, it also has some history of use as a food plant. I have not yet eaten the root. There is always something new to try!

Two species of harebell: *Campanula rotundifolia* (left) and *C. rapunculoides* (right).

Campanula rotundifolia, C. rapunculoides
Harebell Family

Harebells: More than Meets the Eye

You can't judge a book by its cover, and you can't always judge a flower by appearances. It would be easy to dismiss a harebell as just another pretty flower. Neither the flowers nor the foliage suggest food, but get to know the harebells, and you may hit the jackpot. There are many different species, both wild and cultivated, and sometimes they have unexpectedly big, starchy roots.

The rampion bellflower (*Campanula rapunculus*) was once widely cultivated in Europe for its edible leaves and parsnip-like root.

The creeping bellflower (*C. rapunculoides*), also of Eurasian origin, has similarly big roots, and may be growing in your yard already. Our native, wild harebells are less predictable, but also worth investigating. Grab a shovel and start digging!

Notice the united petals and three-parted pistil.

Description, Habitat, and Range

Harebells have widely varying vegetation, but the most common species in the Mountain West is *C. rotundifolia*. The name, "rotundifolia" implies round leaves, which may lead one to double-check the identification of this species, since the obvious leaves are anything but round. The plants have rounded, basal leaves, but they typically whither away before the plant blooms, leaving only slender,

Harebell roots (*Campanula rotundifolia*).

alternate, leaves. While the vegetation varies significantly from species to species, most harebells have milky sap and bell-shaped flowers with five united petals. The triangular petal lobes curve outward. The flowers range from purple to blue or white. Beneath the soil surface, harebells grow a mix of starchy taproots and rhizomes, storing energy over the summer to power new growth the following spring.

Harebells (*C. rotundifolia*) in bloom.

Worldwide there are about 500 species of *Campanula*, with about 30 species scattered across North America, half a dozen of which are found in the Mountain West. Only *C. rotundifolia* is widespread, typically found in pristine, native ecosystems in the hills and mountains, with open soils where there is limited competition from other plants.

Harebells (*Campanula rotundifolia*)

Harebells have potential as survival food. The roots are often thin and stringy, but easily harvested with a digging stick. In Colorado, Kris dug up enough harebell roots for a meal in twenty minutes, while in Montana we have not encountered any roots big enough to bother harvesting. If you do forage for harebells, be sure to leave some root fragments in the ground to give the plant a chance to grow back. The leaves and flowers are also said to be edible, but we haven't tried them.

Creeping Bellflower (*Campanula rapunculoides*)

Creeping bellflowers were introduced for their flowers. They are common in older neighborhoods and sometimes naturalized along roads or trails into the surrounding environment. The plants spread by roots and creep along, so small patches slowly grow bigger and are nearly impossible to eradicate. Mowing or turning over the soil doesn't phase them, they just keep coming back, and that's a good thing in a survival plant.

I dug a well-established cluster of bellflowers out of a flowerbed and in a few minutes harvested all of the roots shown here – enough to make a hearty meal for two people. The roots were readily chewable and nearly tasteless, so they are best added to a stew to take on flavor from meat and vegetables in the pot.

Creeping bellflowers seem like an ideal plant for the survival garden. Start them in a corner of the yard where they can freely invade and take over, then wait for the apocalypse with the smug satisfaction that you have a food supply buried in the backyard!

Creeping bellflower roots (*C. rapunculoides*).

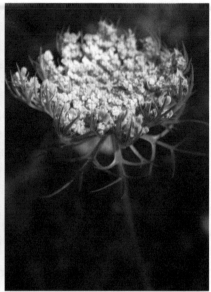

Wild carrot (*Daucus carota*). Notice the distinctive divided bracts beneath the umbels.

Worth Mentioning

Several other plants in the Mountain West have edible roots worth mentioning. These plants are either less common in our area than elsewhere or not overly exciting, or not really productive enough to be considered significant wild food sources. Yet, this guide would be incomplete without some mention of them. All are worth investigating as you encounter them.

Wild Carrot (*Daucus carota*)

Originally native to the Middle East, the wild carrot was cultivated in the first century A.D. for its aromatic, edible leaves and seeds.

The slender white taproot is edible, but generally too stringy to get excited about. Domestic carrots with big, tasty taproots were bred from this species. *D. carota* has become naturalized throughout the continent, but is less prolific in the Mountain West. Our native species, *D. pusillus*, is found throughout

Wild carrot in bloom and gone to seed.

the southern states and up the Pacific coast. Either species would be worth trying.

Be careful to avoid confusing this plant with poison hemlock or water hemlock (see pages 43-44). There are vast differences between these plants, but they are all Parsley family plants with flowers borne in white compound umbels. People have died believing they discovered a wild carrot. It is not enough to be 100% sure of your identification. You also have to be right!

American Bistort (*Polygonum bistortoides*)

American bistort.

There are many species of *Polygonum*, but as far as I know, bistort is the only one with a starchy, edible root. It is common throughout the Rocky Mountains. The raw roots are quite astringent and really pucker the mouth, but the cooked roots are delicious, with a nutty taste. I can collect approximately one cup of roots per hour with a digging stick. (See photo on page 121.) The seeds are also edible. I sometimes snack on the whole flowers. Other species would be worth evaluating.

Arrowhead (*Sagittaria cuneata, S. latifolia*)

Arrowhead or wapato is considered a premium wild edible plant where it thrives in moist, rich environments. Look for the arrowhead-shaped leaves in swampy water. The starchy tubers can be the size of a small egg.

Unfortunately, the Mountain West is not ideal habitat for this plant, and our growing season is too short, so the tubers we've found have been disappointingly small—too small to bother with. Still, it is worth investigating if you find some in your area.

Arrowhead habitat.

Hairy Evening Primrose (*Oenothera villosa*)

There are many species of evening primrose scattered across the Mountain West, some short, some tall, and some locally abundant. None are related to true "primroses." But evening primroses have large, starchy taproots that are theo-retically edible and the plants are occasionally abundant.

In our experience with *O. villosa*, the root crown tases re-markably like beets. The whole, cooked root is edible and would make a prime wild food plant if not for an irritating, itchy sen-sation in the back of the throat – not unlike eating fiberglass insulation! Cooking in three changes of water does not seem to reduce the sensation.

In *The Forager's Harvest*, Sam Thayer reports less of a problem with the nearly iden-tical *O. biennis*, and considers

Primrose roots are big and starchy.

it an excellent wild food. Any species of *Oenothera* could be tried where abundant.

The leaves lose their chlorophyll in winter, leaving beautiful red-purple foilage.

Celebrating summer with a bountiful harvest of wild strawberries.

Fabulous Fruits

We think nothing of eating a succulent tangerine or a delicious kiwi on a snowy January day, but imagine what foraging was like for our ancestors. In winter they ate meat and dried foods. There were few greens or other fresh foods. They must have savored the few leftover shriveled, astringent berries that still clung to the bushes. Springtime brought fresh greens, yet even less fruit. Most of the year, food was nutritious and good, but not necessarily fun and indulgent. Our ancestors must have watched day-by-day every fruit tree and berry bush until that magical mid-summer moment that brought color, fragrance, and sweetness to the world.

Foraging for wild and feral fruits isn't just a matter of survival. It is a cause for celebration! The more foraging you do, the more you will watch and salivate for the first ripe wild strawberry, huckleberry or raspberry of the season. It is an opportunity to participate in the glorious bounty of nature.

Huckleberry / pine nut soup in a primitive clay pot.

Berry-Pickin' Time

Everybody has picked berries at one time or another, so it is not a matter of learning "how to," but of learning how to do it efficiently.

Hand picking is the most simple way to harvest berries, but its efficiency can be vastly improved with the aid of a blickey. Using a belt, center the

A delicious handful of thimbleberries.

blickey just below your belly, freeing both hands to pick quickly.

Run a belt through the wire handle of a small bucket to make an instant blickey. Or cut a large opening in the top of a plastic milk jug and run a belt through the handle. Optionally, cut slits in the side of any bucket, jug, or box and run a belt through the slits. Keep a larger bucket nearby to unload the blickey, and keep on harvesting.

Beating the bushes is another way to pick berries, ideal for shrubs with numerous berries mixed among dense leaves or thorns. Place a tarp under the shrub, and use a long stick to beat the branches, knocking the berries onto the tarp. Too little force will leave the berries on the branches. Too much force breaks the

A blickey on a belt.

branches or sends the berries flying. A six- to ten-foot pole works well, with wide spacing between your hands for optimal control. Experiment to find out what works best for you. Beating the bushes can increase the yield several times over with a lot less effort.

Thrashing the bushes with a stick adds a significant amount of debris to the harvest in the form of bits of sticks and

Beating buffaloberry bushes.

leaves. However, most berries can be sorted easily with the aid of a five-gallon bucket and a hose. Typically, the berries will sink to the bottom of a bucket of water, while the sticks, leaves, and wormy berries generally float to the top, where they can be swept away or poured off.

Apples in January. These apples, stored in a cool, but insulated garage since the fall harvest, are soft and starting to turn brown, but still perfectly good.

Processing Wild and Feral Fruits

When your belly is full and there is still more fruit, then it is time to consider processing and preserving the harvest for future use. What do you choose? Pie? Jam? Jelly? Sauce or syrup? Dried berries, berry cakes, or fruit leather? Can the fruit in jars and decide later? Or put it in the freezer and deal with it another day? There are so many choices, all of them good!

Fruits with small seeds such as wild strawberries, huckleberries, raspberries, or currants, are easy to process. These fruits are ready to work with after picking out any stems, leaves, or other debris.

Some fruits have big seeds that need to be separated from the flesh. Plums or cherries, for example, can be cut open and the seeds removed, which works well if the fruit is big, but can be tedious with smaller fruits, such as Nanking cherries. Optionally, some fruits can be cooked and mashed through a screen, as shown on page 201.

Fruits with medium-sized seeds, such as hawthorns and apples, can be the most challenging, or at least require better equipment. Large apples can be cut by hand and the core and seeds removed prior to cooking,

Serious foraging requires a few good tools, such as this colander attachment to a food processor. In this case, the apples were cooked until soft and the juice poured off into jars. The soft fruit was pressed through the colander to produce apple sauce, with the remaining pulp and seeds discarded out the end of the nozzle.

but for greater efficiency, or when working with crabapples and other small fruit, it is helpful to cook the fruit first, then run it through a hand-powered or electric colander to separate out the seeds.

The other option, lacking a colander, is to boil and press the juice out of the fruit through a cotton cloth. Discard the pulp and make juice, syrup, or jelly. The end product might taste good, but most of the food value is lost with the pulp.

Freezing, Canning, Drying or Cooking?

After resolving the seed issue, or determining that the seeds are not a problem, then proceed to cooking a pie, making jam, drying the fruits, canning, or freezing them for later.

Whole, frozen Nanking cherries.

Whenever practical, it is nice to make the final product right away. Turn that fruit into a delicious pie or jam or dried fruit. Freezing or canning the fruit is fine, but always risks that the treasure might get lost in storage. It is not the size of the freezer or cellar at issue, rather the fact that people are busy and often neglect to finish things in storage. How many years go by before the sweet memories of picking wild berries transforms itself into remorse and regret that nothing ever came from it, and it is time to discard the fruit and move on?

Nonetheless, the dedicated forager will generate more of a surplus than can be utilized short-term, and it is a good survival strategy to have an ample supply of food on hand at all times. Plus, the only thing better than a fresh berry pie in the middle of berry season is a berry pie in the middle of winter!

Some people swear by canning and can everything, but it seems like extra work to me, cooking, cleaning the jars, sealing them tight, and cleaning up the kitchen afterwards.

I prefer a minimalist approach to processing. For example, when saving apples for apple pie, I don't bother to peel them. I cut out the cores and slice the apples into appropriate-sized wedges for a pie, then bag in recycled plastic bags and store in the freezer until ready to use.

Disadvantages of freezing versus canning is that it requires more forethought to thaw the goods prior to cooking, it takes precious freezer space, and there is also a risk that the power could go out or the freezer may break down.

Dried Fruit, Berry Cakes, and Fruit Leather

No need to peel the apples for apple pie. Just core, slice, and make your pie!

The funny thing about fruit is that it is typically full of natural sweeteners, and yet most recipes call for copious amounts of sugar. We don't normally add sugar to meat or vegetables, but we really load it on fruit. It is not uncommon to add a full cup of sugar to a pie. And jams and jellies typically require as much or more sugar than fruit. Therefore, drying fruit can be a nice sugar-free alternative.

While harvesting berries, notice that the dried or partially dried berries clinging to the bush are often the sweetest. Drying most fruits brings out the sweetness, serving as a great ready-to-go snack for camping, hiking, or hanging out at home. Sugar can be added to dried fruit and fruit leather, but it usually isn't necessary, except maybe to bring out flavor when drying leftover pulp after boiling out the juice for something else.

This drying rack has space for multiple trays of fruit leather on a wood stove.

Most berries don't dry well due to their protective skin. Break the skin by mashing soft berries by hand, or run them through a grinder, then dry in the sun or on racks above a wood stove. Optionally, electric food dehydrators work very well for drying berries, either mashed or whole.

We often mash or grind berries and make hamburger-like patties, as shown on page 205, then dry in the sun or in a dehydrator.

To make fruit leather, puree the fruit in a food processor, pour it on a baking sheet lined with plastic or lightly coated with oil, and put it in a warm place to dry. A rack above a woodstove provides ideal warmth to dry fruit leather or berry cakes efficiently, but isn't convenient in the middle of summer. However, a car with the windows rolled up makes a great solar-powered food dehydrator.

Finished fruit leather.

Like many shrubs in the Honeysuckle family, twinberry honeysuckle (*Lonicera involucrata*) and Utah honeysuckle (*L. utahensis*) grow flowers and berries in pairs. The berries are not poisonous, but not very palatable either.

Edible or Poisonous?

Death by berry is one of the greatest fears of would-be foragers and parents of small children. Fortunately, there are relatively few poisonous berries or other toxic fruits, especially here in the Mountain West.

To be safe, the best way to learn to distinguish between edible and poisonous fruits is to learn to identify them properly, according to family and genus. However, identifying down to species is often not necessary. Rather than describing individual species, most of the entries that follow apply to multiple related species with similar characteristics for identification and usually similar uses.

For example, there are about 200 species of gooseberries and currants (*Ribes*) around the world, including approximately 55 species in North America and about 15 or so species scattered across the Mountain West. Every species

Learn the gooseberry-currant pattern and you will be able to recognize dozens of different species without needing to identify and name each one individually.

is unique and different from all the others, with berries varying from yellow-orange to red to deep purple. Most species have small to medium-sized leaves but some species have relatively large leaves. Most grow near moisture, but some are adapted to dry environments. However, most currants and gooseberries typically have palmate leaves and translucent berries with visible stripes running from stem to tip. Learn the gooseberry-currant pattern in the pages ahead and you will be able to recognize dozens of different species as you encounter them, without the need to reach for a field guide every time. As you will discover, some are sweet, some are sour, some are bland, and some are rank and unpalatable. But none are poisonous, which means you can try each species to determine whether or not you like it.

The pages ahead feature many plants specific to the Mountain West, but the associated patterns are broad enough to be utilized anywhere. For example, learn to recognize variations in our local huckleberries and blueberries (*Vaccinium*) and you will be sufficiently qualified to pick totally different species in the wilds of Siberia.

The introduced and cultivated false strawberry looks very much like a regular strawberry, but is pithy and nearly tasteless.

Patterns are not totally bulletproof, but work well enough that mistakes are usually close enough. For example, I ate what I assumed was a novel strawberry (*Fragaria*) in a flower bed, but it was actually a false strawberry (*Potentilla indica*, a.k.a. *Duchesnea indica*) from a different, but closely related genus introduced from the Orient. The fruit was edible, just not very interesting. The bottom line is that it is hard to go wrong if you learn to recognize a few key patterns.

In addition to solid pattern-recognition skills, remember this rule of thumb: **Virtually all blue berries are edible, and the majority of red berries are edible, but most white berries are not.** Even when completely mistaken in plant identification, one is unlikely to be poisoned by any blue, purple, or black berries, especially in the Mountain West.

Be more cautious with red or orange berries. The majority of red or orange berries are edible, including many species that are erroneously assumed to be poisonous. Red fruits are often victims of discrimination as people spread rumors about their toxicity, yet never take the time to properly identify the plants or their actual properties.

The waxy and shiny red or sometimes white fruits of baneberry (*Actaea*) of the Buttercup family are legitimately poisonous, and children have reportedly died from eating the fruits in Europe. There have been no known fatalities from this plant in North America.

Bittersweet nightshade (*Solanum dulcamara*) is also poisonous. A member of the Nightshade family and from the same genus as potatoes, bittersweet contains solanine, the same alkaloid glycoside found in green potato peels. The lethal dose for a healthy adult is thought to be around 200 berries, but

Baneberry has poisonous red or white fruits.

like most poisonous berries, the taste is bitter, and a person is unlikely to try more than one. The bottom line is that there are poisonous red berries, but not many, and they generally taste bad. It would be difficult to be poisoned by eating red berries, except by stubbornly eating a mass quantity of something that doesn't taste good!

As for white berries, most are unpalatable or inedible, and some are poisonous. A very common shrub with white berries is the snowberry (*Symphoricarpos*) of the Honeysuckle family. It is considered mildly poisonous, and can cause vomiting and diarrhea if eaten in excess. Tasting the berries is harmless.

Snowberries are eaten by pheasants, grouse, and bears, although not usually until other food sources are gone.

Bittersweet nightshade is poisonous and could be fatal if consumed in quantity.

Snowberries contain saponins, which have a soap-like quality. Try mashing a few berries between your hands as instant hand sanitizer.

Poison ivy (*Toxicodendron*) of the Cashew or Sumac family also has white or cream-colored fruits. All parts of the plant contain urushiol, a lacquer-like phenolic compound which causes a poison ivy rash. The oil is also harmful when the plants are burned and the smoke inhaled. Many people, myself included, are not allergic to poison ivy, and some people nibble on poison ivy greens early in the spring to build up immunity to it. The risk of consuming it is that an allergic reaction could cause the throat to swell shut and result in asphyxiation. Keep an eye out for the berries to avoid getting a poison ivy rash from the leafless plants in winter.

Snowberries are unpalatable and barely poisonous.

Snowberry / rosehip bear scat.

Urushiol on poison ivy berries can cause the same rash as the leaves.

Black currant (*Ribes americanum*) and desert currant (*R. cereum*).

Ribes spp.
Gooseberry Family

Gooseberry and Currant: Berry Good

My grandmother sparked my interest in plant identification and uses, and my parents like to forage, too. On more than one occasion, Mom and Dad brought tarps, buckets, and sticks into the fields near my grandmother's house to collect gooseberries. Tarps were laid tight around the bushes, and we beat the branches with sticks to knock the berries off.

We brought the berries, leaves, and twigs home in buckets, then cleaned out the debris with the aid of a garden hose. The heavy berries sank to the bottom of the bucket, making it possible to float and scoop unwanted debris off the top.

My mother carefully removed the dried up sepals from the end of each berry, then made gooseberry jam and gooseberry pie. The flavor was intense, delicious, and greatly appreciated after all the preparation effort.

Canadian Gooseberry (*Ribes oxyacanthoides*).

Desert currant (*R. cereum*). Most currant and gooseberry bushes have translucent berries with visible longitudinal lines running from stem to tip.

Description, Habitat, and Range

Gooseberries and currants are small- to medium-sized shrubs with palmate (hand-shaped) leaves and yellow, orange, red, purple, or black berries. The semi-translucent berries usually have visible lines running from stem to tip. Gooseberries and currants all belong to the same genus, but those with thorns are generally considered gooseberries, while those without thorns are currants. Cultivated gooseberries, however, generally have no thorns.

The various species of *Ribes* grow in a wide-spectrum of habitats, mostly where the soil surface is dry, but the water table is within reach of their roots. The golden currant (*R. aureum*) is found at lower elevations along major rivers, while the gooseberry (*R. setosum*) grows along streams in the foothills. Other species can be found along tiny mountain foothill streams, growing in the forest canopy shade. Desert currant (*R. cereum*) is found in more arid landscapes.

Worldwide there are about 200 species of currants and gooseberries, all native to the northern hemisphere. About 55 species are found across North America, common everywhere except the deep South. All species are more-or-less edible, although some are definitely unpalatable. Learn the patterns and variations within the genus as shown on these pages to easily recognize any new species you encounter.

Canadian gooseberry leaf and flowers. *R. oxyacanthoides.* Note the palmate, or hand-like leaf shape, common to the genus.

Diverse in Flavor and Color

The flavor of gooseberries and currants varies as much as the color from one species to another. Gooseberries are distinctly sour, often inciting uncontrollable face contortions. Most currants are modestly sweet, like a treat that could use just a touch more sugar. And a few species are extremely rank in odor and flavor.

Gooseberries are usually sour, yet often addictive. In spite of the face contortions, I reach for another and another, quickly adjusting to the sourness, until I cannot stop eating. Oddly, they are one of the better berries for cooking, especially when sugar is unavailable. Many wild berries taste flat when cooked and require sugar to sharpen the taste, but gooseberries retain their flavor. That said, a little sweetener really classes them up.

In timed studies, I have picked a quart of berries per hour on good bushes. Beating the bushes with a stick, I can collect three or more quarts per hour. The berries sink in water, making it is easy to separate out debris with a bucket and hose. I don't have my mother's patience to pick off the tiny stems and dried-up sepals at each end of the berries, so I just do a quick cleaning and start cooking.

One of the first ripe berries of summer is the golden currant (*R. aureum*), common along major rivers throughout the Rocky Mountains. We often pick them on mid-summer canoe trips, sometimes paddling right up to the bushes to graze. We usually eat the berries on the spot, but if the berries are especially abundant, then we harvest a bunch to make jelly.

Desert currants (*R. cereum*) are not very sweet, but definitely edible, widespread and often very abundant. They make good survival fare when other fruits are unavailable.

When making any kind of currant jelly, boil the flavor out of the fruit and strain off the liquid for jelly, but don't throw away the berry pulp. Mash it into cakes, with or without sugar, and dry it for trail food.

Golden currants (R. aureum) are often prevalent along major rivers.

Red huckleberry (*Vaccinium parvifolium*) is common along the Pacific Coast.

Vaccinium spp.

Heath Family / Blueberry Subfamily

Huckleberry: Worth Dying For

Huckleberries contain flavonoids that help improve night vision. Foraging for huckleberries can improve your day vision and sense of hearing, too, as you watch and listen for bears that might be lurking in the berry patch. That says a lot about just how good huckleberries are. Nobody would admit to themselves or to anyone else that they are risking life and limb to pick huckleberries, but bear encounters are a genuine risk.

See one bear track or a pile of berry-rich bear scat, and your senses naturally go on high-alert. The response is deeply written into our genetic code, memories carried over forward from a time when our species was not at the top of the food chain. But knowing the potential risk is not likely to stop the veteran forager. Today, just as in millennia past, huckleberries are so good that harvesting them is worth the risk of dying!

Huckleberry-flavored bear scat.

Description, Habitat, and Range

Huckleberries are mostly low-growing shrubs with alternate leaves and small, urn- or bell-shaped flowers with an inferior ovary that matures as a red, purple, or blue berry. There is an indentation in the end of the berry, either star-shaped or circular, where the remains of the sepals might still be seen. Since huckleberries and blueberries all belong to the same genus, distinguishing between them is largely a matter of taste. Taste each new species you find. Does it taste more like a huckleberry or more like a blueberry? Either is equally delicious.

Mountain huckleberry (*V. membranaceum*) is prolific throughout the Mountain West.

Huckleberries and their kin are largely adapted to cool, moist habitats of the northern latitudes, high elevation forests, and the Pacific Northwest coast. The size of the bushes and berries varies according to available moisture.

Bog blueberry (*V. uliginosum*) grows in marshy areas, often around the perimeter of mountain lakes.

The dry, sandy soils typical to the granite-dominated mountain ranges here in southwest Montana support grouse whortleberries (*V. scoparium*), or dwarf huckleberries as I call them, which rarely grow more than a foot tall and have tiny berries. Microhabitats with better soil and moisture support larger species with larger berries. The Pacific-like climate of northwest Montana and northern Idaho supports bigger bushes and bigger and more abundant. berries. The biggest huckleberries grow near the coast. Red huckleber-

Dwarf huckleberry (*V. scoparium*) and mountain huckleberry (*V. membranaceum*). A one hour harvest of dwarf huckleberries yielded only one cup of fruit. It is more worthwhile to migrate in search of bigger berries!

ries (*V. parviflolium*) grow so tall that you have to reach up to pick the berries. Worldwide there are at least 50 species of *Vaccinium*, with about 30 species spread across North America. About 10 species are found in variously overlapping territories across the western states.

Sweet Sensations

It is easy to tell when you are in huckleberry country: Just watch for

Collecting huckleberries in the Bob Marshall Wilderness.

signs on every storefront advertising huckleberry shakes, huckleberry pie, huckleberry syrups, jams, and jellies, and huckleberry chocolates. All the hoopla is well justified. Huckleberries are a sweet sensation in any form, and of course, best straight off the bush.

The dwarf huckleberries common to my part of the Rocky Mountains are very tasty but also extremely small. A one-hour study of handpicking produced only one cup of berries. That was an exercise in both patience and abstinence! Using a comb to strip the berries from the plants speeds up the harvesting a little, but takes leaves with it. Fortunately, the leaves are edible and nutritious. I use the stems and leaves in tea.

Otherwise, as a modern hunter-gatherer, I find it far more economical to drive to other parts of Montana, Idaho, or Washington where huckleberries are larger and insanely abundant. On road trips I often dream of bringing home a cooler full of huckleberries to freeze or make into jams and pies. However, I have yet to make it home with any! On one walkabout through Montana's Bob Marshall Wilderness I ate

A spruce bark berry basket.

huckleberries until my teeth screamed in pain from the sweet, acidic juices… and yet I kept eating more!

On a month-long Stone Age trip on the east slope of the Cascades, I literally ate a pint of huckleberries per day during the entire trip. I made a spruce bark berry basket and kept it full all the time. The fructose provided a quick pick-me-up whenever I was hungry or my energy levels were low.

Huckleberry Pancakes

On backpacking and car camping trips it is fun to make huckleberry pancakes. Add some huckleberries and a bit of sugar to pancake batter and fry like regular pancakes. The trick to cooking a good pancake over a campfire or propane stove is to keep the heat as low as possible, and if necessary, intermittently take the pan off the heat to keep it from getting so hot that the outside blackens while the inside remains goopy.

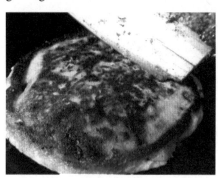

Add a few huckleberries to pancake batter for a delicious treat.

Turning out a perfect pancake over a campfire is the mark of a master camp chef!

To make syrup, add a little water to the berries and cook them down. Mashing the berries speeds up the process. Next, add some sugar, and cook until syrupy, then pour over your huckleberry pancakes, or if dishes are limited, dip the pancakes in the syrup.

Salal (*Gaultheria shallon*). The swollen sepals are part of the fruit.

Gaultheria shallon

Heath Family / Blueberry Subfamily

Salal: Purple Power

Salal berries are sadly overlooked by many people in the quest to find the better-known huckleberries, blueberries, or blackberries. But salal berries are quite abundant in some locations and absolutely worth foraging. On one family camping trip, I picked about a quart of berries, adding some to our pancake batter. I cooked the rest with marshmallows, making a deep purple salal-marshmallow goo that we spread on the pancakes. It was as beautiful as it was delicious. Yes, I do have a sweet tooth!

Description, Habitat, and Range

Salal is an evergreen shrub with alternate leaves, and urn- or bell-shaped flowers that mature into a purple "berry" with a distinct five-pointed star on the end of the fruit. The ovary of the pistil is positioned below or inferior to the attachment of the sepals, so the fruit forms beneath the flower, leaving swollen sepals on the end of the fruit. *G. shallon* is prolific in the moist Pacific Northwest. Smaller species inhabit bogs and subalpine forests in the Rockies from Colorado to Canada.

Worldwide there are about 170 species of *Gaultheria*, with 6 species found across North America. The eastern species (*G. procumbens*) presumably has more flavorful berries and is well-known as a wild food. Alpine wintergreen (*G. humifusa*) is a very small (often only two inches tall) ground-spreading shrub found in open clearings high in the mountain West. The fruits form as a red, berry-like capsule.

Great for Jams and Jellies

Salal berries are mildly flavorful, definitely not as exciting as their huckleberry and blueberry kin, but not bad, either. A little sweetener helps bring out the flavor, making salal berries a good choice for jams, jellies, and pies. In some places salal berries are both large, abundant, and easy to gather in quantity. Native Americans of the Pacific Northwest used these berries extensively, mashing and drying the berries as portable preserved cakes.

A flower or a berry? The swollen sepals and pistil are visible in unripe fruits.

Alpine wintergreen (*G. humifusa*) often grows no more than two inches tall.

Wintergreen Flavoring

Salal leaves are a primary source of wintergreen flavor, methyl salicylate. All species have some wintergreen flavor, but the eastern *G. procumbens* is the primary source. Although unrelated to mints, wintergreen flavoring is often used as mint in chewing gum and candy.

Fresh leaves may not have much of an odor, since the methyl salicylate forms through enzymatic action of a glycoside as the leaves are macerated in warm water. However, the leaves may be added to soups for a unique flavor.

Wild strawberries are similar to cultivated strawberries, but smaller.

Fragaria vesca, F. virginiana, F. chiloensis
Rose Family / Rose Subfamily

Wild Strawberry: Flirting with Desire

Wild strawberries tease the forager with fabulous sweetness and fragrance, yet the delectable fruits are usually too small and scattered to satisfy one's appetite. The plants can be incredibly abundant in the mountains, and a wanderer is likely to encounter ripe berries here and there along the trail. Where you find one, there are likely many more. Stop and rest awhile, crawling around on hands and knees searching for hidden treasures. Strawberries are best eaten this way, one-by-one, grazing along like this is a way of life.

Wild strawberries are packed with flavor!

In all my years, I have encountered only one patch of strawberries abundant enough to truly satiate my appetite! Maybe that is part of the appeal—sometimes our deepest desires are those that are inherently unfulfillable. Wild strawberries tease with the taste and promise of everything you ever wanted, but can never get enough of.

Description, Habitat, and Range

Wild strawberries are similar to their domestic kin, except that wild fruits are smaller and much more flavorful. Strawberries are low-growing plants with trifoliate (three-parted) leaves. Like many other members of the Rose family, the individual leaflets are oval with serrated edges.

Botanically speaking, the strawberry isn't the fruit; it is only the swollen receptacle beneath the floral parts. The true fruits are the dry seeds, or achenes, which are embedded on the surface of the strawberry.

Note the three-parted leaves with oval, serrated leaflets. Strawberry leaves can be added to salads or used for tea.

Worldwide there are about 20 species of *Fragaria*, as well as many hybrids and cultivars. *F. vesca* and *F. virginiana* are widespread across North America. *F. chiloensis* grows in the Pacific coast states, along with some natural and cultivated hybrids.

Packed with Flavor

You haven't tasted a strawberry until you've tasted a genuine wild strawberry. Domestic strawberries were bred in France in the 1750s from a hybrid cross between *F. virginiana* and *F. chiloensis*, giving us a big fruit with unfortunately little flavor. So you will be amazed at the all the flavor packed into one little wild strawberry!

Wild strawberry ashcake pie!

Wild strawberries are not necessarily the most economical food source, but well worth harvesting. In the interest of efficiency, I often eat the little green sepals attached to top of the berry, for a little extra nutrition. If you are able to resist the temptation, then it is possible to gather enough to take home for a small batch of strawberry jam.

An hour of harvesting in a typical patch yields about one cup of strawberries. It is advisable to blend them with other berries, such as raspberries, to get more quantity for less work. On camping trips, try making a delicious strawberry ashcake pie, as detailed in my book, *Participating in Nature*.

Blackberries are most prolific along the Pacific Coast, but also grow on the west slope of the Rocky Mountains in Idaho and Washington.

Rubus spp.
Rose Family / Rose Subfamily

Blackberry & Raspberry: Aggregates

Value is often a function of scarcity. That axiom is especially true of blackberries, which are highly esteemed by those of us who have none, and often disdained as obnoxious weeds by those who have them in abundance. From my perspective, living in Montana, getting to a patch of blackberries is like a pilgrimage to Mecca. I worship blackberries. I submit to their thorny lacerations of my legs and arms as part of the experience. I savor the fruits. It is worth the journey, whether I find enough to bring home, or only enough to fill my belly.

On my home turf, I eagerly seek out the diminutive kin of the blackberries in the form of raspberries and thimbleberries. Although not as big or as abundant as blackberries, they are rich with their own unique flavor. Any of these aggregate-type fruits are equally edible,

Blackcap raspberry or "blackberry" (*Rubus leucodermis*).

190

from blackberries and raspberries to dewberries, cloudberries, and salmonberries. There are 200+ species of *Rubus* across North America. Get to know the aggregates, and you will recognize additional species wherever you go. All are worth trying!

Cut-leafed blackberry (*Rubus laciniatus*).

Description

Botanically, a blackberry or raspberry isn't a single fruit, but an aggregate of many smaller fruits tightly clustered together. The flowers have 5 sepals ánd 5 petals, plus numerous stamens, and typically numerous pistils clustered together on a domed receptacle. The ovary from each pistil matures into its own fleshy fruit with one seed, called a drupelet, clustered together to make up the larger aggregate fruit we call a blackberry or raspberry.

Blackberry (*Rubus armeniacus*, R. *laciniatus*, R. *leucodermis*)

There are many native species of blackberry, however, one is most likely to encounter the introduced and invasive Himalayan (*R. armeniacus* or *R. discolor*) and cut-leafed (*R. laciniatus*) blackberries. These plants grow like weeds along the Pacific Coast from British Columbia to California. They can also be found inland as far as the west slope of the Rockies in Idaho and Washington, typically as brambles along major rivers in lower elevations.

Go decadent! Hot blackberry sauce and ice cream on waffles.

One of my favorite blackberry haunts is Riverfront Park in Spokane, Washington. I consider blackberries my all-time favorite invasive weed!

In my experience, blackberries ripen earlier inland than on the coast. Blackcaps (*R. leucodermis*), for example, ripen along the Columbia River by the beginning of July,

191

followed a couple weeks later by Himalayan blackberries. Himalayan blackberries on the coast may not ripen until the middle of August. I like to collect a winter supply whenever I am lucky enough to be in the right place at the right time.

Fortunately, blackberry season is exceptionally long for a wild fruit. I have picked blackberries as late as Halloween weekend. I often eat a quart of berries while attempting to pick a supply for the freezer. Watch out for the occasional moldy berry that may spoil the taste of a whole handful.

Blackberries can often be gathered in great abundance, making them worthwhile to harvest and process. Blackberries are delicious fresh or dried or made into jams and pies. For a delicious treat, try adding blackberries to your pancake or waffle batter, then top with hot blackberry sauce and vanilla ice cream. If you miss the main harvest and want to extend a scarce supply, try complimenting with apples to bulk up your blackberry pie or jam.

Raspberry (*Rubus strigosus*)

There are many species of *Rubus*, but not very many species of "raspberry." Our wild raspberry is often classified as a variety of the European raspberry, *R. idaeus*, variety *strigosus*, but may be more properly its own species, *R strigosus*.

Raspberries are common in mountains throughout the West, sometimes in damp soil near streams, but also in rocky, sandy soil on south-facing slopes. Unlike blackberries, which typically require a road trip, raspberries invite a walkabout into the backcountry. I love to put my backpack down and forage until I eat every raspberry in sight.

It is uncommon to encounter more raspberries than one can eat, but if you are fortunate enough to bring some home, try making delicious raspberry jam. The berries can be blended with gooseberries for a unique flavor, as well as to stretch the supply.

Raspberry (*Rubus strigosus*).

Note the large, palmate leaf of the thimbleberry (R. parviflorus).

Thimbleberry (*Rubus parviflorus*)

Unlike the divided leaves of other species, thimbleberries have plate-sized, palmate leaves, but comparatively few fruits. Thimbleberries typically grow in dense patches in moist soil in the shade of other trees in the mountains. They are delicious, yet seldom abundant enough to collect more than a handful at a time.

Salmonberry (*Rubus spectabilis*)

Salmonberries are common along the Pacific coast, from Washington north to Alaska. They are less tasty than their kin, but worth trying when encountered. The fruits are edible when yellow like salmon eggs, but may continue to ripen to red and purple hues.

Salmonberry (R. spectabilis).

Related Species

Several additional *Rubus* species may be encountered in parts of the Mountain West, such as the herbaceous dwarf red raspberry (*R. pubescens*), typically found in evergreen forests in moist, Pacific-like habitats. The arctic raspberry (*R. arcticus*) and cloudberry (*R. chamaemorus*) mostly grow north of the Canadian border.

Prickly wild rose (*Rosa acicularis*), flower and fruit. Rosehips vary from moist and fleshy to dry and seedy, depending on the species.

Rosa spp.
Rose Family / Rose Subfamily

Wild Rose: Totally Hip

Rose fruits, called rosehips, are an excellent wild food, in part because they persist on bushes throughout the winter. I love grazing on rosehips on winter walks, sometimes picking and eating all I can fiₙₗ. My body must crave the extra nutrients in winter because I can never seem to get enough!

I grew up on rosehip tea with my grandmother. Grandma Josie collected and dried the rosehips, using a handful whenever she made a pot of tea. The tea was flavorful the first day, and even richer the second day. Soaking softened the rosehips and brought out more of the deep red color. We enjoyed the tea and often ate the softened rosehips, too.

Description, Habitat, and Range

Rose bushes have alternate, pinnately divided leaves with somewhat oval-shaped, serrated leaflets. The flowers have 5 green sepals and 5 petals, plus numerous stamens surrounding a cluster of simple pistils in the middle. The extra petals in cultivated roses were bred from surplus stamens. Botanically speaking, the fruit isn't the fleshy red part, it is the dry seed or achene that develops from the ovary of each pistil. The pistils/ovaries are positioned below the rim of the floral cup or hypanthium where the sepals and petals are attached. This fleshy floral cup swells up around the true fruits hidden inside.

Worldwide there are about 100 species of *Rosa*, including 50 native or introduced species across North America, of which about 10 can be found across the mountain and intermountain west, typically in the hills, meadows, and woods, but not too high in the mountains.

Loaded with Vitamin C

The thin, fleshy rosehip skin is rich in vitamin C, often included in many commercial vitamin products. The seeds contain a great deal of vitamin E. The fruits are easily

Rosehips ripen in the fall and often cling to the bushes all winter.

dried whole and useful for making rosehip tea throughout the year. In a timed study I picked three quarts of rosehips in one hour.

Some rosehips are fleshy and tasty right off the bush, while others are dry and full of hairy seeds. Some people have expressed concerns that seeds from any rosehip could irritate the stomach and intestines or break a tooth, but I have eaten them my entire life without complications. That said, I frequently skip dry, seedy rosehips in favor of fleshier ones. There are subtle differences in the rosehips, such as the shape or texture of the fruit, that help distinguish one species from another. I don't key out individual species, but it doesn't take much experience to figure out which rosehips are yummiest.

Some people recommend separating the seeds from the flesh before eating rosehips. However, with most wild roses, the effort could be tedious enough to squelch one's interest in the plant altogether. Try a few whole rosehips. If they don't bother your system, then try eating them in greater quantity.

Rosa rugosa, native to eastern Asia, is often cultivated in the states. It is worthwhile to split open the jumbo-sized rosehips to separate the seeds, saving the flesh for a delicious edible. If I had access to more of these giant rosehips, then I might consider making rosehip jelly.

Rosa rugosa has very large rosehips.

Chokecherries (*Prunus virginiana*) are small, but often greatly abundant.

Prunus spp.

Rose Family / Almond Subfamily (formerly in the Plum Subfamily)

Cherry and Plum: From Flesh to Pit

If you find a fleshy fruit that appears to have a "seam" down one side and a stony pit in the middle, it is likely a member of the *Prunus* genus of the Rose family, usually a wild cherry or plum. This closely related group of trees and shrubs also includes apricots (*P. armeniaca*), peaches and nectarines (*P. persica*), and almonds (*P. dulcis*). For most species, we eat the fleshy fruit and throw the pit away, but in the almond, we discard the (not-so) fleshy fruit and crack open the pit to eat the nut.

You can experiment with processing and eating the fruits and/or nuts from any species of this genus. However, be mindful that the nuts contain amygdalin, a glycoside that breaks down into benzaldehyde and cyanide. Benzaldehyde is the source of bitter almond flavor, often utilized in cooking. The degree of bitterness is a good indicator of the concentration of amygdalin in the raw nut.

Amygdalin, also known as laetrile or Vitamin B17, is considered beneficial in small doses. But excess consumption of amygdalin leads to cyanide poisoning. Adding to the name game, cyanide may be referred to in other texts as either prussic acid or hydrocyanic acid (its liquid form) or hydrogen cyanide (its gaseous form).

Whatever the name, cyanide prevents cells from utilizing oxygen in the bloodstream, resulting in asphyxiation at the cellular level. A lethal dose is somewhere between twenty and fifty raw bitter almonds (a different variety from the sweet almonds we normally eat).

Anything else in the genus is theoretically less bitter and less toxic than bitter almonds. A typical cherry pit, for example, contains only about .078 milligrams of cyanide, while the lethal dose of cyanide is between .5 to 3.5 milligrams per kilogram of body weight. At that rate, it would take at least 500 raw cherry pits to kill a 180 lb. (80 kg) person, and even then, the seeds are more likely to pass through the gut intact.

In any case, proper cooking, drying, and/or oxidation destroys the cyanide, making the pit – or rather the nut inside the pit – edible.

Description, Habitat, and Range

Like many members of the Rose family, the various species of cherries and plums have alternate leaves with serrated edges. The flowers have 5 separate sepals and 5 separate petals. There are typically numerous stamens surrounding the pistil. The pistil is positioned above or superior to the sepals, which fall away as the ovary matures into a fruit.

The common pattern of this group is easily recognized in the fruit. Big or small, all members of the genus produce a drupe, a fleshy fruit with a stony pit, and they all have what looks like a seam down one side.

Bitter cherry (*Prunus emarginata*).

Chokecherries (*Prunus virginiana*) are the most widespread member of the group, naturally found growing from coast-to-coast. The American wild plum (*P. americana*) is native to the eastern two-thirds of the country, but frequently cultivated in the West and some have gone feral, spreading into new, favorable new habitats. The pin cherry (*P. pensylvanica*) and the well-named bitter cherry (*P. emarginata*) may also be encountered in the Mountain West. Across North America, there are numerous other species of native wild cherries, plums, almonds, and peaches, as well as several imported, cultivated species, for about sixty species in all.

Whole chokecherries are mashed with a rock and made into patties to dry...

Chokecherries (*Prunus virginiana*)

My grandmother picked gallons of chokecherries every year. She boiled the juice out and made chokecherry syrup and chokecherry wine. I loved the syrup on pancakes, and I tried the wine a few times, too. As a survival food, however, chokecherries seemed useless, because we discarded the pulp and kept only the juice.

Then I met a Crow Indian woman named Alma Snell, author of the book *A Taste of Heritage*, who taught me native ways to process the fruits. Put fresh cherries on a metate stone and mash them up, pits and all, then dry. The nut inside the pit has an almond-like aroma. This is no coincidence, since almonds are closely related. The combined

...or put through a grinder and made into chocolate-covered patties!

cherry-almond aroma is rich and exciting to work with while you mash them on a rock. Like most members of this genus, cherry pits contain prussic acid, a form of cyanide, but the compound is unstable and easily destroyed by mild heat and oxygen. Mashing and drying chokecherries renders them safe to eat. Mashed chokecherries are a power-packed wild food, since they include both a fruit and a nut. Alma Snell poured chocolate over her mashed chokecherries to make delicious cherry chocolates!

A basketful of cherries!

In timed studies I've handpicked up to one gallon of cherries per hour, which then took another forty minutes to mash with a rock. The dried chokecherry mash makes a good trail mix, and its crunchy enough that one is unlikely to overindulge and run out of food too soon.

Optionally, cook the fresh mash and use it as a filling in "chokecherry ashcake turnovers," as described in *Participating in Nature*. The pit shells are crunchy, but chewable. Even better, run whole chokecherries through a grinder, which speeds up the process and reduces the shells to a uniformly small size.

Caution: The crushed pit shells are hard and crunchy. My brother cracked a tooth chewing dried chokecherry mash. Chew gently to break up the dried chokecherry mash without crunching down on the shells.

I have also heard that chokecherries can be dried whole and stored for six months or more before eating them. The shells become less crunchy over time, which may be due to some type of time-release mechanism that breaks down the pit shells to facilitate germination.

Nanking Cherry (*Prunus tomentosa*)

Nanking cherries are one of the great-untapped resources of the urban jungle. They are cultivated in many cities and watered frequently enough to produce bumper crops. They grow as a shrub, often pruned to four or five feet tall. The Nanking cherry is about ¾ of an inch in diameter and has a flattened, oval pit in the middle. Nanking cherries were introduced from China. Consider planting a few bushes in your own yard.

Nanking cherries (*P. tomentosa*) are common in the urban jungle.

It is easy to gather several gallons of Nanking cherries in an hour. I place a five gallon bucket on the ground and then, bending a branch over it, run my hands up the branch stripping and flicking the cherries off, which fall into the bucket below.

Nanking cherries are great eaten straight off the bush. They also make a delicious jam, jelly, puree, or syrup. Nanking cherries are delicious in pies, if you have the patience to squeeze the pits one-by-one from every cherry. If pie-making becomes a regular habit, then consider investing in a mechanical cherry pitter.

We have tried crushing whole cherries for fruit leather, but the pit shells were unchewable. A finer grind might help. Optionally, mash and cook the fruit, then screen the pits out, as shown for plums on the facing page. Make fruit leather from the resulting puree.

Nanking cherry pie and syrup.

200

Wild Plum (*Prunus americana*)

Compared to other wild fruits, picking wild plums is like going to the supermarket. A good crop can easily produce more plums than you can use. Ripe plums vary from wonderfully sweet to woefully astringent and sometimes mealy. Quality varies from bush to bush, region to region, and probably from year to year, depending on the growing conditions. They are sweeter after a frost, and often at their prime only when they have fallen off the bush – in which case they may need to be rinsed to remove any grit before processing.

Wild plum (*P. americana*).

Wild plums are most prevalent in the Great Plains and eastward, with natural pockets appearing throughout the Rocky Mountain states. However, they have been planted as windbreaks and hedges, forming dense, self-sustaining thickets of survival food throughout the West. You can plant your own survival hedge around the yard, in the neighborhood, or up the holler.

Wild plums are naturally smaller than cultivated plums. Yet, like their bigger kin, you can slice the plums in half or simply pull them apart at the seam with your thumbs to remove the pit, then dry or cook the fleshy fruit. If, manual pitting is impractical for dealing with larger harvests try cooking the plums

Drying split plums on the dashboard.

Separating the pits with a screen.

Cracking plum pits with lineman's pliers.

with as little water as possible, then rub the resulting pulpy mash through a ¼-inch mesh screen, separating out the pits. This method is very effective at capturing all of the pulp and none of the pits. Dry the resulting mash as plum leather, or add sugar and pectin to make plum jam.

If you can't stand throwing out the pits, or want to do something new and cool, try cracking them open to extract the almond-like nuts. A pair of pliers, especially wide lineman's pliers, work well for cracking pits. Place the pit vertically in the jaws of the tool, then crack down firmly, but try not to completely crush the nut inside. Work inside a box or bucket to catch the cracked shells and nuts. After cracking the pits, do a quick hand sort to pull out the nuts.

The nuts are small, and the reward dubious in practical terms, but cool and worth trying. It is okay to eat a few nuts raw, but roast the rest to break down the cyanide compounds before eating them in masse.

Optionally, if you just want the bitter almond flavor for cooking, simply place a few pits in a plastic bag and crush them with a hammer. Simmer the resulting mash in a bit of water and strain out the debris, then use the tea water in any recipe that calls for bitter almond flavoring.

Plum pit almonds.

Related Species

Apricots (*P. armeniaca*) are one of my all-time favorite foods, probably in part because we had several apricot trees in our yard when I was a kid in California. We ate gallons of apricot jam and hundreds of dried apricots every year. Apricots are harder to come by here in Montana, but we regularly raid neglected and feral apricot trees along driving routes in and out of state.

Apricots and peaches are sometimes segregated into their own genera, as *Armeniaca* (apricot) and *Amygdalus* (peach), but easily hybridize with members of *Prunus*. The pits may be processed similarly to plum pits.

Apricots are less common in the Mountain West, but keep an eye out for neglected urban and feral trees.

All *Prunus* species can be grafted onto one another. I once met a man who grafted peaches onto wild plums that grew on his Idaho homestead.

Picking apricots from a feral tree near Grand Coulee Dam in Washington.

Serviceberries can be prolific and filling for the avid forager.

Amelanchier alnifolia

Rose Family / Almond Subfamily (formerly the Apple Subfamily)

Serviceberry: It's Got Substance

Many wild berries are all juice and sugar, but serviceberries, also known as saskatoons, have substance that a forager can subsist on. Serviceberries are closely related to apples and produce a berry that is both juicy and pulpy.

Bears love to fatten up on serviceberries, as do I. It is easy to eat a quart of berries while attempting to pick a pail full. Serviceberries are also easy to dry and store, and they make an excellent trail food. Native Americans often mashed and dried them in hamburger-shaped patties or mixed them with jerky and fat to make pemmican.

Description, Habitat, and Range

Like many other members of the Rose family, serviceberries have oval-shaped leaves with serrated edges. The flowers typically form in a raceme, and each flower has 5 separate sepals and 5 separate white petals. There are 10+ stamens and a single pistil with five styles.

Like miniature apples.

Like apples, serviceberries produce a false fruit, known as a pome. The fleshy fruit is formed from an enlarged receptacle fused around the ovary, rather than from the ovary itself.

Amelanchier alnifolia is found principally at low to moderate elevation in cooler climates from Alaska to California and east to Quebec. It grows intermixed with other shrubbery in moist, deciduous woodlands and along streams. It also grows in thickets in semi-arid areas that lack sufficient moisture to support other trees or shrubs.

Serviceberries are often infected with rust fungus.

Worldwide, there are about 20 species of *Amelanchier*, with about 10 species scattered across North America, including *A. utahensis*, *A. pallida*, and *A. pumila* in the western states. The berries may not be quite as large or prolific, but they are equally worth gathering when in season.

Watch Out for Bears

If you find a good patch of serviceberries, there is a good chance that bears visit it, too. Watch for sign, such as fresh piles of bear scat, and be alert for possible bears lurking in the bushes. If they have dibs on the patch, then it's best to wait your turn!

Serviceberries are often infected with a *Gymnosporangium* rust fungus, leaving orange spots on the berries or leaves, and sometimes pale little tentacle-like tubes. During the rust's life cycle, it alternates between serviceberries and junipers or cedars. In some cases, the

Grind serviceberries, make patties to dry in the sun, and enjoy all year long.

bushes are so thoroughly infected that good berries are hard to come by. But usually there are just a few berries with orange spots mixed in with the rest. I pick them out as I see them, but I've also eaten many fungal berries without ill effect. Be more cautious if you have food allergies, particularly to mushrooms.

In favorable conditions I harvest two to four quarts of serviceberries per hour of effort. Serviceberries are not as flavorful as other fruits, making it possible to eat more without over-doing it. The berries are good in jams and pies, but the best application of serviceberries is to use them as the natives did—in berry cakes and pemmican. The berries can be dried whole or mashed and shaped into berry cakes for drying. Drying sweetens or concentrates the flavor. These berry cakes are a delicious and nutritious treat on the trail any time of year.

Our dog, Timber, liked serviceberries too!

Related Species

Serviceberries are closely related to apples, hawthorns, cotoneasters, mountain ash, and more. Most of these fruits can be grafted onto one another. For example, apple buds can be grafted onto serviceberry bushes to cultivate apple crops in wild places.

Black hawthorn produces fruits in convenient clusters for easy picking.

Crataegus douglasii

Rose Family / Almond Subfamily (formerly the Apple Subfamily)

Black Hawthorn: Packed with Pectin

The fruit of a hawthorn is technically a pome, like an apple, but informally it's known as a berry. Black hawthorn berries are edible and tasty straight off the bush, but contain such big, hard seeds that one isn't likely to eat more than a handful of fruit. The seeds can be spit out, or a few may be crunched down, if you have good, solid teeth. However, the key to enjoying this fine fruit is to separate out the seeds. Hawthorns are so packed with natural pectin that the juice readily jells moments after it is squeezed out of the fruit.

Description, Habitat, and Range

The inch-long thorns on branches of a hawthorn bush are impossible to overlook. Interestingly, the "haw" in hawthorn is an old word for hedge; these "hedgethorns" were planted as fences to deter trespassers as far back as the Middle Ages.

Black hawthorn leaves are less oval and more pointed than most members

The thorn in "hawthorn."

of the Rose family and generally deeply serrated towards the tips. The flowers are typically clustered in a raceme with 5 separate sepals and 5 separate white petals. There are typically 10 stamens and a single pistil with five styles. The fleshy fruit is formed from the enlarged receptacle fused around the ovary, rather than from the ovary itself.

Picking hawthorn berries in Idaho.

Black hawthorns typically grow in dry ground, near water, often found in canyons or near rivers and streams at low to middle elevations from California to Alaska and across the northern states and provinces to Quebec. Worldwide, there are more than 200 species of *Crataegus*, most of them scattered across North America, with only half a dozen species found in the Mountain West.

Squeezing out Pectin

The best way we know to separate the seeds from the pulp is to mash the fruit by hand in a bowl, mix in a little water, and then squeeze the mash through a clean sock from the rag pile. Squeeze hard to force

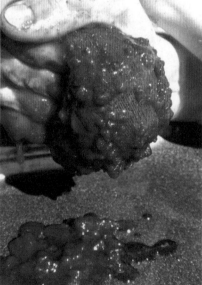

Mash the fruit, add a little water, and squeeze the pectin out through a sock.

out globs of juicy pulp and pectin. In a matter of minutes the pectin will begin to jell on your collecting dish, until you can turn the dish on its side without the mash dripping off. The mash can be made into jam or used to supplement commercial pectin when making jam or jelly from some other fruit. The pulp can also be dried and eaten as a sweet, rubbery fruit leather.

Just like Cranberries

This pectin-rich pulp looks a great deal like cranberries, and can be eaten straight or sweetened. The only problem is that it looks too much like cranberries, so it is difficult to appreci-

The pulp resembles cranberries.

ate the unique and delicious taste of the hawthorn when one's neural pathways are anticipating cranberry flavor.

Intrigued by the pectin, I added egg whites and sugar to a batch and used an electric mixer to beat it into a sweet and frothy, meringue-like foam topping for my hawthorn berry dish. It was delicious!

Hawthorn "ice cream."

Ice Cream?

Yes, you can even turn your pectin-rich hawthorn berry pulp into something greatly resembling ice cream, in taste, texture, and appearance. Combine hawthorn pulp with egg whites, sugar, and milk. Beat the ingredients into frothy foam with an electric mixer. Pour in cups or bowls and freeze until solid.

Naturally, I don't have an actual recipe for the amount of each ingredient, and mine came out excessively sweet. Experiment and see what you can come up with!

Good for the Heart

Medicinally, a tincture of the fruit, leaves, and flowers of various hawthorn species can be taken to increase blood flow to the heart muscle and gently strengthen heart function. Adverse reactions to hawthorn as a medicine include upset stomach, dizziness, headaches, or nausea, but one is unlikely to experience these symptoms from the fruit of the black hawthorn.

Other Uses

Thorns from a hawthorn can be fashioned into primitive fishhooks, typically by lashing the thorn onto a stout little twig to make a J-shaped hook.

Apple buds can be grafted onto hawthorn branches, to potentially turn a hawthorn patch into an apple orchard.

Hawthorn fish hook with a horsehair cordage leader.

Related Species

All species of hawthorn (*Crataegus*) produce edible fruits—black, purple, red, or yellow—and all of them are crammed full of big, hard seeds. Blue-black or purple fruits are generally the most pulpy and delicious, while red ones are more seedy and astringent.

Fireberry hawthorn (*Crataegus chrysocarpa*).

Pacific crabapple (*Malus fusca*) and apple blossoms (*M. domestica*).
Malus domestica, M. fusca, M. pumila
Rose Family / Almond Subfamily (formerly the Apple Subfamily)

Apple and Crabapple: Feral Fruits

In days gone by, children of towns big and small roamed the streets, sampling fruits that hung over neighborhood sidewalks. Growing up in this holdover from the Garden of Eden, kids instinctively became foragers, connecting with nature in their communities.

Unfortunately, architects began modeling buildings with ornamental cedars, junipers, and dwarf pines—trees and shrubs that didn't make a mess of leaves or rotten fruit on the ground. Fruit trees fell out of favor or were relegated to the backyard. The Garden of Eden gave way to a sterile landscape, providing yet another reason for kids to grow up indoors. Fruit trees, where they exist at all, are often neglected, as people prefer driving to the store to buy them already bagged. For the forager, the happy/sad result is that people are often delighted to accept an offer to glean their nuisance trees.

When you landscape your yard, be sure to keep the neighborhood children in mind, and plant fruit trees along a front sidewalk to cultivate the next generation of foragers.

Plant for our young people.

211

Got cabin fever? Try harvesting crabapples and making jelly in mid-winter!

Description, Habitat, and Range

Apples are as easy to identify as fruit from the grocery store. However, store-bought apples are typically larger, more uniform, free of blemishes and worms, and often hard as rocks, since they are bred for shipping rather than for texture and flavor.

Homegrown apples can be sweeter and juicier than store-bought apples, but not always. The best-tasting varieties are often hybrids that produce delicious fruit, yet are susceptible to diseases. Hardier apple trees typically produce tart fruits which are great for making anything from cider to apple pies, but not so great as eating apples.

Crabapples are even smaller, harder, and more tart than the larger eating apples, but some are surprisingly delicious, and sweeter after a frost. Some cling to the trees and can be harvested in winter.

The native Oregon crabapple (*M. fusca*) grows along the Pacific coast from California to Alaska. The acidic fruits are edible raw or cooked.

Feral Trees

Look for neglected apple trees on public or semi-public lands, such as city parks, roadways without too much pollution, parking lots, businesses, and along waterways in urban areas. You can also ask permission from homeowners and businesses to pick their apples. Be sure to rake the ground afterwards, providing greatly appreciated yard maintenance in exchange for the free fruit.

In favorable conditions, apple trees spread on their own from seed. However, the offspring of hybrid varieties may not taste anything like the parent trees. It is fun to find these feral trees, as well as abandoned trees, planted around long-gone homesteads.

Brigham Young University in Rexburg, Idaho maintains an apple orchard museum with dozens of different species, where the public is encouraged to come pick. Every community should have a similar orchard or plant fruit trees in public parks.

I sometimes dig up small feral apple trees and transplant them home, because I know they are hardy enough to survive the intermittent cold snaps, droughts, and diseases that frequently kill off more delicate apple varieties.

Apples, Apples, Apples Everywhere

If I had to live on just one food, I think I would choose apples. I am rarely inspired to eat commercial, pesticide-laden apples, but I gorge myself on homegrown apples and apple cider every fall. The best apples go in the cellar as eating apples. Extending the harvest from October into January is always a thrill. Some apples are trimmed, sliced, and bagged for the freezer to make apple pies all year long. Peeling the apples makes a more refined pie, but for expediency, I skip that step and find the resulting pies entirely satisfying. Other apples are sliced and dried in a dehydrator for mid-winter walkabouts.

Many people make applesauce or the closely related apple butter, but I prefer using apple slices, sugar, cinnamon, and pectin to make "apple pie jam."

Since crabapples are smaller and more labor-intensive to process, most people just dice and cook them down for juice, then strain off the solids and make jelly. Crabapples typically contain a lot of pectin, but additional pectin is recommended to ensure proper jelling.

My parents bought an old-fashioned cider press when I was a kid, because my grandmother had a whole orchard full of apples to process.

Have more apples than you can eat? Consider investing in a cider press.

I still have the cider press, but not many mature apple trees. However, it isn't difficult to find a sufficient supply of apples to fill the freezer with gallons and gallons of delicious cider. It is not a particularly efficient process, as boxes and boxes of pulp are tossed out to the chickens or the compost heap, but it is better than letting the apples go to waste. For expediency, we seldom trim the apples, just hose them off and throw them in the press, worms, bruises, bird pecks and all.

A person could easily start a small-scale apple cider business, selling fresh apple cider by the cup at farmer's markets, or on a bigger scale, by trading apple cider for apple-picking rights. Fresh apple cider that sits around in the fridge or on the counter quickly ferments to become an alcoholic beverage known as hard cider, which tends to have a tangy vinegar taste.

Note that apple seeds contain small amounts of hydrogen cyanide, which can be toxic if consumed in excess. However, the compound breaks down easily in the presence of heat and oxygen, such as through drying or cooking.

Fruit leather, made seeds and all, after cooking down mushy mid-winter crabapples.

How many people grow a flowering crabapple in their yard, yet have never tried the fruit?

Flowering Crabs

Urban landscapes are full of flowering crabs, apple trees that are grown for their flowers rather than their fruits. There are countless different varieties, producing fruits that range from about 3/8-inch up to 1-inch in diameter. The fruits look like miniaturized apples, yet few people recognize them for what they are, and virtually nobody eats them or even knows that they are edible.

The fruits typically cling to the trees all winter long, or until consumed one day by a flock of birds. Some fruits become soft and mushy from freezing. Others slowly dry and shrivel on the trees. Most flowering crabs are tart, but a few are passably sweet.

Most crabapples can be eaten whole, bearing in mind that the raw seeds contain small amounts of hydrogen cyanide, so don't eat too many at once.

The tartness of most flowering crabs will naturally limit how many you want to eat raw. Otherwise, bring the harvest home, add a little water to prevent scorching, and boil the flavor out of the fruits.

Jelly is probably the best choice for flowering crabs, due to the tartness of the fruits and the amount of sugar required to sweeten them. Strain out the pulp and use the juice for jelly-making. Optionally, add a cinnamon stick and try the diluted juice as a tart apple cider.

The cooked fruit can also be run

Straight into the candy bowl. These little crabapples had a nice sweet-and-sour flavor, great eaten whole as a tasty treat.

through a colander to separate out the seeds and pulpy material. Sweeten the resulting applesauce as necessary and dry it for a delicious, tart fruit leather.

Optionally, flowering crab seeds are so small that the fruit of some soft, mushy varieties can be turned into tasty leather without using a colander. Remove the stems, cook the fruit down, and mash it thoroughly. Add sugar as needed and dry. (See photo on page 214.)

Skills such as this could be vital in the event of a civil disaster. It is possible to harvest a great deal of food along city sidewalks, and in an emergency, that might be the only

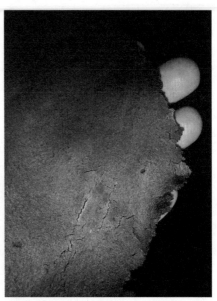

Flowering crab apples can be used to make a delicious, tart fruit leather.

food available. If necessary, a person could live a long time on crabapples!

Take a walk the next time you get the winter blues, and cheer yourself up by bringing home a nice harvest of wild edibles!

Related Species

The Rose family includes many genera closely related to apples with similar-looking, but usually smaller fruits, including the pear (*Pyrus*), quince (*Cydonia*), loquat (*Eriobotrya*), Christmasberry (*Photinia*), chokeberry (*Aronia*), hawthorn (*Crataegus*), serviceberry (*Amelanchier*), mountain ash (*Sorbus*), firethorn (*Pyracantha*) and *Cotoneaster*.

In all of these genera, the fruit is an apple-like false fruit known as a

Firethorn (*Pyracantha*) is often cultivated as a hedge. The fruit can be used to make jelly. The seeds contain small amounts of hydrogen cyanide, but it breaks down easily when cooked.

pome. The ovary is positioned inferior, within the receptacle, and a fleshy fruit is formed from the enlarged receptacle, rather than from the ovary itself.

Given the position of the ovary beneath the flower, the remains of the flower parts can be seen on the tip of the fruit. The petals fall off, but the five sepals remain attached, forming a distinctive five-pointed star. Look at the end of an apple and sometimes you may find shriveled up stamens still in the little gap between the sepals.

As is common in the Rose family, most of these shrubs and trees have more-or-less oval shaped leaves with serrated edges.

All of these fruits are more-or-less edible, but some are highly sour-astringent. Many people erroneously believe them to be poisonous. Like apples, the seeds of some species contain hydrogen cyanide and therefore should be eaten in moderation or dried or cooked prior to consumption, but otherwise, they are not "poisonous."

Cotoneaster lucidus, a native of Siberia, is widely cultivated as an ornamental hedge in the states. The seeds contain small amounts of cyanide, but the fruits are otherwise edible.

Mountain ash, firethorn, and *Cotoneaster* are often cultivated as ornamentals. The fruits often cling to the branches through much of the winter and are enjoyed by the birds. You can also plant them as ornamental survival food!

In my opinion, mountain ash fruits are wholly unpalatable, but some people like them. I've only nibbled on firethorn, and found them tart, but passable.

Cotoneaster jelly.

Cotoneasters are okay, but not overly exciting. The fruits dry as hollow skins in winter, but even then it is possible to collect them, add water, and boil the juice out to make a novel jelly.

Red elderberry blossoms (*Sambucus racemosa*) and blue elderberry (*S. cerulea*).

Sambucus cerulea

Adoxa Family (formerly in the Honeysuckle Family)

Blue Elderberry: The Mother Lode

Elderberries are conveniently bunched for picking. The berries grow in dense clusters that can be readily clipped off or stripped by hand into a container. With multiple berry clusters on a single bush, finding one good elderberry is like hitting the mother lode. You may be able to harvest a year's supply from one bush.

As far as berries go, it's more like striking silver than gold, as elderberries are not the world's most exciting fruit straight off the bush. The berries are not overly sweet and the texture is seedy. But elderberries are great for syrup or jelly, and they can be dried and added to trail mix. Elderberries can even help ward off the flu.

In addition to *Sambucus cerulea*, several other species of elderberry are found in the Mountain West and around the world. The identification, botanical names, and edibility or tox-

Our red elderberry (*S. racemosa*) produces black berries.

icity of each species are highly muddled in literature and in popular culture, but the important points may be readily clarified.

Description, Habitat, and Range

Elderberries are shrubs with pithy stalks and opposite, pinnately divided leaves. The flowers form in a dense, flat-topped cluster, called a corymb. The fruit is a fleshy berry, and the remains of the sepals can be seen attached to the fruit. Blue elderberries are found throughout the western states from Montana to Texas, west to the Pacific coast. They are more abundant in the Pacific coast states and less so in the Rockies.

Photo by Rosalee de la Forêt

White powder on the berries is wild yeast. Read more about it on page 225.

Botanists disagree about whether *S. cerulea* is a species in its own right, or should more properly be classified as a subspecies of the Eurasian black elderberry, *S. nigra*. Other botanists classify blue elderberry as *S. mexicana*. In addition, the most widespread elderberry in the mountain West, commonly found growing at higher elevations, has black fruits, but is usually classified as a variety of the red elderberry, *S. racemosa*. In other words, our black elderberry is actually a red elderberry and our blue elderberry might be a black one! Make sense so far?

Edible or Poisonous?

In popular culture, blue elderberries are considered edible, while red elderberries are often believed to be poisonous. Potency varies significantly from species to species, but most elderberry leaves, twigs, branches, roots, and seeds contain a cyanide-inducing glycoside, meaning that the glycoside produces cyanide when it is metabolized in the body. Ingesting any of these parts can lead to a toxic build up of cyanide in the body. That sounds especially scary for anyone old enough to remember the Tylenol® scare of 1982, when seven people died after taking cyanide-laced tablets.

When we hear that something might be poisonous, we often blow it out of proportion. To put the issue in perspective, consider that cherry pits also contain cyanogenic glycosides and apple seeds contain cyanogenic acids, but how many people do you know who have died from cherry pits or apple seeds? I've certainly swallowed plenty of both, and I often eat whole apple cores, seeds and all. I've also eaten many blue and red elderberries, seeds and all. Your body can detoxify limited quantities of cyanogenic compounds, but you can poison yourself if you consume too much.

Fortunately, cyanogenic compounds are highly unstable and break down easily in the presence of heat and oxygen. Cooking or drying the fruits (of any color) will break down the toxins. Likewise, drying elderberry stems renders them safe to make into whistles, flutes, spoons, or anything else you might like to make from them.

Batter-fried or Berries

Elderberry flowers can be batter-fried for a unique and fun fritter. Dip the flowerhead in the batter and fry one side with the main stem attached. Then use scissors to clip away each of the smaller stems before flipping the fritter over to cook the other side. The cooked fritter may be served with syrup like a regular pancake. Elderberry flowers add surprisingly little taste or texture, so fritters are a good way to intro-

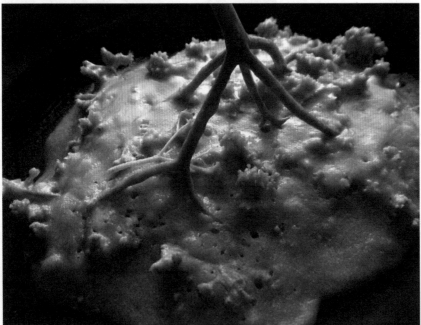

Elderberry flowers make fun pancake fritters.

duce wild edibles and extra nutrition to conventional American food. For additional flavor, sweeten the batter with a little tropical fruit juice mix or some elderberry syrup... if you made some the previous fall.

If you leave the flowers to mature into fruits, you'll likely harvest buckets of berries in the fall. From personal experience, I like blue elderberries, but I usually have to drive farther West to find them. Black elderberries (i.e.: red elderberries with black berries) are more locally abundant, but far less appetizing.

Finding one good bush is like hitting the mother lode.

Blue elderberries are edible raw, but not too exciting. Drying sweetens them some, but the seeds give an unpleasant squeak or crunch. The berries are best cooked down for juice and then made into syrup or jelly. The stems may be left on for convenience, but may impact the flavor of the juice somewhat.

Controlled studies have shown that people can recover from the flu quicker by taking an elderberry extract at the earliest onset of symptoms. I've used the commercial product, Sambucol®, and found it remarkably effective. A home-made syrup, jelly, or tea of the dried berries can have similar benefits.

Related Species

Worldwide there are between 5 and 30 species of elderberry, depending on whether they are lumped together as subspecies and varieties of each other, or segregated out as separate species. Any elderberry would be worth experimenting with.

Oregon grape (*Mahonia aquifolium*) can produce fruit in great abundance.

Mahonia aquifolium, M. nervosa, M. repens
Barberry Family

Oregon Grape: The Ungrape

Oregon grape is not a grape at all, but an intensely tart berry from an evergreen shrub with spiny leaves. Oregon grapes, also known as barberries, include several species with partially overlapping ranges throughout the West, so one is seldom far from the shrubbery. However, fruit production varies according to species and location, especially with the widespread but smaller *Mahonia repens*. Often there is only enough fruit for a jolting taste. But if you are lucky enough to score a good patch or live where the bushes fruit prodigiously every year, then grab a basket and start picking! Cook juice out of the berries to make delicious, tart Oregon grape syrup or jelly.

Flowering Oregon grape.

Description, Habitat, and Range

Oregon grapes have evergreen, holly-like leaves and clusters of small, yellow flowers that mature into purplish, tart berries. Depending on species and location, the plants vary from under one foot tall up to six feet tall. There are often 2 or 3 small bracts masquerading as sepals on the back of the flower, but otherwise there are typically 6 true sepals and 6 petals, often appearing in series of 3 each. The ovary is positioned superior and matures as a sour berry. The inner bark is a brilliant yellow, due to the presence of the intensely bitter alkaloid, berberine.

A basket of berries!

Mahonia repens is the most widespread species, commonly found growing among pine needle debris and sandy soils of open, dry coniferous forests from British Columbia to Texas and California to Minnesota. *Mahonia aquifolium* and *M. nervosa* are locally abundant in slightly moister Pacific climates, ranging from British Columbia to California, east to the continental divide.

Tart to the Taste

Oregon grapes have a unique sour-astringent taste that is mild enough in some species and locations to serve as a pleasant trail nibble. But often the jolt of flavor results in uncontrolled face-contortions while attempting to chew and swallow. The seeds are big enough to be noticeable, but easily eaten with the fruit. In most cases, fresh Oregon grapes are best blended with sweeter berries to tame the fruit. Native peoples of the Pacific Northwest, for example, were known to mix Oregon grapes with salal berries (*Gaultheria*).

On a Stone Age survival trip in northwestern Montana, we extensively foraged and harvest Oregon grapes, and mixed them with mealy kinnikinnick berries (*Arctostaphylos uva-ursi*). Kinnikinnick isn't very satisfying by itself, but somehow the two fruits blend really well together.

Boil Them Berries Down

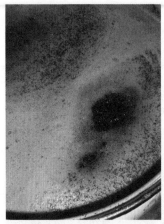

Pectin rises to the top of the pot as a thick white-pink foam.

Oregon grapes make a delicious tart syrup or jelly, when you can find the berries in sufficient abundance. To harvest the berries in quantity, hold the branch in one hand and strip each cluster of berries with the other, dropping them into a container. Expect to get poked and prickled by the leaves in the process.

To separate out any stems, leaves, and bugs, pour the berries in a shallow cardboard box and shake it back and forth to tease the debris to the top where you can pick it off. Sort the remaining debris handful-by-handful as you transfer the fruit to another container.

To make syrup or jelly, add just enough water to the bottom of the pan to prevent burning, then simmer the berries and periodically mash with a potato masher to squeeze the juice out. Cook and mash the berries until the juice has been thoroughly extracted, then strain out the pulp and seeds, saving the juice. Add sugar to thicken into syrup, or follow a conventional grape jelly recipe.

Oregon grapes contain significant quantities of pectin that simmers to the top of the pan as a thick, white-pink foam. Many authors claim that Oregon grapes and other fruits with pectin can theoretically be made into jelly without additional pectin, but I haven't achieved that result. I suspect a person would have to add ten times the normal sugar to basically solidify the syrup into "jelly."

In one super-abundant patch, three of us collected a five-gallon bucket full of Oregon grapes in half an hour. But we didn't have time to sort

We filled a five-gallon bucket in half an hour.

and cook them, since we were also harvesting and processing apricots, plums, apples, serviceberries, and chokecherries. To save time, we ran the Oregon grapes and debris through the cider press, which definitely did not squeeze all the juice out, but did extract about three quarts of juice with little effort. Most of it went in the freezer for winter, and some blended with apple cider for a delicious fresh drink.

Wild Yeast

White powder on the surface of Oregon grapes is airborne wild yeast, which is also highly noticeable on elderberries. Take a look back at the photos of gooseberries, huckleberries, serviceberries, and hawthorn berries and notice a little yeast there, too. Utilizing wild yeast is as simple as mixing flour and water. Since the yeast is in the air, you will inevitably catch some. Leave the bread dough in a bag or pot in a warm spot for a few days, and it will begin to rise and become sourdough. It won't rise as much as it would with commercial yeast, but it will rise.

White powder on the berries is wild yeast.

To assist the sourdough process, try rinsing yeast off Oregon grapes, and use the rinse water. Better yet, blend berries into the dough so the wild yeast can feed on the natural fruit sugars and multiply. Raspberries and blackberries work especially well; I believe the texture may catch extra yeast, and the sweetness of the fruits feeds the yeast well. Crushed Oregon grapes could work, but it might be desirable to screen out the seeds. Read more about sourdough in the section on ashcakes in *Participating in Nature*.

The yellow inner bark of any species contains berberine, a powerful medicine, especially concentrated in the roots.

Big Medicine

Oregon grape twigs and roots contain berberine, an intensely bitter yellow alkaloid. Scrape off the bark and note the bright yellow color of the alkaloid. It is one of the most powerful herbal medicines I know.

Bacterial infections can be life threatening in wilderness situations, especially without access to modern antibiotics. But I once killed a bacterial infection in my finger by soaking it overnight in a tea of Oregon grape root. It was a month-long survival trip, and thanks to the Oregon grape root, I was able to stay for the entire adventure.

Oregon grape root is a good alternative to goldenseal, which is endangered from overharvesting, and isn't native to the West anyway. Read more about the medicinal uses of Oregon grape in *Botany in a Day*.

Related Species

Worldwide, there are about 70 species of *Mahonia*, including 10 species scattered across North America. *Mahonia* is closely related to *Berberis*, which is often cultivated as an ornamental. Generally, *Berberis* includes spiny shrubs with simple, deciduous leaves, while *Mahonia* includes evergreen plants and shrubs with pinnate leaves consisting of 5 to 15 leaflets with spines along the edges. However, neither description works for all species, and plants from the two genera are capable of hybridizing with each other. They are sometimes lumped together as a single genus, *Berberis*. Thus, many species are shuffled back and forth between the genera and may have duplicate names, such as *Mahonia aquifolium* and *Berberis aquifolium*. All species from these two genera share similar edible and medicinal uses.

Red barberry (*Berberis thunbergii*) is often cultivated in the Mountain West.

Kinnikinnick often grows only a couple inches tall.

Arctostaphylos uva-ursi

Heath Family / Madrone Subfamily

Kinnikinnick: Almost Food

Kinnikinnick, also known as bearberry, is almost the ideal survival food. The plant is very widespread, found throughout the mountain West wherever there are open pine forests and sandy soils—places where there is seldom anything else to eat. In addition, the berries often cling to the lowly bushes all through the winter, when food is scarcest. Thus, kinnikinnick could almost pass as the ideal survival food, except that a) the berries are seldom found in abundance, and b) while edible, they are too dry and mealy to be particularly enticing. In short, kinnikinnick qualifies as "almost food."

The berries are available in winter.

Description, Habitat, and Range

Kinnikinnick is technically a woody shrub, but seldom reaches more than a few inches off the ground. It prefers sandy, barren soil where there is little competition. It has thick, shiny, alternate, evergreen leaves, and urn- or bell-shaped

227

Foraging harvest. The left basket contains kinnikin-nick berries, rosehips, and gooseberries. The right basket is all Oregon grape.

white or pink flowers that produce dry, powdery red berries. It grows throughout the American West, across all of Canada, and all of the northern states.

Worth Trying

Kinnikinnick berries are dry and mealy, but edible as a trail nibble. They vary from tart to almost sweet. On a Stone Age trek in northwestern Montana, we found exceptionally large kinnikinnick berries and gathered them in quantity, mixing them with Oregon grapes. The dry, astringent kinnikinnick berries blended well with the sour Oregon grapes. Mixing them made both berries more palatable, and we ate them in quantity.

Related Species

Counterintuitively, the lowly kinikinnick belongs to the same genus as robust manzanita bushes. Look closely and you will see they are different-sized versions of the same type of plant. Worldwide, there are about 66 species of *Arctostaphylos*, most of them native to the American West, south to Mexico and Central America.

Most species are semi-desert shrubs. The tallest are small trees, up to about twenty-five feet tall. The red, peeling park, evergreen leaves, urn-shaped flowers, and dry, mealy fruits

Manzanitas are also included in the *Arctostaphylos* genus.

are all good indicators for this genus. The fruits are generally considered edible, although most are dry and mealy like kinnikinnick.

Buffaloberries can produce big crops and cling to the bushes through winter.
Shepherdia argenta
Oleaster Family

Buffaloberry: Winter Harvest

In winter, when the mountains are buried deep in snow and largely devoid of anything edible, I prefer to hike and camp in the valleys. Snow comes, but melts off or blows away, so I put my tennis shoes on and wander through the fields and cottonwoods along the rivers.

I especially love exploring buffaloberry thickets. The dense, thorny bushes provide shelter for cottontail rabbits, pheasants, and porcupines. Wild turkeys forage around the bushes. Flocks of Bohemian waxwings move from bush to bush, vacuuming up buffaloberries as they go. I take my turn foraging as well, delighted to pick berries in the middle of January.

Description, Habitat, and Range

Buffaloberries are found throughout the northern plains, typically on grasslands where the ground is dry but the water table is within a few feet of the sur-

The leaves appear grey due to fine hairs that reflect sunlight.

Beat the bushes with a stick.

face. The shrub is typically about 8 to 10 feet tall, but can grow up to twice that height. The bark is hard and deeply grooved, giving the appearance that the trunk is shedding its skin. The leaves vary from 3/4 to 2 inches long. They are covered with fine hairs that reflect sunlight and conserve moisture, making the bushes appear grey. The branches are mostly opposite, growing in tangled masses, covered with inch-long thorns. If you ever need to escape from a buffalo stampede, crawl into a dense thicket for protection!

Buffaloberries are dioecious, meaning that male and female flowers are borne on separate bushes. Translation: some bushes are completely barren, while others are loaded with berries. The flower consists of four united sepals and no petals. The ovary is positioned partly or wholly inferior, consisting of one carpel. The fruit looks like a drupe (a berry with a stony seed), but in this case the ovary matures as an achene (dry seed), and the fleshy fruit is really the swollen calyx (the sepals). The fruit is orange or bright red, about 1/8 to 1/4 inch in diameter, drying deeper red as winter progresses. It contains a single seed that is chewable, but can get stuck between your teeth.

Float off the debris and keep the berries.

Picking Versus Beating

In timed studies, I found that I can handpick about one quart of buffaloberries per hour on a good bush. In comparison, using sticks to beat the bushes

Berry picking in January. Repeated frosts sweeten the buffaloberries and make them mushy.

and tarps to catch the berries, three of us working together collected about eight gallons of berries and debris in one hour. We used a bucket and a hose to float off most of the sticks and leaves, and a screen with half-inch mesh to catch the remaining sticks that sank with the berries. This half-hour of sorting left us with nearly six gallons of beautiful buffaloberries!

Harvesting is best done from September to December. The berries slowly dry out on the bushes after that, making it more difficult to float off the woody debris, but lingering berries can be picked all winter.

Face-Squeezers

Fresh buffaloberries are real face-squeezers when first "ripe" in August. A hard freeze helps sweeten them, but like chokecherries, the berries remain tart even with copious amounts of sugar. I once made buffaloberry syrup that was delicious, yet so astringent that it was difficult to get through an entire pancake without losing the ability to swallow! I blended it with maple syrup to make it physically consumable.

Strangely, buffaloberries seem to produce an awful smell if kept in a lidded container overnight, yet they stay fresh for days in an open container.

Buffaloberries can be made into jam or pie, except that the little, flat seeds make an unappealing texture. However, the berries

Mr. Kelly likes buffaloberries, too!

make great syrup or jelly. Consider blending them with apples, crabapples, or some other fruit to reduce the tartness. Add water to keep the fruit from burning, and mash them periodically in the pot with a potato masher. Strain off the juice for the syrup or jelly, and dry the leftover berry mash as trail food, or pass it along to the chickens or compost. To finish the syrup or jelly, add as much sugar as there is liquid. Serve the syrup hot over vanilla ice cream for an amazing treat, or cool it to make jelly. Buffaloberries are theoretically tart enough to jell on their own, but it is sensible to add pectin to guarantee that it jells.

Drying the berries virtually eliminates the astringent quality. Mashing the berries facilitates drying. The dried berries or berry cakes make a good trail food. Dried berries can be ground in a coffee grinder then added to smoothies or oatmeal as a superfood rich in nutrients. Some berries cling to the branches all winter long for a great survival food.

Related Species

The Oleaster family consists of shrubs and small trees with alternate or opposite leaves, primarily found in arid habitats. Silvery hairs on the leaves give the bushes a grayish appearance. Worldwide there are 3 genera and 50 species, native to the northern hemisphere.

The soopolallie or soapberry (*S. canadensis*), grows in northern and western forests. The underside of the leaves are silvery, with a sprinkle of cinnamon-colored dots. The berries contain a lot of saponin, and are not very appetizing, but are otherwise considered "edible."

Roundleaf buffaloberry (*S. rotundifolia*) grows in Utah and Arizona. The fruits are silvery grey and edible… but I've never tried them.

Russian olive (*Elaeagnus angustifolia*) is an introduced and sometimes invasive tree originally cultivated for shelterbelts and soil stabilization. It thrives in fencerows across the Great Plains and in mildly alkaline

The soopolallie or soapberry is common in forests, but doesn't taste good.

soil along rivers and streams in semi-arid western states. The trees have stout thorns, up to two-inches long, which can be fashioned into fishhooks. The fruits are silvery-gray, much like the leaves, and very astringent. They are not related to regular olives.

I repeatedly forget how astringent Russian olives are and grab a handful when passing by. After popping a few in my mouth, I chuck the rest. On the other hand, I once went foraging with a two-year-old friend of mine, and I couldn't stop her from eating them! I wonder if we become so acculturated to a super sweet diet as we grow up that we lose our tolerance for astringent foods. If you can handle the astringency, there is a mild sweetness underneath.

Russian olive (*Elaeagnus angustifolia*) is astringent, but minimally edible.

The native silverberry (*Elaeagnus commutata*) grows in patches, found intermittently through the Rocky Mountains and across Canada. The silvery fruits are edible, although I don't recall how they taste.

Autumnberry or autumn olive (*E. umbellata*) looks much like a cross between a Russian olive and a buffalo berry. Introduced as an ornamental and for erosion control, autumnberries are now widespread across the Midwest and eastern states. It is a prolific berry producer, and apparently quite delicious. See Sam Thayer's book *Nature's Garden* for more information.

Worth Mentioning

Some additional plants in the Mountain West have edible fruits worth mentioning. These plants are less common in our region, not overly exciting, or not productive enough to be considered significant wild food sources. Yet, this guide would be incomplete without mention of them. All are worth investigating when you encounter them.

Twisted Stalk (*Streptopus amplexifolius*)

Twisted stalk berries are edible but not overly exciting.

In most members of the Lily family the "fruit" is a dry, three-chambered capsule, but twisted stalk produces a blandly sweet, edible berry. Like most monocot plants, twisted stalk has parallel veins in the leaves. In this case, the leaves clasp around the stem. The stem zigs and zags back and forth from leaf axil to leaf axil, giving the stalk its namesake twisted appearance. Under each leaf hangs a single red-orange berry with seeds and texture somewhat reminiscent of tomatoes.

Twisted stalk can be quite abundant along mountain streams. The berries are reported to have laxative properties, but I have not experienced this, although my consumption has been limited to a couple handfuls at any one time. The berries taste good as a trail nibble, yet are not exciting enough to collect and bring home for cooking or drying.

Highbush Cranberry (*Viburnum spp.*)

Highbush cranberries belong to the Adoxa family, having been separated from the Honeysuckle family. They are not related to true cranberries, which belong to the Heath family like huckleberries (see page 182).

Our native highbush cranberry (*Viburnum edule*) has tart but tasty fruits.

Our native highbush cranberry (*Viburnum edule*) has tart but tasty fruits.

Bunchberries grow in moist evergreen forests.

It grows in cool, moist forests across Canada, plus the Pacific Northwest and down the Rocky Mountains. However, I have only found it in Alaska, where this photograph was taken.

One is more likely to encounter the European highbush cranberry (*V. opulus*), which is cultivated for its showy flowers. The fruits, however, taste terrible. Several other species are cultivated and some taste good.

Bunchberry (*Cornus canadensis*)

Bunchberry is the diminutive kin of the flowering dogwood tree (*Cornus florida*) of the eastern states. Bunchberry has the same elegant flowers, but packaged in a "tree" only a few inches tall.

The plant is typically found growing in moist soil in shady coniferous forests where the forest floor is otherwise largely barren of competition. It is abundant across Canada and the northernmost states, and present, but uncommon down the arid backbone of the Rocky Mountains.

The fruits are edible and mild in flavor, with large, crunchy seeds. The plants fruit prodigiously in the north country, where the Inuit gathered them in quantity. But don't expect to find more than an interesting trail nibble here in the Mountain West.

Wild Grapes (*Vitis spp.*)

Wild grapes are found throughout the lower forty-eight states and eastern Canada. Various species are found here, there, and pretty much everywhere—with the singular exception of the Mountain West, where grapevines are exceedingly

Wild grapes (*Vitis riparia*).

rare. Nevertheless, expect to encounter them sooner or later, given that wild grapes grow in all the western states.

Wild grapes typically grow in riparian areas at lower elevations, such as along the banks of major rivers. In Montana, grape habitat starts in the eastern half of the state, along the Yellowstone River, east of Billings. This distribution is probably typical in other Rocky Mountain states.

I transplanted wild grapes into my greenhouse years ago, where they grow intermingled with domestic grapes, but the wild ones have not produced fruit. And strangely, I have yet to be in the right place at the right time to pick wild grapes. But I once found a dried up raisin hanging on a vine!

Lemonberry Sumac (*Rhus trilobata*)

Lemonberry or three-leaf sumac has red-orange fruits that are hard and fuzzy and not really food. But they have an exciting lemony-sour taste that is enjoyable to nibble on or for flavoring sun tea. The

Photo by T. Beth Kinsey

Fuzzy red sumac fruits are not really chewable like food, but the lemony taste is great in sun tea or as a trail nibble.

red, fuzzy fruits of any sumac can be used similarly, but only *Rhus trilobata* is native and widespread throughout the West. Look for ornamental species of other *Rhus* species in urban landscapes.

The sumacs are in the Cashew or Sumac family and are closely related to poison ivy, poison oak, and poison sumac. These plants were all formerly classified within the *Rhus* genus. Fortunately, botanists determined that the poisonous species with white berries were sufficiently distinct to warrant their own genus, *Toxicodendron*, leaving the edible, red-fruited species as *Rhus*. Nevertheless, anyone with a severe sensitivity to poison ivy might want to approach the sumacs with caution.

Whitebark pines (Pinus albicaulis) produce delicious pine nuts.

Seeds and Nuts

Seeds and nuts are packed with proteins and oils that are essential for survival. Harvest enough seeds and nuts, and it is possible to survive for a long time without animal protein. Fortunately, there are about a thousand trees, shrubs, herbs, and grasses with edible seeds or nuts in the Mountain West.

Unfortunately, almost all of them are either too small or scarce to economically harvest in any quantity. And many are too small or hard to efficiently break down the outer coating for digestion.

The Mountain West is well-endowed with range fodder to support big game, but practical seed and nut crops are comparatively scarce. As a result, the animals that depend on them, such as the American red squirrel, tend to be lean and scrawny, adding yet another challenge to the determined hunter-gatherer.

Nevertheless, for the curious forager or avid survivalist, there are many seed and nut crops worth exploring and a few that are truly worthwhile.

The Mountain West has abundant forage for big game animals, while good seed and nut crops are scarce.

237

Sweet cicely (*Osmorhiza occidentalis*) and water hemlock (*Cicuta maculata*). The seeds of many Parsley family plants are aromatic and tasty, but can be confused with hemlock or water hemlock, which are deadly poisonous.

Edible or Poisonous?

Of the numerous plants with edible seeds or nuts, the majority belong to a few key plant families. For example, all 11 genera and 220 species in the Pine family produce theoretically edible nuts or seeds, although only a handful of species can be harvested economically (page 255). Any species would be worth experimenting with.

The Grass family is bigger, with about 650 genera and more than 10,000 species around the world. Those that are not infested with ergot fungus are theoretically edible, although most are too small to bother with (page 248). Similarly, the Sedge family includes about 100 genera and 4,500 species, a few of which might be worth harvesting.

Plants of the Mustard family (page 40) also have edible seeds, and many are relatively easy to harvest. However, the seeds are often spicy like mustard and thus better used as a condiment than as a meal in themselves (page 65).

The Parsley family also includes hundreds of species with aromatic, spicy seeds that make a nice trail nibble or spicy addition to a wilderness stew. However the Parsley family also includes a few deadly poisonous plants, especially water hemlock and poison hemlock (pages 43-44). Therefore, do not go blindly grazing on Parsley family plants. Learn to recognize the compound umbels that are characteristic of the family. From there, learn to identify the individual plants. It is important to know what each species is—or at least what it isn't—prior to eating the seeds.

Mint family plants also produce generally edible seeds, including chia (*Salvia hispanica*), which is cultivated for its seeds. It is reasonable to taste and experiment with different species from this family to find a potential food source, or possibly a good spice for camping. As with anything else, use common sense. If something doesn't taste good then stop eating it. Don't harvest anything unpalatable and force yourself to eat it in the name of survival. You may achieve the opposite effect!

Hedge nettle (*Stachys palustris*). Mint family plants have edible seeds.

Plants of the Buckwheat family also have edible seeds, but most are too small to process, and some, like curly dock (page 93), are too astringent to use in quantity.

Rocky Mountain maple (*Acer glabrum*). The seeds are abundant and theoretically edible, but too bitter.

Trees of the Maple family are easy to identify with their winged seeds that form in pairs. The seeds are big enough and clustered enough to make a potentially practical food source. I've tried the seeds small, green, and immature, as well as fully mature and dry. Some are tasty, while others are bitter. Given the abundance of food that could be harvested from a single tree, it might be worth exploring as a potential food source.

The Pea family has interesting wild seed potential, but also includes a number of poison-

Ground plums are a delicious, unexpected prairie treat from the Pea Family.

ous plants. The ground plum (*Astragalus crassicarpus* or *A. succulentus*) has inflated plum-like pea pods that are mostly air, but there are a few tasty edible peas inside, and the young pods can be eaten whole. They are usually found by accident while walking across a semi-arid field of native grasses. Some species in this genus produce swainsonine, an alkaloid which is toxic to livestock.

Some European species of lupine (*Lupinus*) have edible peas, and some have been cultivated for food, but many of our native lupine seeds contain mildly toxic alkaloids. Too bad, because the plants are abundant enough and the pods large enough, that lupines could constitute a major wild food source if a person devised a method to reliably remove the toxins.

Fortunately, nothing in the Pea family is drop-dead poisonous. Although there are many "poisonous" plants that could make a person sick, it would take some effort to successfully kill oneself with anything in the Pea family.

Pea family trees are even safer than the herbs. No Pea trees are native to the Mountain West, but some species are cultivated here, such as the honey locust (*Gleditsia triacanthos*). It has large, edible beans, and the inner flesh of the pod is pulpy and sweet. It is promising enough to warrant additional research.

Longspur lupine (*Lupinus arbustus*). Lupines produce delicious-looking pea pods, but most species are considered mildly poisonous.

Annual sunflower (*Helianthus annuus*) and Nuttall's sunflower (*H. nuttallii*).

Helianthus spp.

Aster Family / Aster Subfamily / Sunflower Tribe

Sunflower: World Traveler

Some cultivated plants have been selectively bred for so long that they retain little resemlance to their closest wild kin. Not so with the sunflower. Cultivated sunflowers typically grow one big flowerhead, while their wild kin often grow dozens of smaller flowerheads on a single plant, but otherwise, look very similar.

Native Americans started cultivating the common annual wild sunflower (*Helianthus annuus*) at least 4,600 years ago, slowly developing plants with fewer, larger flowerheads. Early Spanish explorers brought the seeds back to Europe, where they eventually made their way to Russia.

Sunflowers became popular as a source of cooking oil in Russia because the Russian Orthodox Church forbid the use of many other foods during lent, including butter and lard. The Soviet's ultimately bred sunflower seeds with 50 percent more oil.

Sunflowers came back to America as a resurgent crop due to concerns about transfat-filled, partially hydrogenated soybean oil being used to cook potato chips. Sunflower oil is rich in monounsaturated oleic fatty acids and doesn't go bad when frying potato chips.

II grow both, cultivated and wild sunflowers, yet wonder if they interbreed in my yard or as far as a pollinating bee travels. What genes

Nuttall's sunflower. Every seed is produced by a single flower. The middle consists of tiny five-petaled disk flowers. The big "petals" around the outside are individual ray flowers.

or characteristics are we contributing to the wild population?

Although wild sunflowers are not as easy to process as cultivated sunflowers, it is fun to nibble on wild sunflower seeds, and there are many different species to try.

Description, Habitat, and Range

A sunflower looks like a single flower, but it is actually a composite of hundreds of tiny flowers, and each seed is produced by a single flower within the larger head. As with all members of the Aster or Sunflower family, individual flowers are planted on a pitted disk. You can see this disk after you grow a sunflower and harvest the seeds. You will also see a pitted disk if you blow the seedhead off a dandelion. Almost all Aster family plants have a similar pitted disk, often very small. Be sure to consult *Botany in a Day* for indepth coverage of these flowers.

There are more than 50 species of *Helianthus*, all native to North America, including about 6 species scattered across the Mountain West. The common sunflower (*H. annuus*) typically inhabits disturbed or barren soils, often seen along western roadsides. Other species can be found in a multitude of habitats, including high in the mountains.

Shell and All

Sunflowers seeds are rich in oil and protein. Unfortunately, wild sunflower seeds are much smaller and more difficult to process than those of cultivated varieties. Nevertheless, where there is one sunflower there are often many, so sunflowers can be a good food source.

For starters, pull apart

A small harvest of Nuttall's sunflower seeds.

a mature flowerhead to get out the seeds. Wild sunflower seeds are far too small to crack open and extract individual seeds, so chew them up shell and all. The little green bracts between the seeds have a resinous flavor, as do any flower parts clinging to the seeds, so avoid them as much as possible. Chew the whole sunflower seeds, swallow the good stuff, and spit out

Close-up of seeds from Nuttall's sunflower.

the woody pulp. Take a couple sunflower heads along and pick out the seeds as you walk.

For small-scale production, try harvesting multiple heads and rub each face-down on a flat rock to break out the seeds.

Efficient mass processing is more involved and may have to be spread out over several days. If the sunflower heads are too dry, then most of the seeds will have already dropped to the ground. If the heads are too green, then the seeds won't readily fall out. Sunflower heads often dry out unequally, losing seeds in the middle while still semi-green near the outer edges. The trick to efficient harvesting is to collect whole flower stalks, dry them on a tarp, and then beat the seeds out.

Sunflower seeds were an important food source for many Native American tribes. The seeds were dried by the fire, then powdered, boiled, and eaten as gruel or mixed with grease and made into energy-rich cakes.

Cultivated Sunflowers

Sunflowers are often planted in gardens for their beautiful, grand flowers, but homeowners seldom harvest the seeds. You can offer to pull up and dispose of the stalks in exchange for the seeds. Watch the song birds closely. When you see them hanging out on the sunflowers, you know it is time to harvest!

Cut the heads and bring them home to dry. Kneeling on a tarp, rap the flowerheads with your knuckles or a stick to shake out any loose seeds. Then scrape the remaining seeds out with a stick, your hand, or a knife held perpendicular to the seeds. This work proceeds real quick if the flowerheads have dried long enough. Winnow out the flower parts, and store your harvest in mouse-deterrent containers such as gallon jars or plastic tubs.

Jerusalem artichoke (H. tuberosus) has a starchy tuber.

Sun Tubers

The Jerusalem artichoke, a.k.a. sunchoke or sun tuber (*H. tuberosus*), is native to eastern North America, but often planted in the West. The starchy tubers are high in fructose and become sweeter the longer they cook.

The plants require ample moisture to develop good tubers and grow a self-sufficient patch, but it is otherwise a low-maintenance, perennial crop. Plant some in your yard for a good survival food supply, if the need should ever arise.

Related Species

There are many yellow flowers in the Aster family, a few of which could be easily mistaken for wild sunflowers, especially arrowleaf balsamroot (*Balsamorhiza sagittata*). Fortunately, balsamroot seeds are also edible, as are the seeds of most other yellow, sunflower-like flowers. However, avoid any species that have soft, white fuzz within the flowerhead, such as arnica (*Arnica*) and groundsel (*Senecio*), which could be toxic if taken internally.

Arrowleaf balsamroot seeds may be eaten like sunflower seeds.

In addition to the seeds, arrowleaf balsamroot shoots are also sometimes edible. Familiarize yourself with the plant in bloom and seed stage, and notice the dead stems in winter. The fresh leaves can be harvested early in spring, before they have unfurled. Cut the shoots with a knife and fry them in butter. In my experience, the shoots taste pretty good in the moist Cascades, but are too resinous in the arid Rocky Mountains.

Photo by Sue Smith

Photo by Tom Chester

Amaranthus retroflexus and *A. powellii.*

Amaranthus spp.
Amaranth Family

Amaranth: Grain of the Ancients

Amaranth has been cultivated as a grain for thousands of years in Mexico. It was a major food crop for the Aztecs, who also utilized it in ceremonies. The ground seeds were sometimes mixed with honey or blood from human sacrifices and shaped into religious idols to be eaten during ceremonies. Spanish conquistadors outlawed the crop, but fortunately, the productive cultivars survived as weeds into modern times. Several species are now grown as crops; the protein-rich grain is common in health food products.

Photo by Josh Fecteau

Closely related species are common in disturbed, often manure-rich soils, such as gardens and barnyards, giving rise to the name "pigweed." If you have weeded a garden, then you have probably ripped amaranth out of the ground and cast it aside. Now you will know!

Redroot amaranth (*Amaranthus retroflexus*) is a common garden weed.

Description, Habitat, and Range

Amaranths are mostly annual weeds with alternate leaves, prominent veins, and often reddish stems or roots. Male and female flowers form separately on the same plant. Flowers are small and lack petals, forming tightly clustered around the stem, but each flower is typically enclosed by three green or colored, usually sharp, pokey bracts. The ovary matures as a lidded capsule, called a pyxis, with only one

The young leaves and tender stems are edible as a salad or potherb.

seed per flower. Rub the seed cluster between your palms and blow away the chaff. You will see the shiny black seeds, often with red and pale seeds mixed in.

Rub the seedhead between the palms to free the seeds. Gently blow away the chaff, leaving the heavy seeds behind.

Worldwide there are about 70 species of Amaranthus, including "love-lies-bleeding" (*A. caudatus*), known for its drooping spikes of blood-red flowers. About 10 species of *Amaranthus* are found across the Mountain West, often in weedy lots, gardens and farm fields, as well as disturbed soil along riverbeds and floodplains.

Leaves and Stems

Amaranth leaves and tender stem tips are edible as a salad or potherb and considered highly nutritious. Many people consider the plant to be among the best wild greens. My personal experience with amaranth is limited, however, partly because I fill-up on goosefoots (page 78), which often grow nearby. Moreover, goosefoot tops remain tender and harvestable even when in bloom, while amaranth tops become bristly-pokey in bloom.

Seed Harvesting

The seeds of all amaranth species are edible and may be substituted for store-bought amaranth seed or flour. The seeds are harvested at maturity in late summer or fall. In addition, the dead plants tend to hold the seeds through much of the winter, providing a wide window of opportunity for harvesting the seed.

Use a gloved hand to strip the seed capsules off the stem and de-

Swirling the goldpan and gently blowing is an effective way to winnow small batches of seeds.

posit them in a bag. Better yet, cut whole, dry plants and beat them against the inside of a bucket to knock the seeds free, or place them on

A delicious amaranth and wheat flour pancake with hawthorn berry sauce.

a tarp to beat the seeds out with a stick. Winnow out whatever chaff remains. Be thorough. The prickly chaff can irritate the mouth and throat.

Amaranth seeds are small, hard, and difficult to digest, so it is best to grind them with a flour mill or coffee grinder before cooking. Alternatively, parch the seeds in a pan over hot coals to make them brittle, then grind them with a mano and metate.

Amaranth lacks gluten, so add equal portions of wheat flour to make your baked goods stick together.

Timothy grass (*Phleum pratense*) and crested wheat grass (*Agropyron crista-tum*) flowers in bloom.

Poaceae (Gramineae)
Grass Family

Grass: The Seeds of Civilization

Civilization owes its existence to the grasses. More than half of all calories eaten by our species come from rice (*Oryza*), maize or corn (*Zea*) and wheat (*Triticum*). Other important cereal crops include oats (*Avena*), barley (*Hordeum*), millet (*Echinochloa*), and rye (*Secale*).

Selective breeding has produced cultivars with larger grains and a tendency for those grains to cling to the mature plants, rather than dropping quickly to the ground.

Corn was bred from teosinte, a wild grass found in Mexico. More than 7,500 years of selective breeding has produced a plant that bears little resemblance to its wild kin. Conversely, wild rice (*Zizania*) is unique in that the wild plant was already optimized for cultivation and harvesting. Some grasses have sweet, pithy stems, especially sugarcane (*Saccharum*) and *Sorghum*.

There are hundreds of genera and thousands of species in the Grass family, each as unique as wheat and rye. Alas, most grass seeds are too small to be harvested economically. Most of the promising species were long ago selected for cultivation, radically changing the human diet and facilitating the rise of large-scale civilizations.

Description, Habitat, and Range

Grass is as familiar as the lawn. Neglect the yard for awhile, and the grass will produce flowerstalks and seeds. We don't normally think of grasses as "flowers," since they lack showy petals, but they have stamens and a pistil like other flowers.

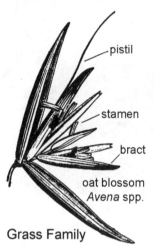

Grass Family

pistil

stamen

bract

oat blossom
Avena spp.

Being wind pollinated, however, they have no need for showy petals to attract insects.

The flower stems are hollow and have knee-like nodes or joints, distinguishing them from the Sedge and Rush families, as noted in this little ditty: "Sedges have edges. Rushes are round. Grasses have joints when the cops aren't around."

node

ergot
fungus

There are about 650 genera and more than 10,000 species of grass around the world, and they are almost all edible. Darnel ryegrass (*Lolium temulentum*) may be poisonous in excess, and a few species produce cyanide in the wilted vegetation, but virtually all other grasses are edible, provided they are not infected with ergot fungus.

About Ergot Fungus

Be sure to inspect the seeds of all grasses for the presence of ergot fungus (*Claviceps purpurea* or *C. paspali*). Ergot consumes the grass seeds, forming a black or purplish powder. Ergot can stimulate uterine contractions and cause abortions. A derivative of ergot is used as a medicine for migraine and cluster headaches. Ergot is also a source of LSD.

Ergot contamination in cereal grains can be very dangerous. *C. paspali* effects the nervous system, causing trembling, staggering, and paranoia. The witch hunts of Salem, Massachusetts, in the 1600s were likely triggered by ergot-contaminated grain; people were burned at the stake by paranoid Puritans running around on LSD.

C. purpurea, on the other hand, restricts blood flow to the extremities, slowly killing the flesh on the fingers, toes, and ears with long-term consumption. Gangrene bacteria, similar to botulism, rots away dead tissues, often forming a foul gas. A religious order was formed to deal with this disease; medics torched the rotting flesh off the victims and prayed they lived. The group adopted St. Anthony as their patron saint, and the disease came to be known as St. Anthony's fire. Federal regulations in 1916 restricted the use of ergot-infested grain to 0.3 percent of weight for making flour, eliminating most ergotism problems.

A nutritious glass of grass juice.

Lawn Juice

Health fanatics often tout wheatgrass juice as a good health tonic. Many people grow their own micro crop of wheatgrass in trays. They clip the wheatgrass when it is a few inches tall, before it becomes too stiff with cellulose, and juice it in a blender. Other types of grass are also edible. Even lawn grass is perfectly edible—except for all the fertilizer, herbicides, and dog crap. Find some clean and tender, young grasses. Chew them up, swallow the vitamin-rich juice, and spit out the fibers. For a more refined product, make lawn juice.

We don't have four stomaches like a cow for fermenting and digesting cellulose, so it is important to seek out the most easily digestible grasses to start with. Avoid wilted grasses, since some species produce cyanide compounds when stressed. Put the grass in your first stomach—a juicer or blender—and add as much water as necessary to process it. Clover can be added to make complete proteins, just as peas or beans are often eaten with grains to make complete proteins. Blend it to a frothy green liquid, then strain the juice through a cloth or screen to remove the fiber.

The final product tastes like the smell of a freshly mowed lawn. It isn't bad, but doesn't really taste like food. Try supplementing the flavor with lemon or berry juice. If nothing else, it is nice to keep in mind that your entire lawn could be eaten in times of emergency, and you'd be healthier for it!

Seeds to Harvest

Most grass seeds are edible, except possbily the aforementioned darnel ryegrass, and anything infested with ergot fungus. Unfortunately, few grass seeds are readily harvestable. Most seeds are too small to harvest or process efficiently. And many grass seeds are too small to grind on a metate or too small to swell and turn to mush when cooked as a hot cereal, and therefore they are difficult to digest.

Reed canary grass (*Phalaris arundinacea*) Cut the grass, dry it on a tarp, and beat the seeds out with a stick.

The best grasses to work with are those with big seeds, much heavier than the surrounding chaff. That makes it easier to winnow the chaff away while keeping the seeds. The following are a few grasses we've found worthwhile to gather. Note that only one or two species from each of the following genera are likely to be worthwhile candidates for harvesting. This is by no means a complete list. Experiment to your heart's content!

Reed Canary Grass (*Phalaris*)

Reed canary grass, different from true reed grass (*Phragmites*), grows tall along many rivers. In a one-hour study, I cut a garbage-bag-full of seed heads. I spread them on a tarp to dry, then beat the seeds

A handful of grass seeds, ready for winnowing.

out with a stick for about fifteen minutes, leaving about two gallons of seed and chaff. Another forty minutes of careful winnowing gave a final yield of about three quarts of good grass seed.

Indian Rice Grass (*Oryzopsis*)

Indian rice grass is known best for its use in the Great Basin Desert, but can be found in the West from Alberta to New Mexico and east to the Cascades. It loves sandy soil and ranges from ponderosa pine forests to desert shrub land. It is often the only plant found in barren flats. The grains are large and easy to process, making them a key crop if they are found in abundance. The plant has been cultivated on a small scale as a gluten-free alternative to wheat.

The Paiute tribe made extensive use of this plant, as described by Margaret M. Wheat in *Survival Arts of the Primitive Paiutes*:

> *"In July, the Indian rice grass (wái) was ready to harvest. Before the nutritious seeds fell to the ground, the women cut great armloads of the grass to be carried to the threshing pads of sun-baked earth. Here, in the cool of the day, old women singed off the little black seeds which clung so stubbornly to the stems. Moistening the sheaves to retard flash burning, they placed handfuls on a small fire. As the grass was consumed, the hard-shelled seeds dropped, roasted, into the ash. Later they were cleaned on a winnowing basket and husked on a flat stone to make meal for gruel."*

Timothy Grass (*Phleum*)

Timothy grass is not a native but it has been wildly planted, even in remote, backcountry settings. The grain is easy to winnow and really quite beautiful. For a one-hour timed study, I hand-stripped the seeds and came up with about one quart of rough yield. Twenty minutes of winnowing left me with a little over a cup of pure seed. The seeds can be boiled and eaten as a hot cereal.

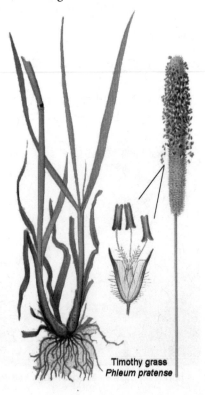

Timothy grass
Phleum pratense

Beat the Hull Out of It

There are several ways to collect grass seeds. The most basic method is to strip the

seed stalks by hand, or beat the seed heads with a stick, catching the seeds in a pan or on a tarp.

For optimal efficiency, cut the whole stalks, place them on a tarp to dry, and then beat the seeds out. Don't have a knife?

Some grass seeds may need to be parched to make the chaff brittle and easier to rub off.

Rubbing seeds between the palms helps break up chaff.

Grab a bunch of grass leaves at their base and push strait down into the ground, breaking the stalks, then twist and pull. This is a very quick and effective method and can also be used to swiftly make a grass mattress or an expedient mouse hut; watch out for grass cuts though. Be sure to wear gloves! The plants can be dried on the tarp to make the seeds drop more easily.

Winnow the seeds by swirling the pan and blowing away the lighter material... its almost like paning for gold!

Next, rub the rough material between your palms to break the seeds free from the chaff. Note that some seeds are encased in a hull or husk that is impossible to rub free of the grain. These seeds should be ground up, hull and all, for a high-fiber cereal.

Some grass seeds can be parched and then rubbed to remove the husk. Seeds that are

A clean batch of Timothy grass seeds.

hairy or sharp should be avoided, or at least parched and ground, as they could otherwise cause irritation or injury in the throat.

Winnowing is the next step, removing the chaff once it is broken free of the seeds. Winnowing is somewhat like gold panning, where weighty gold metal sinks to the bottom of the pan while lighter debris is washed away, and I recommend using a gold pan for winnowing. Swirl the pan, or lightly toss the grain, to bring the light chaff to the surface, then gently blow the chaff away.

Another method is to toss the material in the air so that the seeds fall straight down on a tarp and a light breeze carries away the chaff. I have not had good results with this method, so I prefer the gold-pan / blowing technique, where I can precisely control the flow of wind. In either case, it is difficult to completely remove the chaff. That is okay. It is good roughage for the digestive system.

Cooking

Grains without ergot can be cooked whole as a hot cereal, or ground into gluten-free flour and used for bread. Cooking grass seeds whole reduces the labor involved, but the seeds must be cooked almost to mush or they will pass through the system undigested. Very small seeds may not ever soften enough to become digestible. Another alternative is to sprout the seeds. This makes the material digestible, although it also converts much of the starch and oil content into proteins.

Whitebark pine (*Pinus albicaulis*) and limber pine (*P. flexilis*) are widespread.

Pinus spp.
Pine Family

Pine Nuts: Insanely Nutritious

Mountain country is often barren and largely devoid of anything edible. But sometimes you just have to know where to look. Pine nuts are packed with energy and nutrition, and they are one of few wild plant foods that could actually sustain a person for a time in the absence of meat in the diet.

All pines produce edible nuts, although many species, such as lodgepole pine (*Pinus contorta*) produce nuts that are too small and impractical to harvest. But there are plenty of species with larger pine nuts worth harvesting, found scattered across the Mountain West from deserts to mountain tops.

Several different species are known as pinyon pines, in this case *Pinus edulis*, found in Colorado, New Mexico, Utah, and Arizona.

Description, Habitat, and Range

Pines are mostly evergreen trees and shrubs with spirally arranged, needle-like leaves, typically attached to the branches in clusters of two (red pine group), three (yellow pine group), or five (white pine group) needles per cluster.

Male cones are small and fall soon after dispersing their pollen to the wind. Female cones briefly become elongated, exposing the ovules to the open air to catch the pollen. These cones are aerodynamically shaped to create swirling wind currents to help catch the pollen. After pollination, the scales grow rapidly and cover the ovules, allowing them to mature into seeds.

Male and female cones developing on a lodgepole pine (*Pinus contorta*).

Worldwide there are more than 100 species of *Pinus*, and all produce edible nuts, although only about twenty species produce nuts large enough to bother harvesting. The prime species for pine nuts in North America include the one-needle pinyon pine (*P. monophylla*), found largely in Nevada, and the two-needle or Colorado pinyon pine (*P. edulis*), which grows in Utah, Colorado, Arizona, and New Mexico. Almost as good are the three-needle California foothills pine (*P. sabiniana*), the five-needle whitebark pine (*P. alibcaulis*), found at high elevations near timberline in the northern Rockies and the Pacific states, as well as the limber pine (*P. flexillis*), which grows scattered across foothills throughout the West. Experiment with your local pines to see if you can efficiently extract the nuts.

Whitebark pine (*P. abicaulis*) is a five-needle pine. Young trees have silvery "white" bark.

Pine Nut Power

I have not yet been in the right place at the right time to gather more than a handful of pinyon pine nuts, but here in the Northern Rockies, we are just as glad to harvest pine nuts from whitebark and limber pines.

Whitebark pine grows high in the mountains, mostly above 8,000 feet in Montana. The green or dried cones can be harvested in September and October, but the size of the crop varies tremendously from year to year. When the ground is littered with bear piles crammed full of hundreds of pine nut shells, then you know there are good pine nuts in the trees above. Stay alert and bear aware!

Whitebark pine. Peel back the scales to reveal the nutritious pine nuts.

I once found an extensive grove of whitebark pines that were short like pinyon pines. But the unfortunate reality is that most whitebark pine trees are tall, skinny, and devoid of any good branches for climbing. You will often see an abundance of pine cones hanging from branches forty feet in the air, with no reasonable way to harvest them.

Look around, and you might find a few smaller, younger trees that are climbable, or more likely, younger trees growing beside a large boulder that can be climbed. Extend your reach by lashing a short stick to the end of a longer stick to make a V-shaped hook, used to pull cones down from the trees.

Otherwise, try scavenging cones from the forest floor. Sometimes you can even find a squirrel cache hidden in a hollow log or rock crevasse and raid it like a bear. Don't worry. The squirrels stash far more pine cones than they can use themselves. One good squirrel cache can provide a couple dozen cones and enough pine nuts for a hearty meal.

Green pine cones are typically completely covered in pitch, but somehow lose much of the pitch as the cones mature. Pine cones can be heated by a campfire overnight to loosen the scales, then pried open with one's thumb to extract the nuts. The more the cones dry, the more the scales open up, until the pine nuts can be shaken out. Like many other crops, the season can end abruptly, as the pine cones open up and drop all the pine nuts to the ground.

A ponderosa pine (*Pinus ponderosa*) cone and seedling. The cones are large, but the nuts are comparatively small.

Pine nuts are delicious raw and gourmet roasted. I like to pick the nuts out of pine cones while I walk, giving me pure pine nut power to hike over the mountains. Pine nuts are the richest wild food I've ever eaten!

To separate the shells from the pine nuts, toast them in a pan over the fire, stirring constantly. I often carry a metal gold pan on my camping trips, which works really well for tasks such as this.

Roasting makes the shells more brittle. The thicker shells of pinyon nuts can be gently cracked with a stone after roasting and then winnowed out. The shells of the white-bark pine are thinner, however, and the cracking/winnowing process is less fruitful. I've been able to remove a significant portion of the shells, but far from all of them. Nevertheless, the thin shells are readily edible and add good roughage to the diet, so you can eat them in bulk like a bear.

Strangely, I have not been as successful with limber pines, which typically grow in the foothills and thus are more accessible than whitebark pines. I have harvested immature, green cones in July and heated them to loosen the scales and extract the nearly ripe nuts. But I am somehow never in the right place at the right time to harvest

Pine nuts can be eaten shells and all, but for a more refined product, toast the nuts in a pan, then crack the shells with a rock, and winnow away the debris.

the fully ripe cones in August. By the time I get there, the cones have opened and shed all the pine nuts.

Ponderosa pines (*P. ponderosa*) have big cones, but smaller pine nuts. The pine nuts are too small to shell efficiently, but make a good trail snack, like popping sunflower seeds. The western white pine (*P. monticola*) might also be worth trying.

Under Attack

Whitebark pines, white pines, and limber pines are being deci-mated by white pine blister rust (*Cronartium ribicola*), a type of fungus which was accidentally introduced to North American from Europe around 1900. European and Asian white pines are largely resistant to the disease, but our native white pines are not. At different stages of its life cycle, the rust infects various species of currants and gooseberries (*Ribes*) from the Gooseberry family. This led to a massive campaign to kill off these host bushes with herbicides in our national parks and forests as a means to save the pines. The campaign killed off scores of native plants, but was ultimately deemed to be ineffective against the rust and discontinued in 1971. Fewer than five percent of the trees in any stand are naturally resistant to blister rust, and researchers are now working to harvest cones from these trees for starting seedlings to replace the dying forests.

Unfortunately, the pines are also vulnerable to the pine beetle (*Dendroctonus ponderosae*), which has been equally devastating in recent years. Although native to North America, pine beetles are normally kept in check by frigid winter temperatures. Warmer winters combined with aging lodgepole forests have allowed pine beetles to explode across millions of acres, spreading from lodgepole into whitebark, limber pine, and ponderosa forests. Pine beetles don't attack younger, sappy trees, just trees that exceed about six inches in diameter. Few trees escape this deadly combination of both blister rust and pine beetles.

Whitebark pines are being decimated by a combined attack from white pine blister rust and pine beetles.

259

Whitebark pines are perhaps our most vulnerable pine, in part due to the fact that high elevation trees grow so incredibly slowly. A four-foot tall tree, for example, may easily be thirty to forty years old. Mature trees typically vary from 200 to 800 years old. With climate change shifting habitat ranges higher up the mountains, it will be especially difficult for these slow growing trees to colonize up the mountains in pace with environmental conditions.

Conifers add a ring of branches to the top of the tree every year. To age a tree without cutting it down, count each level of branches. This whitebark pine is approaching four-feet tall and four decades old.

Whitebark pines are keystone species, supplying rich food for black bears, grizzly bears, Clark's nutcrackers, squirrels, and hungry foragers. Eliminating whitebark pines doesn't directly imperil these species, but can make life a lot more difficult. For example, bears won't starve to death without whitebark pine nuts, but they don't reproduce as successfully either, potentially impacting their population over the long haul.

Given all these concerns, some may wonder if it is appropriate for foragers to harvest whitebark pine nuts at all. But in my opinion, harvesting pine nuts (and other wild foods) is essential to saving them. It is a matter of awareness. People who are aware of football, for example, tend to care about football. I care about whitebark pines and other species that are imperiled, because I am aware of them. I am aware of whitebark pines in the mountains, in the news, and in politics.

It doesn't matter where you are. Outside any window is an environment undergroing various stages of cascading failure as we rapidly reduce biodiversity and threaten species with extinction, but most people can't see it and don't get it. We will likely lose half of all life on earth this century, and yet most people are more concerned about the latest sports and entertainment news. Unfortunately, the issues that face humanity are not part of the national consciousness or discussion, and won't be until people become more connected with our natural environment. Harvesting pine nuts is a good place to start.

Pine Needle Tea

The green needles from any species of pine, and anything else in the Pine family, can be used to brew tea. Pine needle tea has a rich but mild flavor. It is a good source of vitamin C, and may be the only available source of vitamin C to prevent scurvy when everything else is buried under snow. That was a bigger concern in the past, when people couldn't obtain fruits and vegetables in the middle of winter, but it is still a good survival tip to keep in mind. Also keep in mind that pine needle tea is resinous, so excessive consumption could potentially plug tubules in the kidneys.

Related Species

The Pine family also includes fir and balsam fir (*Abies*), larch or tamarack (*Larix*), spruce (*Picea*), Douglas fir (*Pseudotsuga*), and the hemlock tree (*Tsuga*). All members of the Pine family produce edible nuts or seeds, but most are not readily harvestable or processable.

Subalpine fir (*Abies lasiocarpa*). All members of the Pine family produce edible nuts, but most cannot be harvested economically.

I once placed a tarp under a Douglas fir tree and beat the branches with a stick to free winged, helicopter-like seeds from the cones on the tree. I collected many seeds, but not enough to constitute food.

In addition, the seeds or nuts of many Pine family species are often highly resinous, or at least difficult to seprate from the resinous material around them. All species are worth trying, provided you are not prone to allergic reactions. On a mountain hike with the local school, I passed around a couple of whitebark pine and subalpine fir cones and suggested that everyone could try the seeds. All was well, except for the science teacher, who broke out into hives.

Photo by Rosalee de la Forêt

Black walnuts have a tough green husk. The young tree has grey, furrowed bark.

Juglans nigra
Walnut Family

Black Walnut: In a Nutshell

Black walnuts are native to eastern North America, not the Mountain West. However, the trees have been widely planted, and they may be encountered along city streets, college campuses, or abandoned homesteads deep in the wilderness.

I learned about black walnuts on an survial trip with friends into the Hells Canyon Wilderness on the Oregon-Idaho border in the mid-1990s. My friends lived on the Idaho side, on a place so remote that they had to walk a footpath a mile down the canyon to get their mail. They had a mailbox on the banks of the Snake River, and the U.S. Postal Service delivered their mail by boat.

Going camping with friends. I'm on the right.

We caught a ride across the river on the mail boat and camped that first night at an abandoned homestead where the ground was littered with black walnuts. It was mid-April, but the walnuts from the previous fall were still good—maybe not totally fresh, but wholly edible. We spent hours cracking the shells and picking out the nutmeats.

Description, Habitat, and Range

The eastern black walnut (*Juglans nigra*) is a tall, straight tree with deeply furrowed grey to black bark. The leaves are pinnately divided, alternate, and aromatic. Male flowers form in drooping catkins, while female flowers form in clusters of two to five at the end of a stem.

The Arizona black walnut (*J. major*) is native from southern Utah east to Texas and Oklahoma.

Black walnuts are most easily identified by their nuts. The fruits ripen in autumn and typically fall to the ground in October, where they can easily be collected in quantity. The hard green husk gradually softens, turning yellowish, then brown and black, making an inky mess that will stain your hands and everything else. The remaining walnut has a thick and tough shell compared to the familiar Persian or English walnut (*J. regia*), but the nutmeat is an amazing, rich food source.

Photo by Rosalee de la Forêt

Black walnuts can be stored for months after the husk is removed.

Worldwide there are 21 species of walnuts, of which 9 native and introduced species are found in North America. The eastern black walnut (*J. nigra*) has been widely cultivated at lower elevations across the Mountain West, while the Arizona black walnut (*J. major*) occurs naturally from southern Utah and Arizona east to Texas and Oklahoma.

Worth Dyeing For

Black walnuts are well-known for the inky dye produced by its rotting husks. People often collect them expressly for dyeing projects, saving the husks and discarding the edible nuts. Although the husks produce a dark brown-black ink, the final dye is typically more of a rich brown.

The hungry forager may have different priorities, but the first step is the same. It is necessary to remove the outer husk, so it is sensible to save this waste material and experiment with making dye.

The soft, rotting husks can be removed by hand, but preferably with gloves on, since the dye can stain your skin for weeks to come. If the husks are sufficiently rotten, then the walnuts can be dried and the husk material flaked off. Just keep in mind that the dripping, leaking dye will stain pretty much anything, including concrete.

To utilize the dye, simmer a pot full of rotten walnut husks and water for an hour or two, then screen off the debris. The dye can be

used on anything from yarn to t-shirts to sweaters to braintan buckskin. Just make sure the dye is adequately cool before immersing wool, buckskin, or anything that might be adversely affected by heat. Buckskins shouldn't be in the dye for more than two

Walnut-dyed braintan buckskin hides, ready for projects.

hours, or the tannins will begin to stiffen the hide. Other fibers can soak overnight, if desired. Whatever you dye, be sure to rinse and rinse and rinse until the rinsewater runs clear.

Getting to the Meat of It

Black walnuts are well armored compared to the familiar walnuts from the store, but the tough shell is easily overcome by placing the walnut on a rock, or other hard surface, and hitting it with a hammer. The trick is to break the shell and access the nutmeat—without smashing it to bits.

Hitting the walnut on one end or the other typically causes it to split open along the seam, exposing the nutmeat as two heart-shaped pieces. Its clean and pretty, but most of the meat remains inaccessible within the shell. Placing the walnut on its side and hitting right on the seam typically produces the same result.

Splitting the walnut on the seam looks pretty, but isn't particularly useful for extracting the nutmeat.

Therefore, it is better to rotate the nut ninety-degrees, such that the seam is crosswise or horizontal, and then bash the walnut just hard enough to break the shell. It is not a precise art, but with a little practice it is possible to get semi-reliable results. Anything that doesn't slide easily out of the shell can be dug out with a nutpick, nail, or sharp stick.

Shelling black walnuts isn't a highly efficient process, so it is no wonder that few people bother with them. I can extract only about two cups of nutmeats while watching a movie. But that is two cups more than I would have if I just watched the movie and did nothing at all!

Black walnuts have a slightly richer flavor than regular walnuts, and can be substituted in any recipe.

It is more effective to hit the walnut on the side, ninety degrees away from the seam.

The nutmeats have begun to dry out a bit by March, but are otherwise wholly edible and delicious.

King bolete mushrooms (Boletus edulis). There are many edible wild mushrooms in the Mountain West, but only a few species that are exceptionally easy to identify and often found in great abundance.

Marvelous Mushrooms

Early taxonomists included fungi within the plant kingdom. That may seem surprising, but fungi sprout from the soil like plants, and they reproduce with spores, as is common among primitive plants.

Granted, mushrooms are not green like plants, because they lack chlorophyll for photosysthesis, but there are many parasitic plant species that also lack chlorophyll. In that sense, it could be argued that plants and fungi should belong to the same kingdom. At least they must be more closely related to each other than to animal life, right?

Not so. Fungi are distinct enough to have earned a kingdom of their own, and the whole kingdom is slightly more closely related to the animal kingdom than the plant kingdom.

Unidentified mushrooms near the edge of a mountain snowbank appear to be generating heat and melting snow.

Coincidentally, people often describe mushrooms as having a "meaty flavor." And while we might talk of *foraging* for edible plants, we *hunt* wild mushrooms. Mushrooms are also rich in protein like meat, and since they don't run very fast, even an unskilled hunter can catch them. The challenge is to find their hiding places!

Finding mushrooms is the key obstacle to identifying and using them, but they appear and disappear like wild things, so one can never truly know when or where they will show themselves.

By comparison, plants are courteous enough to allow a person to observe them from the time they are seedlings until they wither away with old age. But fungi spend most of their lives hiding in the soil, or in dead wood or manure, quietly forming filamentaceous networks of fungal hyphae or mycelium as they consume dead organic matter. They only show themselves when they determine that conditions are right to reproduce and spread their spores. Up pops a mushroom, and with a little luck, the mushroom hunter might stumble across it.

Once a secret location is known, the hunter can return year after year to look for the fungal delights. But even then, one can never know precisely when or exactly where the mushrooms will resurface. Maybe that is why we call it hunting instead of foraging!

Purple coral (*Alloclavaria purpurea*, a.k.a. *Clavaria purpurea*) is considered edible, but is uncommon in the Mountain West.

Getting Started

Variegated bolete (*Suillus variegatus*) is considered edible, but unpalatable.

Many different fungi are found across the Mountain West, enough to justify an entire field guide of their own. On the other hand, fungi are not as abundant here as elsewhere.

Fungi thrive on organic matter, ample moisture, and moderate temperatures. But much of the Mountain West is characterized by poor soils, an arid climate, and temperatures that fluctuate between freezing cold and blistering hot. Some microclimates are favorable to fungal growth, while other places are too dry and sandy to support much biological activity. Be assured, the fungi are here, but they may pass up years of marginal weather conditions before revealing their presence.

The emphemeral nature of mushrooms also makes them challenging to identify. It can take hours to identify a mushroom with total certainty, and that certainty disappears if you don't see the mushroom again for a year or more.

Don't be intimidated by the hundreds of possible species found in many mushroom guides. There are a great many little brown mushrooms, or "LBMs" that are difficult to distinguish from each another in the field guides. Don't bother. Start by learning larger, more distinct mushrooms, and you will be better rewarded for your time.

For the purposes of this book, we are introducing only the most widespread, locally abundant, gourmet-tasting, and easy-to-identify mushrooms found in our region. Get comfortable identifying and using the mushrooms featured on the following pages, and you will have a solid foundation from which to learn additional species. Also look online for a local mycological assossiation or club. You may be able to go on free walks with mushroom experts who can help with identification.

An LBM is any "little brown mushroom" that is difficult to distinguish from all other LBMs in the field guides.

Fly agaric (*Amanita muscaria*) is widely recognized with its bright red cap and white "warts." Here in the Mountain West, however, one is more likely to encounter a yellow-capped variety of the same species.

Edible or Poisonous?

One thing people typically fear more than death from eating the wrong berry is death from eating the wrong mushroom. As is often the case, the fears are overblown, and there are actually very few truly dangerous mushrooms. This guide isn't sufficient to navigate the who's who of poisonous fungi, as the text is oriented towards the easy-to-recognize mushrooms that we utilize ourselves on a regular basis. Nevertheless, a brief discussion of poisonous mushrooms can provide a useful big-picture overview.

People die from eating mushrooms, but *not* from eating the mushrooms covered on the following pages. Nearly all mushroom-related fatalities are caused by various species of *Amanita*. Worldwide, there are about 600 different amanitas, including edible, inedible, and poisonous species. The deathcap, *A. phalloides*, accounts for about half of all mushroom fatalities. Native to the Old World, it was accidentally introduced to the east and west coast of North America, but is unlikely to be encountered in the Mountain West.

One is more likely to find the distinctive and common fly agaric (*A. muscaria*), pictured above and on the facing page. The mushroom is considered toxic, with psychoactive properties that can have depressant, sedative or hypnotic, dissociative, and delirious effects. Fatalities are rare, but possible with excess consumption. The mature mushroom doesn't even look like food, but its immature form could be mistaken for a puffball mushroom, as shown on page 285.

Amanita muscaria. Notice how much variation there can be within a single species.

Unfortunately, fungal field guides can be daunting, especially given the natural range of variation seen in many mushrooms like *Amanita muscaria.* It can take time and determination to figure out that the yellow specimen in hand is the same species as the red one featured in the field guide!

Basic mushroom identification begins with matching the specimen in hand with the photo and text description in a book, as is the case with the mushrooms featured in this guide.

A small step up in identification is to determine the color of the spores. Individual spores are too small to see, but the color can be seen by accumulating a layer of spores. Look around a mature mushroom, and you may see a natural "spore print" on a leaf beneath the cap, or even on the cap of one mushroom underneath another mushroom.

Optionally, you can make a spore print by laying a mature mushroom cap on a piece of paper overnight. There should be enough spores on the paper in the morning to see the color.

More advanced mushroom identification involves a bit of chemistry to form color stains on the fungus, using chemicals such as potassium hydroxide, ammonia, phenol, or an aqueous solution of chloral hydrate, potassium iodide, and iodine.

In some cases, mushroom identification can be challenging enough that taxonomists resort to electron microscopes to examine spore shape and texture to distinguish one species from another. Unfortunately, such methods are not entirely convenient to field identification by the hungry forager!

Fortunately, although there are many "poisonous" mushrooms, very few species are *deadly* poisonous. Dining on the wrong mushroom is likely to trigger gastrointestinal distress, diarrhea, and vomiting, but probably not death. These nonlethal poisonings are relatively common, yet also easily avoidable.

How Poisonous?

Dining on a bad mushroom is far different than merely tasting it. For example, some *Russula* mushrooms are considered edible, while others are inedible or poisonous, but none are considered deadly. There are about 750 different species of *Russula* in the world, and they are often difficult to identify, even for professionals. But, as one mycologist informed me, mild-tasting *Russula* mushrooms are generally considered edible, while those with either a bitter taste or acrid, horseradish-like bite are considered inedible or potentially poisonous. In other words, the method used to determine whether or not a *Russula* is edible is to taste it.

I have tasted a few *Russula* mushrooms myself, but I have not yet made a meal of them. Nor is there any great need to. There are other mushrooms that are easier to identify and far more suitable for dining.

I do know people who routinely taste raw, unidentified mushrooms without hesitation, and they are not mushroom experts. I do not sample random mushrooms, but I might if I were more familiar with the whole range of poisonous mushrooms in our region.

The bottom line is that, yes, there are poisonous mushrooms, and dining on the wrong ones could make you significantly sick, but death is highly unlikely. Moreover, it is easy to avoid poisonous mushrooms entirely by focussing on a handful of species that are easy to identify, often very abundant, and quite tasty.

Fortunately, many choice edible fungi are easy to identify by visual comparison to photos and text in various field guides. Mushrooms featured in this book are unlikely to be confused with toxic species.

There are about 750 species of *Russula*, some edible and some not.

When you have mastered the fungi covered in this book, then watch for mushrooms that are abundant and easy to distinguish at a glance from all other mushrooms in the area. Sit down with a field guide and see if you can identify what it is and whether or not it might be edible. Verify your answer in another book or ask an expert.

Tree mushrooms vary from tender to rubbery or dry, depending on age and weather.

Pleurotus ostreatus
Tree Mushroom Family

Tree Mushrooms: First Rite of Spring

Spring comes slowly to the Rocky Mountains. Here in Montana, cottonwood trees don't leaf out until mid-May. But tree mushrooms, also known as oyster mushrooms, start popping out on dead cottonwood trees or logs starting a week or two earlier. Tree mushrooms also precede and overlap with morel mushrooms, which prefer to wait for those first seventy-degree days. Most people prefer morels, but tree mushrooms make a good consolation prize, and you might bring home a whole bag full.

Tree mushrooms are actually quite delectable when young, and can be considered nearly gourmet. The problem is that tree mushrooms are mostly found and collected when they are already aged and rubbery.

Harvesting tree mushrooms in our video, *Three Days at the River* in *The Art of Nothing Wilderness Survival Video Series*.

Description, Habitat, and Range

Tree mushrooms are easy to identify. You are unlikely to encounter any other mushrooms growing on dead cottonwoods or other deciduous trees in early spring. These are gilled mushrooms with sideways stems, and they form overlapping layers like shelves. The genus name, *Pleurotus*, is Latin for "sideways," and the species name, *ostreatus*, is Latin for "oyster," referring to the shape of the cap. Some people

also claim that the mushrooms taste like oysters. *P. ostreatus* is found across North America and northern Eurasia. Other species of *Pleurotus* are also edible, but are uncommon in the Mountain West.

Cook to your Pleasure

Other mushrooms typically have a more obvious expiration date, becoming mushy and riddled with mushroom fly larvae. Not so with tree mushrooms.

Diced and fried tree mushrooms, bacon, and immature maple seeds, ready to wrap in a grape leaf.

Larvae or not, the flesh becomes rubbery with age. These rubbery masses quickly add up to an abundant harvest, which is great if you enjoy dining on rubber. Otherwise, it helps to be more selective!

Tree mushrooms can be cut off the tree or log with a knife, or pulled off by hand, and trimmed as necessary to clean them. Tender young tree mushrooms may be tasted or eaten raw, although cooking is generally recommended. Young tree mushrooms don't require much cooking and add a pleasant taste to nearly any dish, stir fry, or sauce.

Rubbery old mushrooms are problematic. Dice them into smaller pieces and cook longer to help reduce the rubbery texture. Add mushroom bits to other dishes to add flavor and texture without overwhelming the main ingredients.

Older tree mushrooms are easy to find and collect in abundance, but it is like cooking and dining on rubber!

Taxonomists debate whether there are as few as three or as many as fifty species of morels. Fortunately, there is no need to name them to eat them!

Morchella spp.
Morel Family

Morels: Lose your Morals

Morel mushrooms are among the best known and most sought after fungi, popular for home-cooking, and often picked and sold by commercial harvesters. Morel mushrooms are so good that you may find yourself morally challenged to obey those pesky "No Trespassing"

signs when you think there could be morels beyond the fence. That's understandable, since harvesting morel mushrooms is a traditional and natural activity, dating back tens of thousands of years.

Creating artificial boundaries and locking people out is an aberration of modern culture that should be subverted as a matter of principle. Go on. Break the rules. Sneak in and find those mushrooms. Just don't blame us if you get caught! Optionally, try asking permission. People are often nicer than their signs.

Morchella esculenta.

Description, Habitat, and Range

Morel mushrooms come in many shapes and sizes, and taxonomists still debate whether there may be as few as three or as many as fifty species. Morel mushrooms look sponge-like, varying in color from yellow or golden to dark brown or nearly black, typically with a whitish or cream colored stalk.

The most well-known species is *M. esculenta*, a golden morel typically found growing near cottonwood trees early in the spring, on warm days just after the trees leaf out.

Morchella esculenta has a warm, golden color.

Looking for morels in the grass and leaves is something like an Easter egg hunt. You never know if you are going to find a bonanza or come home empty-handed.

Morel mushrooms can also be found in coniferous forests at times. Forest fires greatly stimulate morel production, probably due to the flush of nutrients washed into the soil. Many commercial pickers follow burns, searching the barren soil in the spring or summer after a big fire.

Get there at the right time, and you may find a great many morel mushrooms. Or you

Every morel is a treasure!

may just find lots of footprints from everyone else trampling the area and compacting the soil. I'm not sure how harmful that impact is, but I greatly prefer hunting morels in the unburned an untrammeled cottonwood groves along the rivers.

Morels can be nearly black in color.

People are often territorial about their favorite morel hunting grounds. They may gloat about their bounty, but they won't always share their secret location!

Watch out for False Morels

False morels include mushrooms from the genera *Gyromitra*, *Helvella*, and *Verpa*, which vaguely resemble morel mushrooms in form. These imposters typically look more brain-like than sponge-like, so there is no reason to confuse them. If it doesn't look like a sponge, then it isn't a morel and don't eat it!

False morels look more brain-like than sponge-like.

Fried, Stir-fried, or Batter-Fried?

Slice or pinch the morels off near the base of the stalk, leaving the dirty base behind. Look for other bits of debris on the mushrooms, which can be easily picked off. Otherwise, morel mushrooms are typically pretty clean and ready to cook.

My grandmother sometimes soaked them in saltwater to bring out any larvae that might be lurking in the mushrooms, but as far as I am concerned, any extra lifeforms are more protein, tasteless, and normally invisible on the dinner plate. Slice the morels lengthwise or crosswise, and cook them any way you please. Morel mushrooms fried in butter or bacon grease is really good. You can also dip them in batter and batter-fry them.

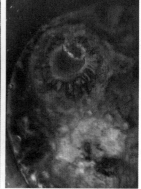

Harvesting morels on a camping trip. We dipped them in a batter of flour and water, then deep-fried them in oil. Delicious!

277

Preparing a springtime stir-fry in a wooden trough.

We are usually camped out among the cottonwoods by the river in morel season, teaching wilderness survival skills to school kids. It is always exciting to find a bunch of morels, which we often add to our stir-fry dinners. The students pitch in to cut up a big pile of carrots, potatoes, bell peppers, chicken and morel mushrooms.

We don't bring dishes, so we cook stir-fry in a wooden trough, mixing hot rocks from the fire into the food until it is cooked. We add water for steam, and sprinkle some teriyaki and soy sauce for additional flavor. We use slabs of bark for plates and twigs for chopsticks. It is always a big hit with the kids and the chaperones!

Cooking a morel mushroom, onion, and wild turkey shish kebab over hot coals.

Horse mushroom (*Agaricus arvensis*). Horse and meadow mushrooms are close cousins of the common button mushroom sold at grocery stores.

Agaricus campestris, A arvense
Agaric Family

Meadow Mushroom: Familiar Favorite

Meadow mushrooms are as familiar as mushrooms from your neighborhood grocery store. The common white button mushroom (*Agaricus bisporus*) found at the store is among the most widely consumed mushrooms in the world. The closely related meadow mushroom (*A. campestris*) and horse mushroom (*A. arvensis*) are similar, so much so that a good way to learn these mushrooms is to start by examining some button mushrooms. Study them carefully. Note the pink gills. Let them age outside the fridge. See how the gills turn brown and the cap flattens out.

If you think you've found a meadow or horse mushroom, take it home and compare it to a button mushroom. It should look like a close cousin.

The pink gills gradually turn brown and the cap flattens out.

279

Description, Habitat, and Range

The name says it all. Meadow mushrooms are found in meadows, typically where the grass is green and the soil is moist. Look for meadow and horse mushrooms in short grass meadows and pastures, not among choking tall grasses.

These mushrooms have thick, white flesh, a thin, cottony veil, and pink gills that turn chocolate brown with age. The gills can be pale in a young horse mushroom, but always pinkish. The spores are also dark chocolate brown. If you find one, there are likely more nearby.

Look for a thin, cottony veil.

These mushrooms can theoretically grow any time the weather is moist and mild, two conditions which are somewhat rare in the Mountain West. Here in Montana, I expect to see them in June or not at all.

Worldwide there are about 300 species of *Agaricus*. None are considered deadly poisonous, but some species can inspire serious vomitting and diarrhea in many people, and even the grocery store button mushroom can have that effect on some people. The species described here stand out for their exceptional resemblance to button mushrooms. Anything that seems close, but not quite right, may be a different species from the same genus. Check it out in a dedicated mushroom guide.

Watch out for *Amanita*

Check the color of the gills on all meadow and horse mushrooms. The gills should show at least some pink color. Any specimen with white or pale gray gills could be an *Amanita* or other potentially poisonous mushroom.

As Good as it Gets

Meadow and horse mushrooms can be used like and substituted for button mushrooms in any recipe. The flavor is mildly richer than store-bought mushrooms, and if there is one disappointment to harvesting and eating them, it is that their store-bought kin may seem disappointingly less appealing after you've eaten the real thing.

Slicing a horse mushroom to cook. Photo from *Canoe Camping: On a Song and a Paddle*, from *The Art of Nothing Wilderness Survival Video Series.*

Meadow mushrooms were common in the pastures near my Grandmother's home up Granite Creek. And while she delighted in finding the first morels of the season, I believe she favored the more substantial, full-flavored meadow mushroom. Unfortunately, both mushrooms were more scarce when she moved to a new home on the other side of the Tobacco Root mountains.

Shaggy mane mushrooms are well-named.

Coprinus comatus
Agaric Family

Shaggy Mane: Self-Destructing

My grandmother taught me about shaggy manes and other "inky cap" mushrooms. We went on walks almost daily, and sometimes we found them growing in cow pastures and meadows near her home. One day we brought a few inky caps home, intending to cook them for

breakfast. The mushrooms were in a bowl in the refrigerator, but all that was left in the morning was a pool of black ink. I dipped a feather quill in the ink and used it to draw on paper.

Shaggy manes don't have much substance like other mushrooms covered here, but they are widespread and common.

The mushrooms release their spores, then produce enzymes that break down chitin in their cell walls, auto-digesting themselves into black ink. The tightly packed gills separate and curl back, facilitating release of spores to the air.

Shaggy manes auto-digest as they age, dripping black ink.

The entire cap can dissolve in a matter of hours.

Description, Habitat, and Range

The shaggy mane is easily inden-tifiable by the shaggy, white, cylindi-cal cap that covers most of its stem. Inside, the gills are initially white, but quickly change to pink and then black. It doesn't last long. The mush-room can grow, cast its spores, and dissolve within a day or so.

Shaggy manes can be found in disturbed ground and along dirt roads, yet also in fields and lawns. They sprout shortly after drenching summer rains. *Coprinus comatus* is common across North America and Europe.

All true species of *Coprinus* have a ring near the base of the stem, remnants of where the cap separated from the stem. Many additional "inky cap" mushrooms were formerly included in the genus, but ge-netic analysis revealed that they were only distant relatives.

Procrastination is for Artists

Shaggy manes are more of a cu-linary curiousity than serious fodder. The flavor is mild and the flesh most-ly liquid. They are good sautéed and served as a dish by themselves. The substance and flavor may be lost by mixing them with other foods.

Whatever you do, do it quickly. When it comes to shaggy manes, or any other inky cap mushrooms, pro-crastinate too long and you will have to exchange your dinner plans for an evening of drawing and painting with black goo.

Of all the inky caps, shaggy manes are easiest to identify. Be sure to study other texts before cooking up any unknown inky cap mushrooms.

Snowy inky cap (Coprinellus nive-us, formerly Coprinus niveus). Genetic analysis shows that most inky caps are only dis-tantly related.

The bigger the puffball, the more exciting the find, but conversely, the less useful the mushrrom may be. The flesh is good if it is pure white inside.

Calvatia gigantean
(formerly *Lycoperdon giganteum*)
Puffball Family

Giant Puffball: Wild Tofu

Giant puffballs are a delight to find, if only because they are so absurdly unlike anything else found in Mother Nature's garden. Wandering through a meadow, you spot what looks like a volleyball in the grass. Take a closer look, you may have found a solid, ball-like mushroom, often so immense that it must be every forager's greatest dream.

Take it home and fry up a slab in butter, and you will discover a food source about as exciting as wild tofu. And that's the disappointment in the puffball. It isn't a wild food to be enjoyed for its own flavor, but to be used like tofu, as a bulk, protein-rich ingredient that needs to be flavored with something else. If you can accept that reality, then you are ready to enjoy puffballs for what they are.

Wild tofu.

Description, Habitat, and Range

There are several genera and many species of puffballs, but only one giant puffball. A mature, but small giant may be only as large as a baseball. Softball- to volleyball-sized puffballs are common. Real giants can be vastly bigger, up to several feet in diameter, but are uncommon. The surface can be either smooth or cracked. Puffballs have no gills. Instead, they are solid and white inside when young, gradually turning yellow and then brown and powdery as they mature. One puffball can contain trillions of spores.

Giant puffballs are common in grassy meadows and sagebrush prairies. In the Rocky Mountains, one is most likely to encounter them in June or July, before the soil loses its moisture.

Watch out for *Amanita*

One danger in harvesting giant puffball mushrooms is that poisonous *Amanita* mushrooms often resemble puffball mushrooms when young. The developing amanita is ball-shaped, before it separates into a distinctive cap and gills. Cut vertically through your puffball specimens, especially the small ones, to check for the developing cap and gills that would signify a poisonous amanita mushroom instead.

Trim and Peel

Puffball mushrooms are easy to prepare. Make sure the inside is fresh, solid and white. Older, yellowing puffballs may upset the digestive system. Trim off any dirt near the point of attachment to the soil, and peel the entire skin. Cut the meat into slabs or cubes, according to your cooking plans. Often, you will discover that you have far more

Amanita muscaria. This mushroom may resemble puffball mushrooms when small, but puffballs have no gills. Slice vertically through puffball mushrooms to make sure they are not amanitas.

Puffball pizza. Here are two slabs of puffball mushroom, slathered with pizza sauce, and topped with cheese, sausage, olives, and watercress.

puffball than you want for one meal. The rest can be frozen for later. Search online for dozens of interesting puffball recipes.

Puffball Pizza

One of the more unique recipes we've tried for puffballs is pizza. Use a slab of a large puffball mushroom as a pizza "crust." Add regular pizza ingredients on top of that, and bake in the oven. The end product is not bad, although not as exciting as it looks. The crust is a bit floppy and better eaten with a fork. But it is a cool innovation to serve to friends and guests.

Related Species

The name "puffball" applies to many different mushrooms spread across several fairly unrelated genera, including *Calvatia*, *Calbovista*, *Lycoperdon*, and *Vascellum*. Most puffballs are edible, but all specimens should be properly identified prior to eating them. Puffballs get their common name from old, dried specimens that are filled with powdery brown spores.

Lycoperdon pyriforme.

Squeeze one, and it will puff out a cloud of brown "smoke." They make great "smoke bombs" to stomp on, kick or throw at each other! The spores can also be applied on an open wound as a coagulant to help stop bleeding. My grandmother used them that way on her horses.

From above, a king bolete mushroom looks somewhat like a big hamburger bun. Underneath, the cap has tube-like pores instead of gills, and it is attached to a fat stem.

Boletus edulis
Bolete Family

King Bolete: Fit for Royalty

The king bolete may be named for its mammoth stature, but it is also a gourmet mushroom fit for royalty. It has more substance than many mushrooms, and a mild, meaty taste, yet it is easier to catch than any four-legged quarry. In terms of wild foods, it is an uncommon combination, to have a food that is both easy to gather and highly desirable.

Be prepared before hiking in the mountains in late summer. You may find there are too many beautiful mushrooms and not enough bags!

I love frying king boletes on camping trips. Best of all, I love finding a surplus to bring home and cook more. To up your status a notch, try frying a batch of king boletes the next time you entertain special guests.

If you find one king bolete, you will likely find more nearby.

287

Description, Habitat, and Range

Bolete mushrooms come in many different shapes, sizes, and colors, but only one is King. The king bolete has a large, thick cap, which often resembles the shape and color of a hamburger bun.

As with all bolete mushrooms, the underside is covered with a layer of long, tube-like pores instead of gills. The pores are whitish when young, turning greenish-yellow with age.

Most distinctively, king bolete mushrooms have a ridiculously fat, bulbous stem. This feature is most obvious in younger specimens, where the bulbous stem may be bigger than the cap.

The cap may be smaller than the bulbous stem in young specimens.

With time, the cap can grow to fit the proportions of the stem, producing a king-sized bolete mushroom, at times exceeding twelve inches in diameter. These monster mushrooms are great for identifying a bolete patch, but are usually too wormy to eat.

King boletes are widely distributed across the northern hemisphere. Here in Montana, we typically find them in the mountains, near water-loving spruce trees in July and August. Find one and there are likely more lurking nearby.

Gathering and Trimming

Discard any king boletes that are too wormy for your taste, and be sure to trim off the dirty base of each one before dropping your treasures in a bag. At your convenience, carefully peel back or trim away

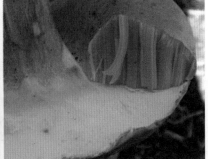

Trim off the dirty base before transporting king boletes. Later, to prepare the mushrooms for cooking, trim off the tube-like pores, then slice the mushroom into slabs.

All trimmed and ready for slicing.

the tube-like pores beneath the cap. The pores are edible, but tend to cook up slimy, so it is preferable to remove them. You may be surprised, however, to find that there isn't much left of the cap after trimming away the pores. Most of the meat is in the bulbous stem.

Into the Frying Pan

King boletes can be sliced and cooked just about any way you please. For simplicity, try frying 3/8-inch thick slices in butter. King bolete mushrooms have a mild, meaty flavor that is simultaneously mild yet exotic. For additional flavor, fry some onions first, then mix in your king boletes and any kind of greens. King boletes can also be added to soups and stews. Look for recipes online and enjoy this wonderful fungus.

Lightly fried king bolete mushrooms with onions, cheese, and parsley.

Related Species

Worldwide there are more than one hundred species of *Boletus*, as well as several other genera that are also known as boletes. All boletes grow in the soil, not on trees. Any one species can vary significantly in texture and color across different parts of its range.

No boletes are considered deadly poisonous, but many species are either tasteless, bitter, slimy, or just not very appetizing, and a few species are poisonous enough to cause vomiting, cramps, or diarrhea. Avoid species with red pores under the cap. Experimenting with unidentified species is not advised. Identify any new boletes you find, and explore them cautiously.

Matte Jack (*Suillus lakei*). There are several genera and hundreds of species of bolete-type mushrooms. Many, but not all are edible.

On my camping trips I have dined on orange-cap boletes (*Leccinum insigne*) and tried both slippery Jack (*Suillus luteus*) and matte Jack (*Suillus lakei*), which are all decent finds, but lack the quantity or class of the king bolete.

An American red squirrel (Tamiasciurus hudsonicus), killed with a rock.

Hunting and Scavenging

Our ancestors started eating meat and marrow about 2.6 million years ago. The protein and fats helped facilitate the growth of larger brains in our lineage. Today, meat is still essential to our diet and health, and sometimes a meal just isn't complete without a hunk of meat on the side.

Rather than hunt, it is likely that our early ancestors scavenged prey killed by other carnivores. For example, vultures circle overhead when leopards or hyenas kill an animal. Our ancestors learned to watch the birds and then run to the kill site to chase away competition.

You can reconnect with our ancestral heritage while speeding down the road in a car. Just watch for a telltale flock of crows or magpies along the road, and you'll know there is a kill site, where an unlucky animal was taken down by a ferocious (and equally unlucky) car or truck. Stop and chase away the birds, then rip and tear into the flesh with your bare hands and chow down right there on the side of the road. Better yet, watch for a fresher roadkill that the birds haven't broken into, and take it home for processing!

Being armed isn't necessary to bring home the proverbial bacon. As it was for our ancestors, hunting and scavenging is about being an opportunist and utilizing whatever is available. On a wilderness walkabout that might involve picking up a rock or stick and chucking it at a squirrel or bunny. It maybe a matter of finding some crayfish or easy-to-catch carp in a river or lake. On a country driveabout, one might pick up a roadkill deer or stop to dig in a grocery store dumpster. Start scavenging, and you may be amazed at all the free food that is readily available.

Thumper and Bambi

Wild animals are cute, and it may seem cruel or savage to slaughter Thumper or Bambi and friends. *It is.*

Killing is bloody business. It is shockingly cruel and savage. One moment a bunny might be happily grazing in the grass, having wandered away from the family for a bit of fresh air. The next moment it is bleeding from the head and writhing in spasms from a well-placed throw of a stick or rock. Is it dead? Maybe. Often as not,

Desert cottontail (*Sylvilagus audubonii*).

you will need to surge forward, grab the animal before it regains its orientation, and bash its head against a rock. Then it is time to skin, gut, and butcher the critter so that you can have one modest meal and live to see another day yourself.

It is easy to forget where meat comes from when it is purchased in the grocery store, neatly packaged on Styrofoam™ trays, wrapped with plastic and labeled. Therefore, it is important to do one's own killing, at least sometimes, if only to fully understand and appreciate the lives that are given up to feed us every day.

It is also important to keep in mind that savagry is the backbone of harmony in nature, and almost every living thing, aside from ourselves, will suffer a brutal death. Cottontail rabbits, for example, can raise several litters every year, with two to seven babies per litter. Unfettered, the population can multiply many times over in a single year. But at the end of the year, there are only about as many cottontails as there were at the beginning of the year. For every rabbit that survives the year, several more died in the claws of hawks and eagles, or in the jaws of coyotes, cats, or snakes. It is highly improbable that even one wild bunny will live long enough to peacefully die of old age in a retirement warren, surrounded by family and friends.

Whitetail deer fawn (*Odocoileus virginianus*) hiding in the grass. Many cute and cuddly newborns never make it to adulthood.

Ditto for deer. Each doe typically has one or two fawns, nearly doubling the population every year. But cute and cuddly newborns die by the hundreds, and those that make it to adulthood are preyed on by mountain lions, hunters, and SUVs. Many starve or fall through the ice and drown while crossing rivers. Dying of old age is so rare that it is almost unnatural. Spend a little time in the woods, and you will notice that the land is littered with bones. Nature is brutal and bloody every day, and it is important to face that reality and the reality of our own savage existence. In order for us to live, something else must die. Responsible killing is about taking ownership of the process. It makes us a little more humane in the way we appreciate the circle of life.

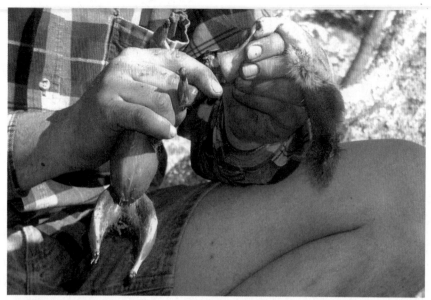

Skinning a squirrel.

Hunting 101: Sticks, Rocks, and Spears

I know of few things more offensive than cocky hunters who boast of using a big gun to blow away a deer, coyote, or rabbit, as if being able to squeeze a trigger somehow makes them manly and powerful.

Sometimes hunting becomes a party, hanging out, drinking beer, and blowing ground squirrels to smithereens. Or the hunters surround a group of deer and everyone shoots randomly into the bunch with semi-automatic rifles. Then they look to see what dropped and pass out the hunting tags. I would love to dump people like that in the middle of the wilderness—with only their bare hands to survive—and see how cocky they are after that.

Learning to hunt without factory-made weapons is a highly effective experience to cultivate deep respect for all life. Try matching wits against a wild animal, and it quickly becomes evident that we are not superior beings. It is a very humbling experience. One can learn to appreciate not only the animals, but also our ancestors, who survived millenia after millenia with only what they could improvise themselves.

Hunting with your hands and wits is an excellent way to start your hunting career if you didn't grow up as a hunter yourself. It doesn't require any special preparation or training, and you can begin at any time. The art of hunting and scaveninging is really a matter of opportunism. If you see potential quarry, at least try stalking it.

Hunting with Rocks

Hunting with rocks is as basic as it gets. Look around for a nice rock, about golfball- to baseball-sized, and chuck it at the prey. Our ancestors hunted with rocks all the time, and they were highly adept at it. If you didn't grow up throwing rocks for a living, then you may need practice. Fortunately,

Rabbits often freeze and pretend to be invisible, rather than running away.

many animals are patient enough to let you try again and again.

Learning to skin a bunny.

Cottontail rabbits, for example, often freeze and pretend to be invisible. Sometimes they patiently let you throw several rocks or sticks at them before they dash for cover.

Tree squirrels may allow multiple tries as well, often retreating higher and higher up a tree until they have determined your maximum throwing range. One time, some friends and I tried to hit a squirrel in a tree. Rather than leaping from tree to tree, the squirrel identified a safe spot where we couldn't hit it from any side. It was clearly visible and within our range, but the three of us threw at least a hundred rocks each, and none of us ever hit the squirrel. Nevertheless, it was good practice. Seeing another squirrel the next morning, I picked up a rock and chucked it, killing the squirrel the first try.

Grouse often fly to a tree when startled and perch on a branch. Sometimes they stay put, no matter how many rocks go whizzing past. There are several genera of "mountain grouse" in the coniferous forests of the West, including spruce grouse (*Falcipennis*), blue grouse (*Dendragapus*), and ruffed grouse (*Bonasa*). It helps to have patient prey if you are not an experienced hunter!

Roasting rabbit on hot coals.

The Throwing Stick

One of the best hunting weapons ever invented is the stick. Unlike a rock, which is thrown overhand (over the shoulder), the stick is usually thrown side-armed (from the hips). The stick travels helicopter-style, parallel with the ground, cutting a wide swath that is much wider than the narrow trajectory of a rock. As with all throwing, lead and aim with the foot and arm opposite of the one holding the stick for the best accuracy and power.

Demonstrating how to use the throwing stick in a wilderness survival class.

Grouse often fly up to a perch and stay there—no matter how many sticks and rocks go whizzing by.

This stick, also known as a "rabbitstick," should be shorter than your arm, solid, and the right size for a good hand grip. Basically, look for a heavy boomerang. Watch out for any nubs on the end, as they have a penchant for ripping off flesh when releasing the stick. The throwing stick is probably the most successful hunting tool in human history, and yet, like the rock, it is not likely to be found or recognized in an archeological dig.

The stick doesn't fly as fast as a rock, but it improves the chance of hitting the prey. It is ideally used for targets on open ground such as a rabbit. It is more difficult to use in brush or trees, which may deflect the stick. Nevertheless, the stick can be thrown vertically (overhand) to hit a squirrel on a branch beside a tree trunk. It also works well for grouse.

It takes practice to develop proficiency and accuracy, but the throwing stick works well on prey animals that allow multiple tries. Chucking sticks and rocks is all-consuming—even our vegan friends get caught up in the primal calling!

Roasting grouse over hot coals.

Hunting with Spears

Making a spear takes a bit more work than picking up a stick or rock, but a spear is ideal for some quarry, especially porcupines. Look for a long, straight, sturdy, stick, and carve a sharp point at the tip.

Porcupines are often found in trees, but also spend a great deal of time on the ground, grazing on plants or hiding under logs and brush. It is often possible to stalk or

Porcupines are best hunted with spears.

walk within a few feet of them, close enough to thrust a spear. But as slow as porcupines are, they can move astonishingly fast when moti-

Skinning a porcupine with stone tools. From the video *Three Days at the River.*

vated to do so. If the cover isn't too thick, then it is usually possible to follow them to a protective thicket and spear them there. Skin the animal carefully from the belly side to avoid the quills.

See our video *Three Days at the River: Volume One in The Art of Nothing Wilderness Survival Video Series* for more on hunting and eating porcupine.

Legal or Not?

Hunting and wildlife laws vary greatly from state to state, so be sure to research your local state laws before hunting. For example, tree squirrels are protected in Washington state, and some may be endangered in parts of that state, but they are not protected in Montana.

Grouse are huntable, but only with a hunting lisence and only in season. Moreover, Montana law dictates that *"Grouse may be taken with a shotgun not larger than a ten gauge; a long, recurve or compound bow and arrow; a rifle; or a handgun. All other means of taking are prohibited."* Hunting grouse with sticks or rocks is more challenging and authentic, but not legal due to omission from the written law. I doubt the rule-makers considered sticks or rocks when writing the rules. I hope to see the laws updated someday to respect ancestral hunting methods.

Alive or dead, crayfish can seem just a little bit scary.

Crayfish: Inland Lobster

As a lifelong landlubber, I cannot say I've eaten a lot of seafood or ever really acquired the taste for it. But once in awhile we'll encounter a section of river where the crayfish are reasonably-sized and crazy abundant, and how can we possibly pass that up? Crayfish, also known as crawfish, crawdads, or mudbugs, are like miniature lobsters, and the closest thing to seafood in the Mountain West.

Description, Habitat, and Range

Crayfish are easy to identify. There is nothing to confuse them with. Armed with a pair of big pinchers in the front, the crustaceans crawl forwards when foraging, but retreat backwards, propelling themselves to astonishing speeds with their tails. They eat dead insects, fish, and vegetation, and any small, live creatures they can catch.

In the Mountain West, crayfish are typically smaller than in warmer environments. Four inches from nose to tail is a good-sized crayfish, and anything smaller isn't worth collecting. Expect to go crayfish

A crayfish with eggs.

hunting in late summer, when the crustaceans are largest and the water is lowest. Look for them hiding among rocks in shallow and warm val-ley bottom rivers and streams, not in chilly mountain waters.

Worldwide there are hundreds of species of crayfish spread across numerous genera over three families. Only a few species of native and introduced crayfish are found in the Mountain West, mostly from the genera *Pacifastacus*, *Orconectes*, and *Procambarus*. Crayfish should never be transplanted from one water body to another, as they can become highly invasive and destructive.

Fearless Hunter

There is nothing so fun as spending a lazy afternoon chasing crayfish. But with those

Like lobsters, crayfish turn red when cooked.

big, scary-looking pinchers, the most challenging part is controlling one's own fear. Fortunately, crayfish are too small to cause any real harm. Nevertheless, who wants to risk getting pinched?

Given that crayfish look forwards, but retreat backwards, it is best to sneak up behind them with one hand. Grab the body just behind the pinchers with the thumb and index finger, pinning them to the river bottom while adjusting your fingers for a good grip. From this angle, your fingers are out of reach of their pinchers. Lift out of the water and drop them in a bucket of water to keep them alive until cooking time.

Boiled Alive

Like lobsters, crayfish are boiled alive. Boil the water, then add the crayfish, killing them almost instantly. Crustaceans turn red when cooked. The red color, a carotenoid pigment called astaxanthin, is there all along, but mixed with other colors that break down when heated, leaving only the red.

A nice chunk of tail meat.

Eating crayfish is like eating lobster, but on a smaller scale. Bend the tail backward, cracking it off, then pry it open and eat the meat. Smaller tidbits can be extracted from the claws. Crayfish are a fun treat, but may have a slightly muddy flavor. Don't expect to get much from each critter.

Carp spawn in shallow water where they can be easy to catch.

Cyprinus carpio
Carp Family

Common Carp: Disdained but Delicious

Common carp, also known as Asian carp, are esteemed as a traditional Christmas Eve dinner in central Europe. Carp have been introduced to waterways worldwide as a productive source of food. Today, aquaculture operations produce more carp than any other species, totaling about three million tons annually. Carp are considered a valued food source just about everywhere except in America, where the fish are often denigrated as "trash fish" and "bottom feeders."

Carp were originally introduced here for food, but culturally fell out of favor. Few people look for carp, and fewer try eating them. Millions of dollars are spent trying to eradicate carp, or control their population, which could be much more effectively accomplished if anglers were enticed to catch and eat the fish.

We have discovered through first-hand experience that carp are delicious, often insanely abundant, and generally easy to catch, even without a fishing pole.

Showing off the catch.

Description, Habitat, and Range

Carp are large, fast-growing fish with coloration that ranges from muddy brown to olive-green on top and brassy yellow or golden along the sides and bottom. They have large scales, which are outlined in black, and a single, long dorsal fin. The mouth is sucker-like, with big, kissable lips adapted to bottom feeding. They have no teeth, rendering them gentle to catch and handle. Two fleshy barbells form a fashionable and harmless mustache, which appears to be an unused holdover form another time. Carp congregate in groups, particularly in spawning season, so if you see one there are likely many more.

Carp thrive in typically warm, nutrient-rich waters where they feed on fast growing aquatic vegetation and invertebrates. They typically spawn in late May and early June in shallow backwaters and along the shores of lakes and rivers. Females can lay up to 300,000 eggs at once, which stick to vegetation and debris along the bottom. Eggs hatch within three to ten days and mature to adulthood in two to four years. Adults typically range from 12 to 24 inches long, weigh 8 to 10 pounds, and live to be about 15 years old, but can grow much bigger, heavier, and older. The biggest carp ever recorded in Montana measured 38 inches and weighed 40.2 pounds.

Ancestral carp originated in drainages of the Black, Caspian, and Aral Seas, dispersing east into China and Siberia, and west into the Danube River. Romans constructed massive aquaculture ponds to cultivate carp as food. Fast-growing descendents of these Roman carp have been introduced to waterways worldwide as a food source, and are now considered an invasive species in many habitats. With their vacuum-like snouts and prolific numbers, carp consume subsurface vegetation and muddy the waters, competing with or impacting the habitat for many native species. Ironically, the original, wild carp are now imperiled in their native range.

Carp *seem* like easy targets for predators, given their tendency to swarm in

Carp often congregate around boat docks on warm-water lakes, these at Lake Mead, near Las Vegas, Nevada.

shallow waters. Yet, adult carp are generally too big to be easily killed by North American predators, such as pelicans, eagles, or other fish. Bears would likely kill them if they discovered when and where to find them, which may be miles away from their usual habitat.

Young carp and small adults do fall victim to predation, but carp grow so fast in nutrient-rich waters that they are only vulnerable for a short time. Being hyper-prolific and invulnerable, carp numbers can swell into the millions. The most effective predator to balance the ecosystem may be the hungry forager!

Shooting Fish in a Barrel

Carp hunting can be ridiculously easy. The first carp I caught were on the Verde River in Arizona, while guiding troubled teens on wilderness expeditions. I spotted a group of seven or eight carp mingling half out of the water along the bank, protected by a wall of tall reeds along the water's edge. I grabbed an overhead tree branch and swung myself over the reeds, landing feet-first on the carp!

In the mayhem, I threw two big fish up on the bank. I've since caught many more by hand (sometimes by sitting on them), as well as by net, spear, and bow and arrow. I'm not much of a fisherman, however, so I haven't tried using a fishing pole. My first

Bowfishing with a compound bow and attached reel.

carp encounters were happenstance, but now I look for them. Here in Montana, I like carp hunting in late May or early June, as the water warms up and the fish start spawning, but just before the mosquitoes emerge in full force.

Hunting carp with a primitive bow and arrow.

Bow Fishing: I find primal pleasure in wandering along murky backwaters, bow in hand, searching for carp. Carp hunting provides reasonable assurance of success, making it possible to truly "live off the land." An afternoon stroll can yield a half dozen carp as big as your thigh; more than you will be able to eat. Your calories acquired, you can spend the rest of the day gathering milkweed shoots, picking a salad, exploring, and hunting for mushrooms.

Bow fishing is loads of fun and good practice for anyone who might later want to hunt bigger game. Laws vary from state to state, but in Montana it is legal to hunt all "non-game" fish, such as carp and suckers, with a bow and arrow, except where otherwise noted. Just be sure to use a powerful bow and sharp arrows, since carp are heavily armored with large thick scales. Modern recurve and compound bows often have a threaded hole where a fishing reel can be added. Fishing arrows have barbs that open up after passing through the flesh, so the arrows don't slide back out as you reel in your catch.

I prefer to use my hand-made, sinew-backed chokecherry bow and my own arrows. But without a line and reel, I can only hunt in shallow waters. I have found that nail-tipped arrows penetrate carp really well, while sharpened wood tips bounce right off.

To hunt for carp, wander along shallow banks during the spawning season and look for them wallowing in the muck, often half out of the water. Hitting a big carp is pretty easy. But once you strike, you must jump into the water, grab the arrow, and drive it down into the carp, pinning it to the mucky bottom. Then slide your other hand under the fish, pick it up and make your way to shore before removing the arrow. Be ready to swim though, because sometimes they make a run for it, and you have to follow your arrow until you catch the fish.

Improvising: Carp can also be hunted with a crude, improvised spear. Spear through the fish with a single-prong spear, or use a double-prong spear to pin the fish to the bottom while you reach in and grab it. Find a spear that is straight and sturdy, but

Head shot.

Shot with a primitive arrow.

Totally satisfying!

303

don't waste too much time on refining the tips, since you will be jabbing it into the ground. Strangely, fishing laws are often more restrictive about hunting with spears. In Montana, for example, spear fishing is allowed only for specific species on designated lakes and reservoirs. Rubber- or spring-propelled spears can only be used while swimming or submerged, and only hand-propelled spears may be used for ice fishing. I suspect that the laws are not written to protect the carp, which are considered a nuisance fish.

Tom's son Donny nailed one with a spear.

If you find yourself without a weapon at hand, try catching carp by hand. They do not normally swim backwards, so bring one hand down in front of the face to stop them from swimming forward and the other hand straight down on the back to pin them to the bottom. For insurance, sit on them to hold them between your legs, or do an all-out belly flop to hug them to your chest. Then work your fingers in the gills and even the mouth to hold them securely before picking them up.

Although carp instinctively swim for deeper water to escape, sometimes they can be herded through shallow riffles or part way on the bank, where they are easier to catch. Get the fish onto dry land, then smack it in the head with a heavy rock and all the force you can muster, or the rock will just bounce off.

Interestingly, catching fish by hand is considered illegal, or at least unlegal, in Montana and many other states. There isn't any particular law against fishing by hand, but technically, it is only legal to catch fish by whatever means are specified in the regulations, which makes fishing by hand illegal through omission. In practice, there isn't much difference at times, between walking up to a carp with a bow and arrow versus just reaching down and picking it up.

Given that carp are considered an invasive species and a threat to native fisheries, do take as many as you can reasonably use.

Roasted Over Hot Coals

The simplest, but not the fastest way to cook carp is to gut them as you would any fish, then roast whole on top of the hot coals, or on green willows on top of hot coals. Cooking can take a long time, and the hot coals gradually lose heat, taking longer and longer to cook the closer you get to being done. Sometimes we have cooked carp for hours this way, until long after sunset, before we could finally descend on the fish and pick them apart like vultures. You know the fish is cooked when the meat separates easily from the bones. A large carp makes a great communal meal where everyone digs in by hand. Sometimes we bring barbeque sauce along for dip.

Carp can be slow-roasted directly on hot coals, then picked apart and eaten as a group meal.

Served on a plywood platter.

Fillet O'Carp

To fillet a fish, carve off the meat on both sides and discard the rest of the carcass. Filleting always seemed wasteful to me. I grew up on pan-sized brook trout, which were too small to fillet, supplemented occasionally by a bigger rainbow, brown, or lake trout, which were too valuable to justify wasting even a morsel. But carp are big, often very abundant, and disdained by nearly everyone, so it is easier to justify the waste. Besides, filleting a carp transforms a good fish into a great fish, enabling many more culinary options. And anything you toss out will be eagerly consumed by seagulls, raccoons, and other scavengers.

There is no need to gut a carp if you intend to fillet. Lay the fish on

Cut the skin and peel it back.

One side skinned and ready to fillet.

Trim off the meat.

a clean surface and skin one side, cutting around the fins, so that only the skin is removed from the body. Poke a knife in under the skin and slide forward along the inside, slicing the skin much like opening an envelope with a letter opener. Cut the meat as little as possible at this stage, if only to make a neater fillet. Cut around the perimeter, then start behind the gills and pull the skin away. A knife may be needed to separate the meat from the flesh at first, but once started, the skin will peel right off. This is a slippery task at first, but it is easily learned, halving the skinning time by the second fish.

With the skin out of the way, start at the backbone, behind the gills and trim away the meat. Cut down to the ribs and skim across them to remove the flesh. The bulk of the meat is found along the spine, but you should be able to remove meat all the way out to the belly for a nice fillet. Some small bones will remain inside the finished fillet, which must necessarily be removed while eating. Having finished one side, flip the carp over and fillet the other side.

Cut down along the ribs.

A beautiful carp fillet.

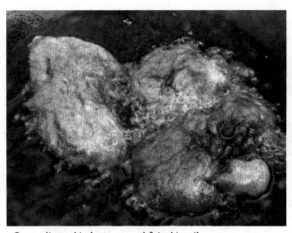

Carp, dipped in batter and fried in oil.

With carp fillets in hand, take the opportunity to experiment with a variety of cooking methods and recipes. Try pan frying carp fillets in butter and lemon pepper, or dip chunks of meat in batter and fry them in oil. Carp fillets can also be slow cooked on a rack over an open fire. Try adding green willow, mesquite, or apple wood to the coals for smoking the fish in the cooking process, and you will have the most delicious fish you could ever imagine!

Fresh, Not Frozen

Some of my most memorable, savory wilderness meals consisted of fresh carp cooked over an open campfire. Those were all caught by hand, prior to starting bow fishing. Then I heard about the Montana Bow Hunter's annual Carp Safari, held at Canyon Ferry Reservoir near Helena each June. I wanted to learn about bow hunting, so Kris and I drove up to check it out.

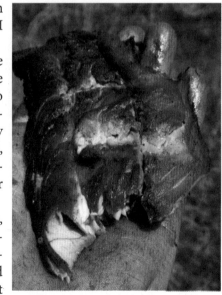

Bowhunters register for the event then fan out across the lake for the day, competing to see who can bring back the most and the biggest carp. At the end of the day, they check in, count, and weigh the fish, and discard all into a great big construction dumpster. In a good year they can nearly fill the dumpster.

Carp are considered a nuisance, because they've disrupted the natural balance of native and transplanted fish. The Carp Safari is intended to help deal with this problem, yet the population is so extensive that

A delicious willow-smoked carp fillet.

307

Drying carp in the sun. Leave both fillets attached at the tail for hanging the meat neatly to dry.

the effort is more symbolic than substantive. In an attempt to not completely waste the resource, the MBA seeks partnerships with ranchers who compost the carp for their fields.

Kris and I showed up at the Carp Safari with a couple coolers and a bunch of ice, begging the bowhunters to donate their carp to us, rather than heaving them in the dumpster. Most just looked at us as if we were utterly subhuman, but a few people gave us their carp, which we cleaned and froze.

Unfortunately, we discovered that carp doesn't freeze well, turning the meat to mush when thawed and cooked. It was quite a disappointment, especially in comparison to our delicious fresh cooked carp experiences. Researchers have found that quantities of adenosine triphosphate and creatine phosphate in the flesh decrease very rapidly when the meat is frozen slowly, while compounds such as inosine monophosphate increase greatly. Translation: the meat turns to mush unless you can get it fresh and freeze it quickly. Perhaps filleting the meat would speed up the freezing process. We'll have to try that next time!

Related Species

Worldwide there are 22 species of *Cyprinus*, as well as several other genera that are commonly known as carp, several of which are found in North American waterways, including grass carp (*Ctenopharyngodon idella*), bighead carp (*Hypophthalmichthys nobilis*), silver carp (*Hypophthalmichthys molitrix*), and potentially black carp (*Mylopharyngodon piceus*). All belong to the Carp family, also known as the Minnow family. To the forager, they are all food. Goldfish (*Carassius auratus*) are also in the Minnow family, and sometimes hybridize with various species of carp.

A roadkill moose calf: tender, organic, and free.

Roadkill: It's What's for Dinner

An estimated 1.5 million deer are mowed down by cars every year on America's highways. There are also elk, antelope, moose, bear, rabbits, pheasants, grouse, geese, coyotes, foxes, porcupines, snakes and more—to the tune of about a million vertebrate casualties *every day*! It makes me wonder sometimes: How many animals are killed by commuters rushing off to work at a boring job, working in a cubical all day to earn enough money to swing by the grocery store and pick up a feedlot-raised beefsteak from a cow pumped full of growth hormones and antibiotics? Wouldn't it make more sense to skip the job, enjoy the day, then go scrape some nice organically grown wild meat off the pavement?

Scavenging for roadkill is easier than hunting for wild game. You don't need to buy a gun. You don't need to take hunter safety classes, purchase a permit, drive a hundred miles, hike around for days, shoot an animal, and then wonder how to get it back to your vehicle. You just have to be willing to sieze the opportunity to pick up fresh meat when the opportunity presents itself. In some states it is even legal to do so.

My grandmother mentored me in processing roadkill game. She didn't believe in wasting valuable resources. I've since butchered enough roadkill to become comfortable and proficient at the process, and I know enough about battered meat and bloated carcasses to provide guidance where other texts on hunting and butchering leave off.

Description, Habitat, and Range

Roadkill is easy to identify. Just watch for bloody masses of flesh and fur and feather that line our highways from coast to coast. Roadkill can be found almost anywhere there is pavement and speed limits higher than 35 mph. If a carcass is not too badly damaged then you might even be able to identify what type of creature it was, and critically, whether or not it is salvageable and edible.

Roadkill deer are most common in fall, when they switch from summer routines, alone with their fawns, to winter routines, wandering as herds. Hunting season also scares deer back and forth across the highways, increasing the number of kills. Drive slowly at night to avoid an accident.

A *Canada goose* roadkill in prime condition.

Green Roadkill or Ham?

Finding meat on the side of the highway is one thing, but is it edible? Trust your senses. If it looks green and the smell makes you want to barf, then leave it alone. Sometimes even the freshest roadkills are foul. Once, when following a big pickup truck pulling a fifth-wheel trailer, I watched as the driver hit a deer, then rototilled it underneath every set of tires. The driver wasn't sorry about hitting the deer, just totally pissed since he was driving the rig home from the repair shop where they undid the damage from the last deer he hit. As for the deer, it was as fresh as could be, but with the stomach contents exploded everywhere, it was one of the more foul roadkills I've encountered. I dragged it off the road before it caused another accident and left it for the vultures.

We have picked up a few other deer that were killed only minutes before. But more often, animals are killed on the highway sometime during the evening, night, or morning, when wildlife is most active and visibility is limited. If you see a carcass along the road that wasn't there yesterday, and nighttime temperatures were cool enough, then it might be worth checking out.

Animals that are hit in the head are ideal, since the body itself is left undamaged, but most roadkills have some broken ribs or legs and deeply bruised and bloodied meat that must be trimmed off. That's okay. Hunting with rifles can have a similar effect on the meat too.

It is also okay if the carcass is a little bloated. Bacteria in the gut continue digesting food long after the animal is dead, but the carcass doesn't have working elimination muscles and thus can't fart it out. The more bloated it is, the more likely you are to encounter out-gassing during transportation or butchering, although the meat may still be good. Proceed cautiously and bring home only the freshest

Free meat. Just load it and go.

roadkills, or experiment around a little with some roadkill dissection to find out what is and isn't fresh until you find your comfort zone.

Yes, But is it Legal?

Roadkill laws vary from state to state and change from year to year, so it is sensible to research your local laws via the internet before shopping your local highways. In general, there is a trend towards legalizing roadkill harvesting, with each state having a different set of rules about how to proceed.

In Montana, the legislature passed a law in 2013 legalizing the harvest of roadkill antelope, deer, elk, and moose, following rules and guidelines administered by the Department of Fish, Wildlife, and Parks. Prior to this law, it was illegal, or rather, unlegal, to pick up roadkill game in Montana. There was no specific law against it, but there was no law allowing it either, which technically made it an illegal taking of game.

It didn't make sense. Hunters could be charged with a crime if they let a hunted animal go to waste, but we were letting 10,000+ deer go to waste along our highways every year. Meanwhile, 20 percent of Montana's children were classified as undernourished, living in households without enough money to buy quality food. Many people went ahead and harvested roadkill anyway. It wasn't legal, yet nobody really cared, either, as long as one kept the activity

Roadkill should not be gut-ted by the road, so I often bring the carcass home, then hang, skin, and gut it.

Cut from the anus up to the throat.

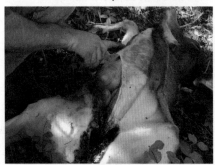

The deer is slightly bloated already.

Use a mallet and knife to split the pelvis.

The pelvic bone has been cut open to pull out the intestines.

below the radar. The legislator who introduced the roadkill legislation previously worked as a police officer and sometimes brought roadkill game into his local foodbank, thereby breaking the law himself, but only with good conscience.

The deer shown here was not a roadkill per se, but a "fence kill." Sometimes when deer jump over a fence, they catch a back leg between the top two wires, tightly twisting the wires together around their leg. This deer was stuck in a fence, with three legs on the ground and its back leg sticking straight up in the air. I hoped that I could untwist the fence wires and let it go, but the leg was completely broken and held together only by skin and tendon. The compassionate thing to do was slit its throat and cut the tendon to let it drop to the ground. At that point I had a freshly dead deer, and I could not ethically walk away and let it rot. So into the car it went.

Gutting a Deer

The first step in processing a deer is to remove the innards. Most people call this "field dressing," and do it immediately after the kill. First they cut the throat to allow the animal to bleed out; then they slice it open and remove the insides. I don't normally do field dressing because the animal has typically been dead from one to several hours before I find it, and I won't gut it on the side of the road. I put the carcass in the car and haul it away to process it. And I don't bother to bleed it, since the blood has usually congealed by then anyway.

After hauling, I gut the animal as soon as possible to prevent bloating and to cool the carcass to avoid spoiling the meat. To gut the animal, slice from the anus all the way up to the throat. Then go back and cut through the thin layer of fat and meat on the belly to expose the guts, being careful to avoid rupturing anything inside. The more bloated the carcass, the more careful you have to be. In the second photo you can see that the stomach is slightly bloated and the pressure is forcing the stomach out as I work.

To remove the intestines without spilling the contents, it is helpful to cut through the pelvic bone. This is easily done where the two halves are sutured together. You will feel a ridge of bone with your fingers. Put your knife blade on the ridge and use a wooden mallet or stick to tap the knife through. Cutting through the bone on either side would be much more difficult.

Next, alongside the breastbone to open the chest cavity. Force the knife through if you can, or use a wooden mallet on the back of the knife. Also cut across the throat to release the esophagus. Then grab the esophagus and pull the innards out toward the rear end. In the pictures here I have the deer on a slight incline with the head up, so that the guts are already slumping down with gravity.

Below the heart and lungs is a thin membrane called the diaphragm. Cut through the diaphragm when you get to it. Then continue rolling the whole

Cutting the breast bone.

Start at the esophagus and pull everything out.

Pulling out the heart and lungs.

Lifting the end of the intestine out of the pelvis.

mass of innards out of the body. Take some care at the tail end to avoid squeezing pellets out the anus, but it is no big deal if you do. Even if everything goes wrong and you rupture the stomach, intestines, and/ or bladder, it can still be washed clean, so don't sweat it. Everyone has their own system for gutting, skinning, and butchering, but all paths lead to the same end.

Skinning a Deer

Many people like to age a carcass after gutting it. They hang it up, with or without skinning it, and prop open the chest cavity and pelvis to allow air circulation. The meat is left hanging for a couple of days or up to a couple weeks, depending on the weather and the size of the critter. Don't let the hide freeze to the body, or the whole carcass will have to be thawed to get it off. Cool weather, about 40°F, is ideal for aging. Flies can be attracted to the carcass in warmer weather to lay eggs, so it should be tightly wrapped in a sheet for protection. The cloth also helps keep the meat from drying out, particularly if it's skinned. Aging the carcass can help tenderize the meat, but it is hardly necessary. I prefer to finish the job and get the meat into the freezer.

While it is possible to skin flat on the ground, I find it easier to do the job in the air. Hanging the deer also helps keep the meat out of the dirt. Some people like to hang a deer by the back legs, but I prefer to hang it by the neck, as shown in photos A and F. The hide seems to come off more easily that way. I used a scrap of baling twine to tie this one to a tree branch. A come-along is helpful for hoisting heavier anim ls. In photo A, I have cut around the circumference of the neck, and I am using my knife to free the hide above the front shoulders.

Remove the lower half of the front and back legs either before or after hanging the deer. Flex the legs back and forth to find the joint, then cut through it with a knife. Photos B and C illustrate cutting through the joint on a front leg. The joint is more convoluted on the back legs, but cut through as far as you can, then break it apart over your knee, as shown in photo D.

Next, use a knife to split the skin open along the inside of the legs, as shown in photo E. Now, set aside your knife and avoid using it to separate the hide from the meat, or you risk cutting into the skin, making it less valuable for tanning. You can tan the hide yourself, following directions from my book *Participating in Nature: Wilderness Survival and Primitive Living Skills*, or you can take the hide to a recycling center (during hunting season), where it will be shipped to a commercial tannery.

Peeling the skin off. The hide has a thin layer of meat on it, but no knife scars.

Most holes in a finished piece of buckskin are knife slips from skinning. You won't need a blade after making the initial cuts. The rest of the skinning job is like peeling a big, fuzzy banana. Grab the hide and peel down, as shown in photo F. Lean into it with your body weight, and use your fists and elbows as needed. You may be amazed at how quickly and cleanly you can skin a deer this way. I usually cut the tail off, but this time the hide peeled right off the tail, as shown in photo G.

There will be a thin layer of meat left on the hide, as shown in photo H, but that is okay. These muscles are used for twitching the skin to scare away flies. It isn't useful for table meat anyway, and it is a real treat for the dog when you flesh it off the hide during the tanning process.

Peel the skin off, and then you are ready to proceed with butchering. I usually fold the hide up and set it aside and flesh it after the meat is in the freezer, but in this case I laid it out flat to hold the meat while I did the processing.

Butchering Basics

Butchering is the process of cutting the carcass into pieces small enough to fit in the frying pan or freezer. A body is broken down into easily sectionable parts and the only tool you'll need is a strong sheath knife. As with any skill, there are a zillion ways to do it, and even I don't do it the same way every time. The process shown here is substantially different than what a professional butcher would do with power saws.

This style of butchering works well when the only tool you have is a knife. The objective is to package the meat cuts as various steaks, roasts, boiling bones, and stew meat. The process is somewhat different if you are doing the job primitively with intent to dry or smoke the meat.

Cut through at the shoulder joint.

To start, pull the front leg out and cut through at the shoulder joint. This is an easy cut and the knife goes right through. Place the front quarter on a cutting surface and split it apart at the joints. The lower section or foreshank has tough meat riddled with sinews that is good for a use as a "boiling bone," but not much else. The next section up, the arm, is more tender, but still not very fleshy, so it too makes a good boiling bone. The third section is the shoulder. Bone and all, it makes a good roast, although this one was fairly small.

Cut the front quarter apart at the joints.

Freezer wrap is nice, but hardly necessary. We recycle leftover bread bags and plastic grocery bags for the job, being careful to place the print side out, since there may be toxic heavy metals in the ink. I double-bag each portion to help prevent freezer burn and close the bags with a twist tie. I write on the bags with a permanent marker, or sometimes stick labels on them. Each portion is given an appropriate label such as "V-Shoulder Roast." The V

Remove the hind quarter at the ball joint.

Cut the hind quarter apart at the joint.

317

Remove the bone, then cut steaks.

Cutting steaks.

Pull or cut the backstrap meat from along the vertebrae. This is some of the choicest meat on the animal.

stands for venison. Some people date the packages so they know how long the meat has been in the freezer, but we go through it fast enough that it doesn't matter. After the front quarters are cut up, move to the hind quarters.

The hind quarters are cut off the carcass much like the front quarters, but the ball joint is a bit more difficult to find in the meat. Cut close to the pelvis and flex the limb back and forth to guide you. Once released, move the meat to a cutting board and cut it apart at the joint.

The lower shank makes another good boiling bone. The big chunk left over makes great roasts or steaks. Butchers leave the bone in place and cut across it with an electric saw to make round steaks. You can do the same thing at home with a sharp meat saw, but it is less work to trim out the bone before cutting the steaks.

The bone is closer to one side than the other, so cut through from the shallow side and trim around the bone leaving the meat behind. When the bone is out, go back and cut the meat into nice rump steaks. Cut across the muscles rather than with them. Optionally, leave the bone in place for a nice big rump/sirloin roast. You will develop your own preferences as you gain experience.

For simplicity, we mostly cut and package steaks, stew chunks, roasts, and boiling bones. Hamburger is great, too, but you'll have to drop a few bills to get a good meat grinder.

After the four quarters have been processed and put away, it is time to work over the ribs and backbone. With a meat saw, you can cut down the ribcage to make short ribs. Then you can cut across the vertebrae to make T-bone steaks. The ribs can be cut even with a dull sawblade, but the vertebrae requires a sharp blade.

I stripped meat off the ribs and left the bones.

In practice, I usually skip the T-bone steaks and simply trim out the backstrap meat with a knife. These long backstraps are among the most tender cuts on the whole body. Use a knife to slice the backstraps away from each side of the backbone, then cut across the backstraps to make steaks. To make larger steaks, cut them twice as thick, then cut them in half, but stop before cutting all the way through. Let the two halves lay down flat, still connected in the middle to make a "butterfly steak," as shown here.

Like backstraps, but closer to the tail and inside the body cavity, are the much smaller but highly prized tenderloins. Slice them away from the vertebrae in a similar manner.

After cutting off the prime meat, I trimmed off the thin layer of meat covering the rib cage. This layer would

Cut the backstraps into double-thick steaks, then cut the steaks again, but not all the way through. The two halves make a "butterfly steak."

normally be left on the ribs and the ribs cut into sections, but on this day I only had a knife, so I stripped off the meat and diced it into small pieces for stew meat.

I do feel that it is important to salvage as much meat as you reasonably can. It seems like dishonorable waste to see hundreds of pounds of meat thrown in local dumpsters every hunting season. Hunters often strip off only the choicest cuts and discard the ribcages and more in the garbage. It seems sacrilegious to me to kill any living being and dispose of it as trash, instead of utilizing the resource and allowing the scraps to compost back into nature.

Note that there is often impact damage on a roadkill animal, usually to one leg and one side of the rib cage. The worst pieces with broken bits of bone are best given to the dog. It was especially nice working on this "fence kill" since there was no damage to this meat.

I usually cut through the joints between the vertebrae at the neck to make one or two "neck roasts." On the lower end, the pelvis often has enough meat left on it to make a decent roast or at least a boiling bone.

Otherwise, leftover bones can be cracked to extract the marrow or sawed up for bone broth. A day of boiling in a pot and you'll have a delicious and nutritious broth. Use it for cooking, rather than instant bouillon cubes, which lack important nutrients.

The tongue is also very edible. Cut the cheeks open between the jaws to open the mouth wider. Reach in with a knife to get to the back of the tongue.

If the internal organs are good condition, save the liver, heart, and kidneys, too. The liver and heart can be washed and soaked in salt water overnight before slicing into relatively thin 'steaks'. The organs are the most nutritious portions and should ideally go straight into the frying pan or into the fridge to be eaten in the next couple of days. Organs that land in the freezer may be forgotten.

Many people laud the noble savage who used every piece of the deer, and imply that you are dishonoring the deer if you don't. Yes, hunter-gatherers had the ability to use every piece of an animal, but that doesn't mean they did. They were not capable of carrying or storing more than a limited amount of food and gear, so there were typically unused parts left behind to feed the wildlife.

Working with roadkill, it is honorable to salvage the meat, and it is a big enough job just to gut, skin, and butcher a deer to get the meat in the freezer. So don't feel guilty if you trim off a lot or give half of a deer to your dog.

Actually, there is surprisingly little meat on a deer after separating out the guts, hide, and bones. Chances are that it will fit into even a small freezer with room to spare. You'll enjoy many tasty and healthy meals over the weeks and months to come, especially knowing that you put a roadside carcass to good use.

Slice the cheeks open between the jaws to get to the tongue.

Home-Made Jerky

It is nice to have a supply of jerky for camping trips and as trail food for day hikes. Store-bought jerky is ridiculously expensive and loaded with pre-servatives, while home-made roadkill jerky is easy to make, all natural, and free.

At its most basic, jerky is just dried, raw

Drying deer meat on branches in the sun.

meat. Slice meat into quarter-inch thick strips as big or as small as you like, and hang the strips up to dry. Jerky can be oven dried at the lowest setting with the door cracked open for moisture to escape, but we prefer sun drying. I have a couple of old screen doors that make great drying racks, and it is easy to tilt the doors towards the sun for optimal drying. Be sure to avoid placing meat on anything that may leach chemicals into the meat.

Be prepared for guard duty. Neighborhood dogs and other scavengers will help themselves if they can. For that reason, and to avoid dew, it is sensible to bring the meat inside for the night, returning it to the sun the following day.

Dried meat is good, although admittedly not overly exciting, especially when accustomed to seasoned, storebought jerky. Spice up the

Screen doors make an instant drying rack.

meat with a sprinkling of salt and red pepper, which also helps to repel flies, or any other spices of your choosing. I often soak the raw meat in leftover pickle juice for an hour or so, and then dry it, for pickle-flavored jerky. Discard the pickle juice afterwards.

321

Almost dry.

Optionally, willow smoke adds a nice primordial flavor and also helps to keep the flies off. However, timing and intensity of the smoke and heat has to be carefully monitored. Too much heat will cook the meat, increasing the risk of spoilage, especially if the outside sears and traps moisture inside. Heavy smoke can also seal the outside of the meat, trapping moisture inside.

Place the drying frame over a bed of coals and keep the willow wood spread apart to encourage smoke rather than flame. To speed up the process, drape a cotton/canvas cloth or some hides around the frame to trap and concentrate the smoke, but be careful to not catch it on fire or get it so hot that it cooks the meat instead.

To make jerky in winter, I prefer to use an oversize needle and thread to hang the raw meat on a string over a woodstove. Again, it is important to monitor the heat to avoid cooking the meat.

Working without preservatives, the end product should be completely dry and brittle, without the residual moisture and flexibility of store-bought jerky. Store the dried jerky in a paper bag inside a plastic bag, either in a cabinet, or better yet, in the freezer. It will be there when you are ready to hit the trail!

Dumpster diving can provide many unexpected treasures!

Dumpster Diving: Living the High Life

The experienced forager knows how to make a wild salad, dig up starchy roots, gather delicious wild fruits, pick mushrooms, and fill the freezer with free wild meat. So why not also dine on free food foraged from grocery store dumpsters?

Food in dumpsters is rated as perfectly edible one day, but is discarded the following day due to an arbitrary "sell by" date stamped on the package, as if the contents suddenly become poisonous. Grocery stores also discard perfectly edible fruits and vegetables with minor blemishes. It is good food, and all you need is your eyes, nose, and a bit of common sense to watch out for any food that might be past its prime.

Between farms, factories, transportation, and grocery stores, about 40 percent of America's food is wasted without ever reaching the table. Dumpster diving is one way to help prevent senseless waste. It is a great adventure and treasure hunt, often yeilding hundreds of dollars worth of free food.

About forty percent of America's food is wasted without ever reaching the table.

Description, Habitat, and Range

Dumpsters are easy to find. Look behind the local grocery store, and there will be either a dumpster or an oversize trash compactor.

From cheese and yogurt to fruits, vegetables, and orange juice, its all good.

Unfortunately, big grocery stores usually have trash compactors, and they dispose of hundreds of dollars worth of food every day. It seems like a crime when that food could be distributed to people in need.

On the other end of the spectrum, the owners of ultra-small mom and pop grocery stores in small towns are usually so budget-conscious that they bring the leftovers home for their own use.

We have the best success with medium-size grocery stores in towns of a few thousand people, where there is a lot of food waste and no trash compactors. Small grocery stores in bigger towns can also be a good resource. In addition, be sure to check bakery dumpsters, dollar stores, and even the local organic food store. It is a great sport. Check all kinds of dumpsters to see what you can find! I especially enjoy dumpster diving when traveling, and I often arrive at my destination with the entire car packed with food.

On the other hand, dumpster diving can be frustrating after encountering empty dumpsters, locked dumpsters, or dumpsters full of actual garbage. Be persistent. Get to

The bounty from checking a few dumpsters along a 500-mile roadtrip.

know your neighborhood and you can often find more food than you can carry. More than anything, it takes a little nerve to brave snooping and digging around in dumpsters or to admit to your friends where you acquired your groceries!

Yes, But is it Legal?

The U.S. Supreme Court ruled in the case of California vs. Greenwood in 1988 that when a person throws something out, that item is now the public domain. According to the court, *"It is common knowledge that plastic garbage bags left on or at the side of a public street are readily accessible to animals, children, scavengers, snoops, and other members of the public."* However, that alone doesn't translate to open-season on all dumpsters.

According to the www.freegan.info website, *"Dumpster diving is legal in the United States except where prohibited by local regulation... However, if a dumpster is against a building or inside a fenced enclosure marked "No Trespassing," you could be questioned, ticketed or even arrested by the police."*

Legal or not, dumpster diving can feel clandestine enough to make the heart pump with anxiety and thrill while trying not to get caught even for humility sake. On rare occassions we have been reprimanded by grocery store managers, but it was no big deal. We didn't try to provoke them, but merely listened to the lecture and agreed to go away and not come back (at least for awhile). For this reason, and more critically, to avoid prompting stores to install trash compactors or locks on their dumpsters, we often skip lucrative bins when passing through at the wrong time of day.

Sometimes I plan my cross-country trips to hit highly-visible dumpsters in the dark, after business hours, to avoid any chance of confrontation. It is also important to be a courteous dumpster diver. Don't make a mess, and better yet, clean up around the dumpster and make a positive difference.

We often haul home fancy brands and non-essential foods, that we would not likely buy when shopping.

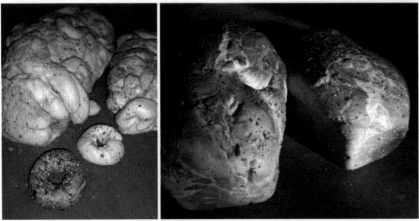

Dough from a bagel store dumpster was baked into delicious "bagel bread."

Dining on Garbage

Dumpster diving isn't about scraping mushy tomatoes out of a pile of goo at the bottom of the bin. Be a choosy shopper, and select only the nicest garbage you can find. Grocery store dumpsters are often full of sealed containers and boxes of food, along with fruits and vegetables that require little more than a pyschological rinsing before consumption. If there is goo in the dumpster, it is typically from a container that broke open while being heaved into the bin. For example, if you score a dozen quarts of yogurt, you may need to rinse off the containers to clean up the one quart that splattered over the rest. That's not a bad price to pay! Indeed, dumpster diving saves money, so the more you scavenge, the less you'll need a real job.

Use your eyes and nose and some commonsense to look and smell the food and determine whether or not it is fit to eat. You have undoubtedly encountered far scarier dishes in the back of your refrigerator than you will ever find in a dumpster, so be brave but smart, and assess each item on its own merits.

If it is night or you are in a hurry, then gather all that can be carried, and bring it home for a thorough inspection at your own leisure. Rejected foods can go to the compost pile, or feed the chickens or other critters you may have.

Even meat can be found in dumpsters. Meat is often perfectly good when discarded, but it doesn't last long, especially in warm summer weather. On occassion, we have brought home hundreds of dollars worth of bacon, whole chickens, and steaks. But do be cautious. Pass by anything questionable or feed it to the dog, and thoroughly cook anything you decide to keep.

We bring home a literal truckload of essentially free wheat every year.

Gleaning: An Age-Old Tradition

Gleaning is the act of cleaning up leftovers after a farm field has been harvested. The practice is deeply rooted in European cultural customs, and still protected by law in many countries today. In biblical times, farmers were even encouraged to leave food behind intentionally, as dictated by Leviticus 19: 9-10, *"When you reap the harvest of your land, you shall not reap your field to its very border, neither shall you gather the gleanings after your harvest. And you shall not strip your vineyard bare, neither shall you gather the fallen grapes of your vineyard; you shall leave them for the poor and for the sojourner."* One purpose for establishing the Sabbath as a day of rest was to allow an opportunity for the poor, thrifty, and wandering to gather their food.

Nowadays, nearly a quarter of all food grown on farms is either left behind during harvesting or sorted out and rejected before the harvest is taken to market. Any local crop grown is worth looking into. You may be able to obtain permission to glean-up the leftovers.

Description, Habitat, and Range

What grows in your neighborhood? Farms of any kind may have a surplus in one form or another. Here in southwest Montana, farming and ranching consists primarily of wheat, potatoes, hay, and cows. We have successfully gleaned all of the above in one form or another.

327

In a broader sense, gleaning can include *anything* that is produced in your area. We have, for example, gleaned free cinderblocks off a scrap pile at a local block plant and free insulation panels off a scrap pile at another local factory.

Ask Around

A free cow, gutted and ready to skin.

The key to successful gleaning is to be bold about knocking on doors and asking questions. I know, it's easier said than done! But ask away, because the worst anyone can do is to say "No."

We bring home a full truckload of wheat every year, a literal ton of food, from one local wheat farm. The farm uses machinary to separate the wheat from the chaff before sending it to market. We get the "screenings," consisting of mostly broken grains of wheat mixed with a bit of chaff. The farmer holds the wheat screenings in a grain silo. We park the truck under a spout and flip a switch to fill a big bag or the truckbed itself. The owners don't ask for payment, but we give them $50 anyway. For that price, we have an entire year's supply of food for our flock of chickens, which often provide us with more than a dozen eggs per day. Sometimes we run the wheat screenings through a grinder to make our own fresh flour.

Numerous potatoes are often left in the fields by harvesting equipment, or are later rejected in the sorting process. My brother once brought home hundreds of pounds of potatoes from a local farm, which were then shared among many different households.

We've never gleaned hay from a farm, but we frequently pick up broken bales along the road, where they have fallen off a truck. I have also picked up onions and sugar beets along the interstate, which roll off of over-loaded trucks as they rumble through from distant farms.

One time we even gleaned a cow, after it broke its leg on an icy creek. The ranchers shot the cow, and would have left it to waste, as is the normal custom, except that a ranchhand knew my friend Katie and asked if she wanted to help butcher it. Being an expert at such things, she cleanly and swiftly skinned and butchered the cow while three of us guys mostly just gawked and tried not to get in her way. We all receieved a generous share of the meat.

Look around your neighborhood, inquire, and in time you could be gifted with great abundance!

We constructed this 10 x 10 foot guest castle and play fort with mostly scavenged and recycled materials. The cinderblocks were factory rejects. The concrete dome was cast over an old fiberglass satellite dish. The windows were ordered new, but the door was purchased secondhand, and the plastic lumber used to frame and trim the openings came from a dumpster.

A Foraging Lifestyle

Foraging is more than survival, it is a way of life! Discovering our regional plants, fungi, and animals as a hunter-gatherer is a means to experience exotic flavors not available at the grocery store. The process of foraging educates and enables individuals to become more native to our region. Foraging also empowers a person to reduce the demand for and dependency on unsustainable industrial agriculture and multinational corporations. Yet, foraging for food is just the beginning.

It is possible to "forage" many other resources, from furniture to house-building materials, conserving the environment and saving money. Foraging can help free people from a drudgery of meaningless work.

Insulating a garage with free fiberglass.

We check our local community dumpsters when passing, and yet, typically bring home a couple thousand dollars worth of useful goods and materials every year. Looking around my house, I see a coffee table, log frame bed, two desks, an office chair, a widescreen TV, and a couple of bedside tables that all came from dumpsters. We are pretty choosey, so we don't pick up anything we don't like. We also bring home many useful materials, such as lumber, insulation, paint, concrete dye, ladders, drain pipes, fence posts, wire, garden hoses, and lots of firewood, already cut to length. My publishing company, HOPS Press, LLC, depends on boxes and packing material scavenged from dumpsters.

In addition, we pick up copper pipe and wire, car batteries, aluminum, brass, and scrap metal, recycling all of it for extra spending money. For example, cutting the cords off of electric appliances adds up quickly. Recycling copper helps reduce the cost of copper products for everyone and prevents needless additional mining. It isn't difficult to gather enough recyclables to pay for a tank of gas, and that adds up over time.

Beyond dumpster diving, we have gleaned many other useful resources, including enough cinderblocks rejected by one factory to build a garage and enough beadboard insulation from another factory to super-insulate a 2,300 square foot house.

Rocks are often piled up in farm fields, free for the asking. We've

gleaned enough rocks from hills and roadsides to build three stone houses. Pallets can be turned into firewood or used to frame an entire house. Look around and inquire wherever you go, and you may be astonished at all the free resources. Find what you can, and many other resources can be bought second-hand at a discount.

Hunting and gathering conserves resources and money. Conserve enough resources, and it may be possible to dispense with a regular job. For example, as a young man, I minimized the need for conventional employment by avoiding expenses, living cheap, buying land, and moving into a tent while build-

My house is built of free local rocks and many salvaged materials.

ing a house. It is a passive solar stone and log home, built with local rocks and many salvaged and secondhand materials. Building cheap and paying out of pocket eliminated the need for a mortgage and interest payments. Designing for solar gain and energy efficiency made such a low electric bill that it wasn't difficult to install enough solar panels to produce more electricity than the house consumes. Having few expenses enabled me to follow my dreams and launch a successful writing and publishing career. It would have been nearly impossible to follow my own path if I were trapped working for someone else!

Path to Freedom

The goal of the foraging lifestyle is not to merely substitute one form of work for another, but to live free like deer. We have the right to live like any other species, to forage when hungry, to sleep when tired, and to play when the moment feels right. Our species is unique in that we also work and create useful products and services, such as houses, cars, movies, and books. There is nothing wrong with work, as long as it is meaningful employment and we choose to work because it is satisfying to do so.

We founded Green University® LLC to cultivate a new way of living, playing, working, and being. Our internship program connects the dots from wilderness survival to sustainable living in the modern world. Through primitive living skills, we immerse participants in the natural world and deal with sustainability issues at an intimate level. The acts of finding shelter, harvesting wild foods, making clothes, and keeping warm reproduces issues of modern sustainability on a model scale as we journey to meet our needs.

Green University® LLC cultivates a new way of living, playing, working, and being: www.GreenUniversity.com.

Conversations started in the wilds are continued at home as we mentor students in building with local materials and scavenged resources from the industrial waste stream. Students can learn how to establish a self-sufficient rural or urban homestead without getting stuck in a meaningless job, working to pay a life-long mortgage and utility expenses. We begin with self-sufficiency and look outward towards global sustainability.

Letting go of Fear

If we are going to save our planet from ourselves, we must first get our feet back in touch with the earth. We need to see our planet, not as something to be feared, but as something that is as close as our own skin. We need to feel the dirt between our toes. We need to learn to drink from mountain streams. We need to forage like wild animals.

As your toes slip from their shoes and detour from a city sidewalk and up a mountain stream, allow your mind to stretch too. This planet was not meant to be carved up with pavement, fences, and artificial boundaries. Stretch beyond the realm of schooling, careers, and drudgery. The plants and animals outside the window are not aliens, and neither are we. Become more knowledgeable about what lives and breathes outside the front door. Accept nature's gifts and share yours. Celebrate freedom, and spread seeds of a better tomorrow.

The journey you have started through the pages of this book can become your path to freedom. It is the freedom of letting go of fear, of discovering that we are part of this planet and we belong here. It is the freedom to follow your heart and live your own dreams.

This world is our Eden. Step into nature's playground and dance to the rhythm of your soul. Every breath is a chance to make the world a better place for all.

Kris Reed, living and drinking like a native.

A lovely spring salad of chickweed, violets, and dandelions.

Bibliography

_____. "Interview with Tom Brown, Jr. and Larry Dean Olsen." March 10, 1998. http://www.hollowtop.com/spt_html/interview.htm. Accessed March 15, 2014.

Beauchamp, R; Boyce D. Foragers of the Terminal Pleistocene in North America. University of Nebraska Press: Lincoln, NE. 2007.

Brown, Tom Jr. The Search. Berkley Books. New York, NY. March 1983.

Brown, Tom Jr. Tom Brown's Guide to Wild Edible and Medicinal Plants. Berkeley Books. New York. 1985.

Bryan, William L., Jr. Montana Indians: Yesterday and Today, 2nd Edition. American & World Geographic Publishing: Helena, MT. 1996.

Craighead, John J., Frank C. Craighead, & Ray J. Davis. A Field Guide to Rocky Mountain Wildflowers. Houghton Mifflin Co: Boston. 1963.

Dorn, Robert L. Vascular Plants of Montana. Mountain West Publishing: Cheyenne, WY. 1984.

Elpel, Thomas J. Botany in a Day: The Patterns Method of Plant Identification, 6th Edition. HOPS Press: Pony, MT. 2013.

Elpel, Thomas J. Participating in Nature: Wilderness Survival and Primitive Living Skills, 6th Edition. HOPS Press: Pony, MT. 2009.

Elpel, Thomas J. Roadmap to Reality: Consciousness, Worldviews, and the Blossoming of Human Spirit. HOPS Press: Pony, MT. 2008.

Elpel, Thomas J. Shanleya's Quest: A Botany Adventure for Kids Ages 9 to 99. HOPS Press: Pony, MT. 2005.

Gibbons, Euell. Stalking the Wild Asparagus. David McKay Company, Inc.: New York. 1962-1973.

Gillaspy, James, Ph.D. *"Purslane: A Personal Perspective."* Bulletin of Primitive Technology. Vol. 1. No. 7. Spring 1994. Pgs. 54-55.

Hart, Jeff. Montana: Native Plants and Early Peoples. Montana Historical Society Press: Helena, MT. 1976, 1992.

Harrington, H. D. Edible Native Plants of the Rocky Mountains. University of New Mexico Press: Albuquerque, NM. 1967.

Kallas, John. Edible Wild Plants: From Dirt to Plate. Gibbs Smith. Layton, UT. 2010

Kallas, John. *"Amaranth—Staple Food Source for Modern Foragers."* The Wild Food Adventurer. Vol. 3, No. 2. July 1, 1998.

Kallas, John. *"Edible Blue Camas—Preparation Old & New."* The Wild Food Adventurer. Vol. 3, No. 2. July 1, 1998.

Kallas, John. *"Infant—Nitrate Caution."* The Wild Food Adventurer. Vol. 6, No. 1. April 1, 2001.

Kallas, John. *"Oxalates Schmokulates."* The Wild Food Adventurer. Vol. 6, No. 3. August 28, 2001.

Kallas, John. *"Wapato, Indian Potato."* The Wild Food Adventurer. Volume 1, No 4. Dec. 10, 1996.

Kallas, John. *"Wild Spinach: Delicious, Nutritious and Abundant"* The Wild Food Adventurer. Vol. 1, No 2. June 30, 1996.

Kirk, Donald R. Wild Edible Plants of the Western United States. Naturegraph Publishers: Healdsburg, CA. 1970.

Lincoff, Gary. The Joy of Foraging. Quarry Books: Beverly, MA. 2012.

Malone, Michael P. and Richard B. Roeder. Montana: A History of Two Centuries. University of Washington Press: Seattle. 1980.

Morton, Julia F. *"Cattails (Typha spp.) – Weed Problem or Potential Crop."* Economic Botany. Vol. 29. January - March, 1975. Pages 7-29.

Moulton, Gary. The Definitive Journals of Lewis & Clark, Vol. 8. Bison Books/University of Nebraska Press: Lincoln, NE. 2002.

Olsen, Larry Dean. Outdoor Survival Skills. Brigham Young University: Provo, UT. 1967, 1972.

Olson, Miles. The Compassionate Hunter's Guidebook. New Society Publishers: Gabriola Island, BC. 2014.

Runyon, Linda. Essential Wild Food Survival Guide. Wild Food Company: Dorchester, MA. 2009

Snell, Alma. A Taste of Heritage. Bison Books - University of Nebraska Press: Lincoln: NE. 2006.

Thayer, Sam. Nature's Garden. Forager's Harvest: Ogema, WI. 2010.

Thayer, Sam. *"Nettles: The Good, The Better, and the Ouch."* The Forager. Vol. 2, No. 1. Spring 2002. Pages 9-11.

Thayer, Sam. The Forager's Harvest. Forager's Harvest: Ogema, WI. 2006.

Tilford, Gregory L. Edible and Medicinal Plants of the West. Mountain Press Publishing Co.: Missoula, MT. 1997.

Wheat, Margaret M. Survival Arts of the Primitive Paiutes. University of Nevada Press. Reno, NV. 1967.

Index by Genus

A
Abies 261
Aconitum 16
Actaea 177
Agaricus 279
Agropyron 248
Allium 157
Alloclavaria 268
Amanita 270, 280, 285
Ambrosia 83
Amelanchier 24, 204
Amianthium 138
Anticlea 125, 138
Apocynum 59
Arctium 148
Arctostaphylos 223, 227
Aronia 216
Artemisia 21
Asclepias 57
Asparagus 55
Atriplex 29, 82
Avena 248

B
Barbarea 65
Berberis 226
Boletus 267, 287
Bonasa 295
Brassica 64, 116
Brodiaea 155

C
Calbovista 286
Calochortus 119, 120, 151
Calvatia 284
Camassia 136
Campanula 163
Carassius 308
Carduus 100
Centaurea 103
Chenopodium 78
Cicuta 43
Cirsium 100
Clavaria 268
Claviceps 249
Claytonia 131
Conium 44
Coprinellus 283

Coprinus 282
Crataegus 207
Cronartium 259
Ctenopharyngodon 308
Cydonia 216
Cymopterus 161
Cyprinus 300

D
Daucus 166
Dendragapus 295
Dendroctonus 259
Dichelostemma 155
Duchesnea 176

E
Echinochloa 248
Elaeagnus 232
Eriobotrya 216
Erythronium 143

F
Falcipennis 295
Fragaria 176, 188
Fritillaria 146

G
Gaultheria 186, 223
Gyromitra 277

H
Helvella 277
Hesperocnide 87
Hordeum 248
Hypophthalmichthys 308

I
Iva 83

J
Juglans 262

L
Lactuca 74
Laportea 87
Larix 261
Leccinum 290
Lepidium 65

Lewisia 127
Lolium 249
Lomatium 161
Lonicera 175
Lycoperdon 284

M
Mahonia 222
Malus 211
Mimulus 115
Morchella 275
Mylopharyngodon 308

N
Nasturtium 112
Nuphar 126

O
Odocoileus 293
Oenothera 168
Opuntia 105
Orconectes 299
Oryza 248
Oryzopsis 252

P
Pacifastacus 299
Perideridia 159
Phalaris 251
Phleum 248, 252
Photinia 216
Phragmites 251
Picea 261
Pinus 255
Plantago 98
Pleurotus 273
Polygonum 167
Portulaca 109
Potentilla 176
Procambarus 299
Prunus 196
Pseudotsuga 261
Pyracantha 216
Pyrus 216

R
Rheum 90
Rhus 236

Ribes 175, 179, 259
Rorippa 113
Rosa 194
Rubus 190
Rumex 90
Russula 272

S
Saccharum 248
Sagittaria 167
Sambucus 218
Saxifraga 96
Secale 248
Shepherdia 229
Silybyum 101
Sisymbrium 63, 113
Sonchus 72
Sorbus 20, 216
Sorghum 248

Stellaria 116
Stenanthium 138
Streptopus 234
Suillus 269, 290
Symphoricarpos 177

T
Tamiasciurus 291
Taraxacum 66
Toxicodendron 21, 178, 236
Toxicoscordion 125, 138
Tragopogon 75
Trifolium 88
Triteleia 155
Triticum 248
Tropaeolum 113
Tsuga 261
Typha 47

U
Ulmus 45
Urera 87
Urtica 84

V
Vaccinium 11, 182
Vascellum 286
Veronica 115
Verpa 277
Viburnum 234
Viola 94
Vitis 235

Z
Zea 248
Zigadenus 125, 138
Zizania 248

Index by Common Name

A
almond 196
amanita 270, 280, 285
American bistort 167
antelope 309
apple 211
apricot 196, 203
arctic raspberry 193
arrowhead 167
artichoke 101
Asian carp 300
asparagus 55
avalanche lily 144

B
balsam fir 261
baneberry 177
barley 248
bear 309
biscuitroot 161
bistort 167
bitter cherry 197
bitterroot 127
bittersweet nightshade 177
black currant 179
black hawthorn 207

black walnut 262
blackberry 190
blackcaps 191
blue camas 136
blue dicks 155
blue elderberry 218
blue grouse 295
blueberry 11, 183
bolete 267
breadroot 161
broadleaf plantain 98
broccoli 116
brodiaea 155
brook saxifrage 96
brooklime 115
brussels sprouts 116
buffaloberry 229
bull thistle 100
bunchberry 235
burdock 148
button mushroom 279

C
cactus 105
camas 136
Canada thistle 101

canaigre dock 91
carp 300
carrot 166
cauliflower 116
cherry 196
chickweed 116
Chinese elm 46
chives 157
chokeberry 216
chokecherry 38, 198
Christmasberry 216
cloudberry 193
clover 88
collard greens 116
common camas 136
corn 248
cotoneaster 217
cottontail rabbit 292, 295
coyote 309
crabapple 211
crawdad 298
crayfish 298
creeping bellflower 163
creeping thistle 101
crested wheat grass 248
curly dock 93

currant 175, 179
cursed thistle 101

D
dandelion 66, 117
death camas 125, 126, 138
deer 293
desert cottontail 292
desert currant 179
dock 90
dogbane 59
dog-tooth violet 144
dogwood tree 235
Douglas fir 261
dwarf huckleberry 183
dwarf red raspberry 193

E
elderberry 218
elk 309
elk thistle 104
ergot fungus 249
evening primrose 168

F
false morels 277
false ragweed 83
fawn lily 144
fir 261
firecracker lily 155
firethorn 216
flowering crabapple 215
flowering dogwood 235
fly agaric 270
fox 309
French sorrel 92
fritillary 147

G
garlic 157
geese 309, 310
giant puffball 284
glacier lily 143
golden currant 181
goldfish 308
gooseberry 175, 179
goosefoot 78
grouse 295, 296, 297, 309
grouse wortleberry 183

H
harebell 163
hawthorn 207
hedgethorn 207
hemlock tree 261
highbush cranberry 234
honeysuckle 175
horse mushroom 279
huckleberry 11, 182

I
Indian fig 106
Indian rice grass 252
inky cap mushrooms 282

J
Johnny-jump-up 94

K
kale 116
king bolete 267, 287
kinnikinnick 227
knapweed 103
kohlrabi 116

L
lambs quarters 78
larch 261
lemonberry 236
limber pine 255
lobster 298
lodgeple pine 255
loquat 216

M
maize 248
manzanita 228
mariposa lily 151
meadow mushroom 279
milk thistle 101
milkweed 57
millet 248
miner's lettuce 134
monkey flower 115
monkshood 16
moose 309
morel mushroom 275
moss rose 110
mountain ash 20, 216
mountain grouse 295
mudbug 298

N
Nanking cherry 200
narrowleaf plantain 98
nectarine 196
nightshade 177
nodding thistle 102
nopales 105

O
oats 248
onion 157
orache 29, 82
orange-cap bolete 290
Oregon grape 222
oyster mushroom 273

P
pansy 94
papago lily 155
patience dock 92
peach 196, 203
pear 216
pepperweed 65
pheasant 309
pin cherry 197
pinyon pine 255
plantain 98
plum 196
poison ivy 21, 178, 236
poison oak 236
poison sumac 236
pond lily 126
porcupine 297, 309
prickly lettuce 74
prickly pear cactus 105
primrose 168
puffball mushroom 284
purple coral fungus 268
purslane 109

Q
quince 216
quinoa 80

R
rabbit 295, 296, 309
ragweed 83
rampion bellflower 163
raspberry 190, 192
red clover 88

red elderberry 218
red squirrel 291
reed canary grass 251
rhubarb 90
rice 248
rice grass 252
rose 194
ruffed grouse 295
Russian olive 232
rye 248

S
salal 186
salmonberry 193
salsify 75
saskatoon 204
saxifrage 96
sego lily 119, 120, 151
serviceberry 24, 204
shaggy mane 282
sheep sorrel 90
Siberian elm 45
snowberry 177
soapberry 232
soopolallie 232
sorrel 90
spotted fritillary 147
spring beauty 131
spruce 261
spruce grouse 295
squirrel 291, 294, 295, 296, 297
stinging nettle 84
strawberry 188
strawberry goosefoot 83
subalpine fir 261
sugarcane 248
sumac 236

T
tamarack 261
thimbleberry 193
thistle 100
Timothy grass 248, 252
tree mushroom 273
tumble mustard 63
tumbleweed 63
tunas 105
twisted stalk 234

V
variegated bolete 269
veiny dock 90
violet 94

W
walnut 262
wapato 167
watercress 112
wheat 248
white clover 88
whitebark pine 255
whitetail deer 293
wild asparagus 55
wild broccoli 63
wild cabbage 116

wild carrot 166
wild cherry 196
wild grape 235
wild onion 157
wild plum 201
wild rice 248
wild rose 194
wild strawberry 188
wintercress 65
wintergreen 187
wortleberry 183

Y
yampa 159
yellow pond lily 126
yellowbell 146